Design for Independent Living

Design for Independent Living

The Environment and Physically Disabled People

**by Raymond Lifchez
and Barbara Winslow**

Whitney Library of Design
an imprint of Watson-Guptill Publications/New York

The Architectural Press, Ltd.
London

First published 1979 in New York by Whitney Library of Design,
an imprint of Watson-Guptill Publications,
a division of Billboard Publications, Inc.,
1515 Broadway, New York, N.Y. 10036

Library of Congress Cataloging in Publication Data
Lifchez, Raymond, 1932-
    Design for independent living.
    Bibliography:
    Includes index.
    1. Architecture and the physically handicapped—
United States. I. Winslow, Barbara Strong,
1941-   joint author. II. Title.
NA2545.P5L5   643   78-21273
ISBN 0-8230-7140-5

First published 1979 in Great Britain by The Architectural Press Ltd.,
9 Queen Anne's Gate, London SW1H 9BY
ISBN 0-85139-156-7

Manufactured in U.S.A.

First Printing, 1979

For the Center for Independent Living

It is not without reason that the world of physically disabled people in our society is cloaked in mystery. It is a historic truth that a society will isolate those who jeopardize the collective image of what is desirable in life, and physically disabled people are a case in point. They raise the specter of our own frailty and, in America, create a certain guilt that with all our belief in community we cannot contain them, with all our technology we cannot "heal" them. The authors believe that much of this anxiety can be alleviated by demystifying that world, for it is a fact that fear is largely born of ignorance. It is toward this end that this book is dedicated.

Contents

Acknowledgments

The authors thank the Wallace Alexander Gerbode Foundation of San Francisco and its Executive Director Thomas Layton for their confidence in us and for the major grant that supported our research during 1976–1977. We thank the Center for Independent Living (CIL) in Berkeley, which gave locus and social centering to all our activities related to this work since 1975. Without CIL there would have been no Berkeley story to tell. We are grateful to Richard Bender, dean of the College of Environmental Design, and Joseph Esherick, chairman of the Department of Architecture, at the University of California at Berkeley, who have unequivocally supported our interest in this subject and our approach to it. They made it possible to research and teach in ways that greatly contributed to the development of our understanding and method of presentation.

We owe special thanks to Anselm Strauss of the University of California Medical School at San Francisco, who reviewed our first efforts and who not only urged us to continue but gave us a research plan for doing so; and to Dennis George Williams, who assisted us in carrying out this plan. For their incisive and detailed reading of the manuscript, we are also grateful to Irving Kenneth Zola, Brandeis University; Sandra Howell, Massachusetts Institute of Technology; Eric Dibner, Center for Independent Living; Peter Trier, the Disabled Students Union; and Susan O'Hara, the Physically Disabled Students Program. To John Parman, who coauthored with Raymond Lifchez another manuscript, "Teaching an Awareness of the Needs of Physically Disabled Persons," parts of which have been incorporated into this book, is due particular mention.

We are especially grateful to the seven people who allowed us to present them as spokespersons for the physically disabled population we are reporting on. But we are equally grateful to the more than two hundred individuals, from all manner of professions and walks of life and with specific knowledge of the physically disabled community in Berkeley, who agreed to be interviewed, often more than once, and whose reports were invaluable. The ease with which we moved through the disabled community network gave us direct knowledge of its benefits and strengths. We thank Carmen Paz Anderson for the generous use of her large and accessible house, an important crossroads within this network, where many hours of group interviews took place over eighteen months.

Photography has been instrumental in all aspects of our research, teaching, and consulting reported on in this book. We have been fortunate to have the assistance of photographers with a special interest in our subject. Jane Scherr especially contributed substantially in both the making and the selecting of photographs. Her point of view about what pictures would be necessary coincided remarkably with our own, but she was able to go out and make them. Henry Bowles, George Dibble, Dyche Emory, Pat Goudvis, Michael Henry, Deborah Hoffman, Barbara Knecht, Judith Stronach Lifchez, Colleen Mahoney, Lydia Mechanic, and Bonnie Wudtke also contributed. Ken Okuno, official photographer, and Lynn Kidder, archivist, at the Center for Independent Living were extremely helpful in making new photographs and finding old ones and in furthering our mobility within the Berkeley network. We were supported in making our photographic collection by Susan O'Hara and Frank DiOrio, who permitted us to incorporate selections from their excellent manual, "Guide to Independent Living for Disabled Students." We are also indebted to Robert Tarr and his staff at the Multimedia Center, School of Optometry, University of California at Berkeley, for their technical advice and assistance.

We also wish to acknowledge a Faculty Summer Research Fellowship and four Teaching Grants to Improve Instruction awarded to Raymond Lifchez over the past three years by the University of California at Berkeley, which have made it possible to investigate aspects of our subject in relation to architectural design. We are indebted to Bruce Miller, who handled our accounts, for keeping us in the black.

Finally, we would like to thank Joanna Taylor for her care in editing the manuscript; Sarah Bodine, senior editor of The Whitney Library of Design, who from the outset believed in our subject and convinced others of its worth and timeliness; and Susan Davis, editor of The Whitney Library, who with consideration led us through the tedious process of turning a manuscript into a book.

A Word on Words

The use of terminology referring to physically disabled people in this book has been the subject of much discussion. The terms most commonly used in Berkeley are not always those people use in other locations or in the literature of disabled people. In some cases terms employed in Berkeley, such as *independence,* have meanings that do not precisely match the accepted definitions in other usages.

In Berkeley, for example, *independence* is the term applied to living a self-determined lifestyle. It is not reduced in any sense by physical dependence upon other individuals or environmental aids. Despite such inconsistencies we have chosen to use the local terminology because it has special significance to those we have worked with and is used liberally in quotations of their thoughts.

The terms *disabled* or *physically disabled* are used rather than *handicapped* in referring to people; a disabled person may be handicapped by his environment, but is not himself handicapped. However, a further distinction is necessary. Often disabled people are referred to as "the disabled." It is preferable to use *disabled* not as a noun but as an adjective, as in "disabled people" or "people with disabilities." While this may seem artificial, the point is to make readers think of the person first; it is akin to the push to change language patterns to effect women's liberation.

People often unthinkingly refer to those who are wheelchair bound as "wheelchairs," meaning wheelchair cases. This is truly inappropriate, for it labels the person as an appliance, thereby focusing only on the prosthetic, and denies the person his or her right to individual identity. Such labeling is truly, if subtly, stigmatizing. We have therefore used such terms as *people in wheelchairs* or *wheelchair users,* as these are the terms preferred by those we know.

The term *crip* is much used in informal conversation; it is an in-group term that may be offensive if used by outsiders. We have used this word when it appears in quotations and when it is the commonly applied label, as in "crip humor" or "crip lib." The term *quad* is often used when referring to a quadriplegic (one who has lost some use of all four limbs) and *para* in referring to a paraplegic; other abbreviated terms are less common and have been spelled out.

Finally, some note must be made of our use of the pronouns *he* and *she.* For simplicity and clarity we have chosen the convention of using *he, him, his,* except where the subject is in fact feminine. Where the masculine terms are used to refer to either or both possibilities, we ask the reader to think *he/she, him/her,* or *his/hers.* To assist this way of thinking, we have indicated this choice--or attitude—in the first pages of the text.

Foreword

In this book we are introduced to a group of physically disabled people who, escaping lives of safety and isolation, are seeking independence and community. Raymond Lifchez and Barbara Strong Winslow liken them to immigrants coming to a foreign country. Berkeley, California, is the land of the free; it offers a fair degree of accessibility and an unusual degree of social services. A community of people has grown up whose members travel in electric wheelchairs and live their own lives in their own self-determined lifestyles. In a city of many cultures, they have formed another.

The book has an unusual approach to environmental design, in that it overlaps with sociology and anthropology. It builds empathy with a group of people with whom most designers have no familiarity. This not only can increase our respect for wheelchair-bound disabled people and stimulate an intention to include them in society and the built environment, but can also promote an attitude of awareness towards special groups in general—children, the poor, the elderly. Our definition of the norm is enlarged.

I recommend this book to those who are politically and sympathetically interested in making better environments for disabled people. These would include the general public, as well as architects and planners, social scientists and medical professionals.

Sarah P. Harkness, AIA
The Architects Collaborative, Inc.
Cambridge, Mass.

Prologue

There is a television ad for a popular cigar where the pitchman winks slyly at the audience and says, "We're gonna get you!" The TV audience may resist and reply, "You're not going to get me!" but such a response is not possible for the readers of this book. *Design for Independent Living* only looks like a treatise about disabled people and how *they* can be integrated into mainstream American society. It is, in fact, a book about all of us—about what we all *will* at some time have to face. Note that I did not say "may." I quite consciously said "will."

My certainty is based on statistics. At this moment, the U.S. Department of Health, Education, and Welfare estimates that there are over thirty million Americans suffering from some physical condition that limits their full participation in society. In reality, it is not their condition that limits their participation, but the world we have created—a world that excludes all but the most able-bodied people and lets the rest fend for themselves. Our private and public buildings lack elevators, escalators, ramps, and even railings. Our mass transit is only for the most agile and prevents easy access for anyone on crutches, canes, or in a wheelchair. Our very sidewalks and curbs are difficult for those with vision impairments, hazardous for those with mobility and balance problems, and impossible for anyone in a wheelchair. These are only the most obvious examples. Once in a place, a disabled person may find the chairs too unstable, the doors too narrow, the floors too slippery, and the toilets impossible to use. The list is endless. It's as if disabled people are confronted with a world of signs saying, "Stop! Danger! Keep Out!"

But to think of these as problems that only a limited number of people face is deceptive. While at any given moment the number of physically disabled people is finite, in the long run every reader of this book will be counted in their number. Thanks in large part to high-technology medicine, few of us die of old age any more or of what was once called "natural causes"; rather we enter an increasingly lengthy period of the terminal stages of one or more disorders. Yet this seems to be a reality that we never tire of denying. And it seems to be a denial that cuts across all classes of income, education, and even sophistication. This was illustrated to me recently by a friend, a psychologist, who with great enthusiasm was showing me pictures of his retirement home—a lovely condominium in Southern California. Instead of showing appreciation at the panoramic view it offered, I gasped at the two flights of winding external stairs it took to get there as well as at the balconies and the many flights of stairs inside the building. Aware of my shock, he looked at me and shook his head. It was the first time it had dawned on him that he might not be in the same physical shape at age 70 that he is now at age 43.

This sort of denial is likely to make all of us triply cursed. First, by denying the real economic, physical, and social deprivations that inevitably accompany aging and disability in our society, we feel like "has-beens" and "less-thans" when they eventually do occur. Second, by denying that it could happen to us, we lose the possibility of preparation. We thus neglect to marshal the necessary social, psychological and economic resources until we are forced to face the issue, and then it is often too late. Finally, the denial leads to a kind of collusion. For in not fighting for disabled people but neglecting, or even misunderstanding them, we too often feel that we have lost the right to protest and make demands when we ourselves are in that position. In a sense we are left with the feeling that we deserved what we got. The first step in freeing ourselves from these curses is to open our eyes and our minds and acknowledge that disabled people, even severely disabled people, are not *them* but *us*.

Towards this end, Lifchez and Winslow have provided an apt beginning. Although they are architects and have written a book about the physically disabled and their physical environment, theirs has risen far above the usual treatment of such topics. While practical suggestions do abound, this is primarily a book about people and how they manage to live life to the fullest. Instead of focusing on what is unique to people with a severe disability, the authors write about the needs that are common to all people. Eating, sleeping, grooming, working, mating, and playing are activities that all of us engage in. The authors delineate the adaptations necessary to allow all people to continue these activities regardless of their age or physical ability. Gradually as a result, we see the lives of physically disabled people unfold as constituted not of the great achievement of herculean tasks but of the difficult accomplishment of mundane ones. Theirs is a story about the joy of self-sufficient acts where needing help does not mean one is helpless; where being alone does not mean one is lonely; where being in touch with one's body does not mean one is hypochondriacal; and where life is lived for its potentiality not its precariousness, though being alive, well, and active can never be taken for granted.

But to read the stories with awe and admiration is a mistake. If the reader stands in awe it should not be of their courage, but of a society that makes their daily lives so awesome. I have a recommendation with which the authors might quarrel: yield to your curiosity and jump first to the photographs; look at them until the shock of their disablement fades; and then look at their faces so you can remember them as real people as you read. That is all we, the handicapped, ask for—a chance to be seen as real, with the same needs and wants as everyone else.

Irving Kenneth Zola, Ph.D.
Professor of Sociology
Brandeis University
Waltham, Mass.
and Board of Directors and Counselor
Boston Self-Help Center
Brookline, Mass.

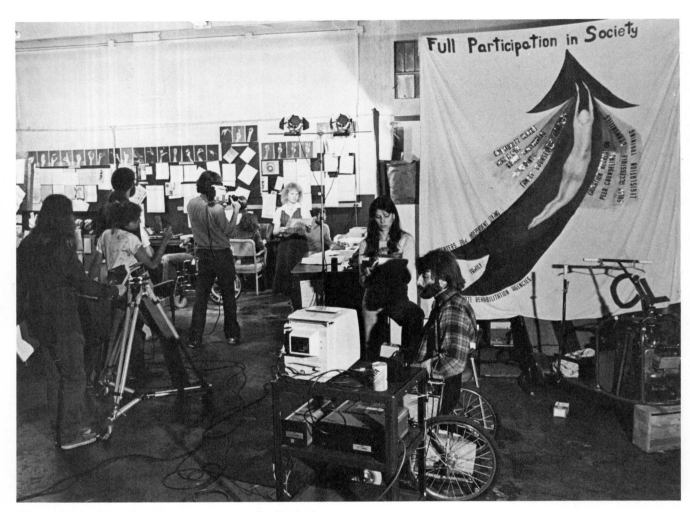

Center for Independent Living: a center for Berkeley and an emerging center for the physically disabled coalition in the United States.

Introduction

Berkeley, California, is a much talked about community: an important resident center of counterculture in this country, the home of an internationally known university, a focus of liberal thinking and liberal lifestyles. Under sometimes foggy skies, it sports a year-round temperate climate in an attractive physical setting of bays, views, and hilly landscapes. As an inhabited place, it resembles more-rural communities in that small businesses still outnumber large concerns or chain operations in the shopping districts and individual homeowners in individualized dwellings outnumber those in multistoried apartment complexes. But Berkeley has certain similarities with large cities in the assortment of cultural and social events and activities available, in the mixture of ethnic and subculture groups, and in the general urban pace of public life. It is a special place where one can drink very good espresso, learn Zen meditation, and phone one's political representative all at the same time. As Charlotte Painter put it in her book about Berkeley, *Seeing Things*: "Paris it is not, but also it is not foreign. Or Godforsaken like New York. Some say rather that it is God-infested."[1]

Geographically, Berkeley consists of two distinct districts: the hills and the flatlands. The center is the university—the University of California at Berkeley. Demographically, a further distinction can be drawn between areas south and north of the university. The area south of the campus is occupied primarily by students. There is more low-cost rental housing, a higher crime rate, and many people who identify with a counterculture lifestyle. The heartbeat of the area is Telegraph Avenue—a strip of small shops, inexpensive restaurants, bookstores, coffeehouses, and so on.

The area north of the campus is primarily occupied by more conventional families. The population is older, mainly professionals and professionally oriented people. Many students attend the various religious institutions located on this side of the campus. Here, the terrain is hilly, the foothills of the "hills" section to the east and north. Shopping and services are dispersed, and both are more expensive than on the south side of the campus.

Of particular interest is that Berkeley, with its counterculture reputation, liberal attitudes, hills and flatlands, is also a center for physically disabled people. This disabled population is concentrated on the south side of the campus and toward the flatlands. Here the terrain is more suited to those with impaired mobility; the housing is cheaper and older, more easily modified; shopping is concentrated; the able-bodied population is younger and consists, in general, of a mixture of students and others with a certain counterculture spirit and lifestyle. Perhaps these attributes provide a more appealing attraction for the predominantly young, disabled population that lives there. Disabled people often point out that they come to Berkeley precisely because varied and deviant lifestyles are accepted. They feel that this society will be open in accepting them; that they can, in a sense, go relatively unnoticed in this environment of "freaks."

There has been no exact census of the disabled population in Berkeley. The Research and Evaluation Division of the Center for Independent Living (CIL) determined in 1973 that there were about 12,000 disabled people between the ages of eighteen and sixty-four in Berkeley at that time.[2] These people live predominantly in an area of approximately 2 square miles (5 square kilometers), with Telegraph Avenue its center.

It is along Telegraph Avenue that disabled people are most visible in numbers. There the obvious, taken-for-granted freedom and independence of disabled people is quite astonishing. With the help of electric wheelchairs, prosthetic devices, and good attendant care, many of the disabled population go everywhere and do everything. And, perhaps what is more significant, once they get where they are going, they become an integral part of the activities of urban life. They are present in coffeehouses, restaurants, parks, theaters—drinking coffee, dining, sunning, passing time in conversations.

If one views street and city life as a visitor, this presence and integration of disabled people into community life might only be a matter of passing interest. However, if one is concerned about the environmental adaptation and accommodation for and by disabled people, this phenomenon is of paramount importance. Here is a population commonly thought of as shut-in or institutionalized, living a free and active life in the public world.

What has happened in Berkeley? What is the role of the environment in determining this phenomenon? Are there environmental or social approaches characteristic of Berkeley that would work as effectively in other communities? Can knowledge gained about Berkeley be used to help create more communities offering full access to disabled people? And, more important, since the disabled population appears to be so well integrated, leading full social, work, and political urban lives, what can be learned from Berkeley that would encourage or enable other disabled people to have richer experiences in the world?

If one is planning environments or policy for physically disabled people, the Berkeley of today is an appropriate place to learn about these environmental needs. But for Berkeley to serve as an example, it must be approached conscientiously. Aspects or attributed meanings of Berkeley that are unique should not be stressed. For example, physical or climatic conditions indigenous to Berkeley should not be accented because their applicability is limited. Such conditions are exclusive and cannot be altered or changed by the exertion or desire of those who live there. That which makes Berkeley special as a place is what people have accomplished or are in the process of accomplishing there. What must not be suggested is that to become independent, disabled people must come to Berkeley. Nor do places have to become exact copies of Berkeley to assist disabled people. Independence can be pursued and achieved in many places. It must, like all human acts, originate in the individual. Berkeley is only an example of what can be achieved and what the process of achieving may entail.

The aim of this book is to aid designers, planners, students, and others concerned with the design or planning of the built environment in developing an approach to integrating physically disabled people into the fabric of their communities. It is also intended to give others who are not specifically concerned with this issue some perspective on what it means to live as a disabled person in a world that has been conceived as a setting for able-bodied people.

This book originated in 1975 with a course in the Department of Architecture at the University of California at Berkeley. For some time we had been concerned with issues related to environmental access for special populations, such as the frail elderly

and physically disabled persons, and we decided that major problems of access were confronted by those who use wheelchairs. We therefore set aside an eight-week period to look at this question closely in the company of those who use wheelchairs.

The "client" for that course was the Center for Independent Living, which was examining the possibility of building barrier-free housing in Berkeley to ease the severe shortage of accessible facilities and accommodations. The project was assisted by a dozen disabled consultants who spent a great deal of time and energy discussing, evaluating, formulating, and communicating their environmental needs, both spatial and psychosocial. The information gathered in this process proved, as expected, very useful in the design task for which it was intended.

It was, to say the least, a consciousness-raising experience for all. The consultants, often for the first time, examined the spaces they occupy, their environmental values and biases, and the emotional as well as the physical demands that they placed upon their surroundings. The designers found themselves involved in a process that demanded an understanding of the whole person and his or her interaction with others. The screen through which we usually filtered our view of those different from ourselves became a real barrier to effective design. Solutions that were based on dimensional or purely physical requirements were rejected as inadequate. And attempts to find useful sources to guide the design process were fruitless—the only effective resource was the consultant group.

Like all people, the disabled consultants wanted to influence their lives and their physical, lived-in worlds. They wanted their lives and their environments to say something about themselves—to say what they valued. And what they valued was independence, deinstitutionalization, and freedom from the stereotypical images that they felt limited their hopes and growth. Each had had experiences of living in places, rooms, and buildings that said little to them, or nothing worth listening to. Each had had to exert considerable effort to determine how the environment should be altered and changed so that it afforded an opportunity and a potential for living a fuller life.

At the end of that summer we who taught the course began to see Berkeley through new eyes. We assume that the same desires for an independent, fuller life exist throughout the country: that given the opportunity, everyone, disabled or not, would prefer a lifestyle that offers not only choices but also a sense of belonging, that is, a sense of being a meaningful part of all that is taking place in any physical location. Making this happen for disabled people requires an understanding of their environmental needs that goes beyond meeting government regulations, building ramps, or adapting bathrooms and kitchens. This understanding—how it can be disclosed and incorporated into the designed world—is what this book is about.

Part 1
Disclosing an Ongoing World

There are very few communities in the United States that give disabled people the resources necessary for independent living. Berkeley, however, has become identified with a social, political, and physical environment that is highly supportive of this goal. The Berkeley image has grown measurably over the past several years, and each successive newcomer confirms that this image remains strong in the eyes of others across the nation. And by coming to Berkeley, each successive newcomer confirms that the Berkeley image is genuine.

In each case those who have come have altered their own environments in order to support their way of living independently. Independent living and the environment are made congruent. Thus Berkeley has been given additional meaning as a place because physically disabled people have chosen it and by their choice have affected it.

Mainstreaming in Berkeley

Over the years, programs and informal service shops have been developed in Berkeley by disabled and other interested people to assist those who wish to become independent. In the early 1960s a residence program for severely disabled students was initiated in the student health center, Cowell Hospital, at the University of California. Although the program was located in a medical facility, it was not completely devoted to medical care. The disabled residents lived separated from the wards and were obligated to find their own attendants among the community and, in general, to regulate their own lives. The hospital was there when needed. Around 1970, however, those living in the Cowell facility began to move out and to live in the community, for it was unavoidable that living in the health facility would eventually be seen as a compromise solution to full independent living. In 1975 Cowell was closed, and today those severely disabled students new to the campus who prefer a period of transition between institution or home and a fully independent university life may spend their first year as

Paris–Vienna–Berkeley: the coffeehouse continues its historic role in planning and shaping society.

Berkeley students in one of the regular residence halls among able-bodied students. This transition period is made possible by a university back-up system of attendant care within the residence hall. Through this route perhaps a dozen severely disabled individuals begin their first experience of independent living each year.

One of the first students in the Cowell program and several of his classmates founded the Physically Disabled Students Program at the University of California to further assist disabled students. It was predominantly this same group of people who later founded the Center for Independent Living, Inc. (CIL), in 1972 after they had graduated from the university. CIL functions as a workshop and growth center for the physically disabled people of the east San Francisco Bay area. With the university, CIL is the most important aspect of the Berkeley image. At some point in his or her life in Berkeley, every disabled person enters the CIL, and at almost every point each one benefits by the presence of this organization in the city. For example, when the city of Berkeley and the university began programs to make the town and campus environments more accessible, much of the political impetus and knowledge for doing so stemmed from CIL's activities.

What is significant is that these social and environmental changes and movements have been brought about by the physically disabled population itself expressing its own needs. That disabled people have effected such changes, not just in their own lives but in society at large, is impressive. It forces one to speculate on the changes that other physically disabled people, who for whatever reasons live institutionalized lives, might effect on their environments if given some model for doing so.

The authors believe that *mainstreaming*—a term commonly interpreted to mean that disabled people should have opportunities similar to those of the nondisabled—has a broader meaning than just noninstitutional living. In fact a significant insight gained from writing this book is that our perception of mainstreaming has changed. We now perceive that mainstreaming can be as much a state of mind as a way of acting in the world, and it may, under the right conditions, be carried out anywhere. Of the disabled informants who made this book possible, all had some history of institutional care before coming to Berkeley. They believe that disabled people who require long-term care in residential facilities can also mainstream, though they feel that the impetus to do so may have to come from the institution itself.

Long-term care facilities are not exactly known for their social and political programs. In fact, they seem to be devoted to only one purpose: maintaining biological life. And in this society, which places great emphasis on social and political involvement and productivity as aspects of the whole life, biological care is indeed a reductive program. To focus only on the maintenance of physical health is too narrow a program for the development and sustenance of human potential. So that those who are institutionalized can mainstream, the institution must have the avowed purpose of keeping its residents in the world: the capability for productivity must be enhanced by real programs related to the marketplace (not reduced to arts and crafts); and interest in the affairs of society must be operationalized by allowing the residents to take part in these affairs (not reduced to voyeurism via television sets). The requirement for mainstreaming is that people be truly in the world, spiritually and mentally, even though they may not be on the street or entirely on their own. No matter what an institutional program is, if it does not have this avowed purpose and the means of implementing it, it becomes nothing more than a warehouse. And it is largely for this reason that all the disabled people who contributed to this book have rejected institutional life.

In certain cases, by choosing to mainstream informants also rejected homecare by relatives. But that choice was not based so uniformly on the same jaundiced view as that of institutional life. While living at home, a disabled person is not necessarily a shut-in; there is always the potential for mainstreaming if the caring can accept such a role for their disabled relative. Effort needs to be directed toward the maintenance of social and political ties with the outside world that parallel those of the family itself. However, it is important to recognize that mainstreaming works both ways: both parties—those cared for and those caring—must continually look outside their immediate environment for interests and relationships. Families often keep their disabled relatives at home at great financial and emotional cost, but this kind of heroism is only acceptable when it does not disable the caring

themselves. When caring for the physical well-being of the disabled person becomes an exclusive pursuit, then the act of caring can become a damaging sacrifice that may prevent any of the people involved from mainstreaming. In many instances the informants chose to leave home—to mainstream—so as not to jeopardize their family's potential for mainstreaming as well.

The Interactionist Position

The research orientation that provided the theoretical and practical framework for this book is the stance in the social sciences that is called *interactionism*.[1] What is most applicable in interactionism is that the individual is regarded as an active agent, determining the nature of his or her world by giving meaning to it through his or her interactions with it. Interactionism is a commitment to seeing and accepting meaning in the physical environment in terms of the ongoing dialogues and acts of human beings.

The interactionist position is synonymous with an empathic commitment to understanding another person. Interactionism is not observing; it is being with. An important aspect of the stance is that through empathy one conveys that one values the other person and his or her world. As Carl Rogers has said, "It is impossible accurately to sense the perceptual world of another person unless you value that person and his world—unless you in some sense care."[2]

The research strategy for this book has been mainly a form of the psychosocial interview; we talked with disabled people and have been present in their world without using a prescribed formula to interpret it. A portion of the material was obtained by participants who were physically disabled. However, we chose to collect most of the data as able-bodied individuals and not by posing as disabled people. Role playing would have been a limiting experience; and those who are physically disabled do not confine their activities to events or situations with others who are disabled. In view of the aim—to disclose the meaning of the physical environment to its inhabitants—the researcher's relationship to the world into which he is looking should be one of *empathic presence.* If the researcher is genuinely concerned about the lived experience of disabled people and honestly respects it, then his or her picture of that world will be very close to the world as it is experienced by disabled people.

From among the many disabled people interviewed, seven were singled out who were designated the *key informants*.[3] Part 2, Profiles, is devoted to these people. The selection of the key informants was an instrumental step in uncovering environmental needs that have implications for proposed and planned environments for the physically disabled population. For, as with any other population, disabled people who use wheelchairs do not share the same personality. Nor are they a group or a gang with corresponding traits and characteristics. Some are determined, some are not, and others represent all the stages between the two extremes. The key informants had to be those whose acts and biographies revealed active wants and the accomplishment or the state of accomplishing personal goals. They pointed the way by their adeptness in identifying, constructing, and using meaning in their environment.

From the seven profiles and many other encounters with the disabled community and the community at large comes Part 3, Networks. This section recognizes the more formal networks, principally those of government and private agencies, which provide disabled people with social services, but it focuses on the other contacts that assist or contribute to the social life of disabled people. These contacts are most evident in grassroots organizations initiated and maintained by disabled people themselves. When viewed as a network, these indigenous organizations and their linkages are the context in which Berkeley is distinguished by disabled people from any other place.

In Part 4, Places, the environmental supports necessary for living independently are reported. Environmentally, this is the most significant section.

Disabled people historically have been subject to environmental deprivation. Physically and socially, they have been confined to a limited number of settings. In Berkeley disabled people are expanding their horizons, introducing new environments as well as changing old ones for new needs. This section is organized according to the framework of archetypal places developed by Mayer Spivack, who has proposed thirteen places that he feels must be accessible for one to lead an optimal life.[4] This schema has been employed not only to organize the data but also for purposes of comparison, so that disabled people can be seen in relation to an optimal human schema.

In Part 5, How to Research, we pose some questions to ourselves as designers: beyond taking a position, what can we tell other designers who wish to design environments that are truly barrier free? What tools and methods are available for understanding those who are different from ourselves, so as to proceed with that understanding in our professional work? In Part 5 four ways of gaining an awareness of the environmental needs of others unlike ourselves are described, using physically disabled people as a case in point. We discuss techniques and methods for gaining an awareness which we feel comfortable with and which we have used in our professional work and teaching.

The Epilogue contains a few essential thoughts that came to mind only after the study was completed. Finally, a photographic Catalogue gives some clues about how simple it is to alter the environment to make it work if time is taken to observe how people do it for themselves.

Part 2
Profiles

The life story of each disabled individual is unique; each faces different problems and has made slightly different adjustments with the able-bodied community in order to find a personally satisfying life. It is not possible to draw conclusions about this population as a whole from the profiles of a few individuals. However, it is much easier to understand the cumulative effects of varied situations, the development of attitudes and beliefs over time, and the intensity of feeling for the psychological and physical environment if selected individuals are profiled and their responses to the social and physical environment are seen in the context of each life history. The seven key informants give this depth to the analysis.

In addition, the profiles of key informants serve two other, important purposes. First, they provide a sense of human reality and human continuity. Statistical data, case studies as anonymous examples that fulfill theoretical assumptions, or laboratory tests set a distance between us and disabled people. This distance, from a humanist position, cannot be bridged. Such information separates *us* from *them*. Second, the profiles eliminate many of the mysteries of being disabled. However brief, they let us see whole human beings in the world, acting in and determining that world. We see more than the disability or the wheelchair. There is a person behind the disability and in the wheelchair whose presence can be blurred or forgotten if we focus on attributes that separate us from him or her.

The subjects of the profiles were selected for a variety of reasons. One is that they all share a number of experiences and characteristics. Each is severely physically disabled and confined to a wheelchair with limited use of arms and legs. Each came to Berkeley from another environment, aware that this community offered them supports and opportunities available in few other places. They are all active, verbal people who have come to grips with their disability and who have and are continuing to define a place for themselves in the world. Living independently, controlling their own surroundings, and defining their own values are important to them. What is equally important is that they are actively pursuing and accomplishing what they value. Although the threads of their lives differ, the directions are similar to and typical of the lives of the hundreds of others who were also interviewed.

These individuals, as a group, are representative of the young, severely physically disabled population in Berkeley. The several students in the profiles and their relative youthfulness are typical. Men do outnumber women; those confined to wheelchairs are more numerous. Because Berkeley is a community in which many appear to freely try on alternative lifestyles to find what is most personally rewarding, it is a natural setting for those who are actively engaged in altering and changing their lives, which is typical of the disabled people who have come to Berkeley.

Each profile, however, is that of a selected individual. Their differences are important too. Each individual has had to face a unique set of circumstances, and each has had to develop a satisfying personal life. To do this, each had to persist in exerting the determination to make a world. Their stories are also told in the hope that others, even those who are not physically disabled, will find useful models among them. The seven subjects are

Peter Trier, disabled since birth, is a doctoral candidate in philosophy who has become actively involved in the physically disabled rights movement. His experience in Berkeley has broadened his interests and given him confidence in the possibility of stimulating real change.

Mary Ann Hiserman has been disabled since childhood; she grew up in a very protective environment, as many disabled women do, and overcame both her own and her parents' reservations in order to come to Berkeley. Mary Ann is now a graduate student in architecture, with a special interest in the environments of disabled people.

John McLaughlin has had hemophilia since birth, but did not know it until he had the accident which confined him to a wheelchair when he was a teenager. As a peer counselor to the disabled, he uses his personal experiences in conjunction with his training in psychology to help others make satisfactory adjustments in their lives.

Peter Trier.

Gary Peterson is both confined to a wheelchair and blind. He has developed ways to cope with both disabilities and work toward a career goal that is uniquely suited to his interests.

Lennis Jones is a traumatic quadriplegic with very limited functions. By skillful management of his environment and his attendants, Lennis attends school and leads an active life. He is extremely dependent upon his surroundings and approaches them innovatively.

Carmen Anderson is the disabled mother of three children. Since the accident that left her a quadriplegic, she has both managed a household and launched a career as a "disabled capitalist."

Tom Dempsey, also a quadriplegic as the result of an accident, is a novelist-journalist who has created an environment in which he can manage without the help of attendants. For him, independence implies not relying on others.

The seven individuals profiled here will be followed throughout the text. Their environments will be examined and their feelings presented. They are, however, only a very small percentage of the more than one hundred disabled individuals and their attendants who were interviewed and observed. The concepts presented and the experiences described were taken from this much larger group and discussed with other disabled people to assure that a wide variety of experiences and outlooks were considered.

Peter Trier

Peter Trier, twenty-six, has been disabled since birth with hereditary muscular atrophy. Although this disease is not progressive, the effects have become more pronounced with age because his weakened muscles have had to support an increasing load. At twenty-six, Peter does not expect to grow, and there is no further potential for muscular development, so his condition is stable. Peter has limited use of his arms. He can use a push chair in a very limited indoor area, but requires an electric chair for all other activity. He requires help in transferring (for example, from chair to toilet), getting in or out of bed, or changing position. Peter also requires a strap to remain erect in his chair while traveling. One of his early fears of living independently was that his head would fall to the side and he would be helpless. The strap does not entirely prevent this occurrence, but his fear of its likelihood has vanished.

Peter is a member of a traveling family. His father was in the navy and moved regularly throughout his early life. The effects of frequent moves on small children—changes of school, lack of parental knowledge and power in the school situation, no stable social group, no predictable future activities or associations—were even more pronounced on Peter, who was not in a position to overcome these disadvantages independently. He feels that he was overprotected by his parents, who were hesitant to let him leave a sheltered environment—a fear he grew to share.

During childhood, his home environment was very limited in order to unobtrusively regulate freedom and to offer greater security. Peter's parents tried to minimize the risks and frustrations in his immediate (controllable) surroundings; the effect was to enable him to lead a relatively normal existence within this shell. Parental expectations clustered around academic achievement, where Peter experienced no limitations. His success reinforced the apparent normalcy achieved in his limited surroundings. He was able to use the telephone, move about indoors in a hand-powered chair, converse, eat, and otherwise participate in family activities.

The freedom within the home also implied security. The carefully controlled environment tended to increase anxiety in noncontrolled settings outside the home. Peter feels now that both he and his parents overemphasized the risks. His approach to new or challenging situations was passive. Barriers were accepted as the natural state of things in the world outside, and because of his reluctance to impose on anyone, he was unlikely to seek help. As a result he lacked the knowledge or willingness with which to approach new situations; an excess of caution kept him at home or on familiar routes when unaided.

The absence of either accessible public transportation or an available source of attendants as he grew up led to continued dependence on his parents to meet his needs for outside activity and contact. Consequently, he either gave up the things he wanted to do or did them less often than he would have liked.

In his early years Peter was never part of a regular social group. The first two schools he attended were specifically for disabled children; when they no longer offered him a satisfactory education, he attended a regular school. His first school in St. Louis was "all right." While limited to disabled students, it did offer some learning opportunities. The next school, however, just gave up. The physically disabled children were grouped with students who were retarded or had learning disabilities. The role of the teacher was simply to babysit. It took a personal appeal by his father to the school board to enroll Peter in a public school where he could learn at a normal pace. Environmental barriers and inadequate staffing for the special needs of disabled students were the reasons given to his parents for keeping Peter out of a "normal" classroom. In his case, the problems were solved by the assistance of his mother.

In Peter's early school years, his mother did everything that made it possible for him to be in school. She drove him to school every day as there was no transportation, then carried him up the steps into the school, placed him in a seat, arranged all his materials, located reference materials and library books, and otherwise assisted. The school environment provided no support for his needs, and few were met by his hand-powered chair since he lacked the strength to move it more than a few feet. Peter learned at an early age that to succeed in the academic goals set by his parents and himself would require extensive dependence on others to meet his physical needs.

Peter's decision to leave home and seek a more independent lifestyle was tied to his desire to continue his education. He had received an undergraduate degree in philosophy from the University of Arizona while living at home. His parents always encouraged him in academic pursuits, and going away to graduate school was a logical extension of his education. Anticipating that his parents would find this break hard to accept, Peter made elaborate plans with his brother long before he revealed his intentions to his parents.

His approach was to describe going away to graduate school as one of many possibilities under consideration. He wrote to several schools, investigated many programs, and selected the University of California at Berkeley based on the program available at Cowell Hospital and on the educational options. Having made this choice, he drew up extensive lists of everything that could possibly go wrong: he could not find an attendant, he would not be able to get into the buildings his classes were held in, his head would fall to the side in an out-of-the-way place and he could not get help, he would not be able to get to places to complete assignments. Peter then made a visit to Berkeley with his parents. List in hand, they investigated all the foreseeable risks. The major problems Peter anticipated were environmental (barriers, hazards, absence of transportation) and social (how to meet specific needs in

a community unknown to him). The Cowell residence program provided an excellent temporary answer to all these issues. He could live in and operate out of a protected environment with no more risks than he faced at home, while simultaneously investigating the best way to seek a still more independent life in the larger community.

For Peter, the semisheltered environment at Cowell was important for two reasons. First, it allowed him to leave home, assuring his parents that he would be cared for as long as necessary. Second, it gave him a sheltered situation in which to overcome his dependency on his home environment and find new role models for an independent life.

Peter sees the Cowell program as having been rehabilitative in a very limited sense. It essentially placed disabled individuals in contact with one another and provided a place to stay while "you got your act together." The important lesson that it taught him was "If I couldn't do it, it was due to my hang-ups and not to my disability." Having disabled friends whom he cared for and respected increased his self-respect. He could not devalue himself because of his disability if he valued others with similar limitations.

Peter is now a doctoral candidate in philosophy; he has completed his qualifying examinations and is writing his dissertation on Spinoza. He is well-suited to the academic life and is considering a career as a teacher at the university level. Yet the major benefit from his years of education is independence and a commitment to work actively for disabled rights.

Peter is extremely articulate and presents himself well in public. As a result, he has become a spokesperson for groups seeking disabled rights and has become friendly with a wide assortment of people. His participation in the 1977 sit-in at the San Francisco Department of Health, Education, and Welfare (HEW) office to demand passage of the Rehabilitation Act of 1973 was the culmination of an increasing awareness of and involvement in the movement. For him, it was a beautiful experience characterized by shared emotions and loving concern; the depth of commitment of a group who were willing to take serious risks with their health and well-being for the sake of a shared belief moved him profoundly. It created a closeness with others that Peter had not previously experienced. The signing of federal regulation 504 was a victory, but for Peter only a small part of a continuing battle.

In his personal life as well as in his public involvements, Peter is actively seeking to increase awareness and acceptance of disabled people as valued members of society. He stresses the potentially liberating aspects of disability. "When you are disabled you just don't have time for all the false values, the materialism, the 'modesty.' You have to define your values and devote your energy to the things that are important." This philosophy is evident in his way of life.

Peter has chosen to be very direct about his disability. His environment reflects all his special needs, and he makes no effort to disguise special equipment. He has fully accepted his disability, it is part of the only self he knows, and he expects his friends will accept him with whatever supportive devices he requires. He distinguishes between "friends" who come to his home, understand his limitations, and offer assistance when needed and "acquaintances" whom he meets in the world outside and with whom he maintains a fairly normal posture to avoid embarrassment. The boundary between the two types of relationships is a difficult one for Peter (and many other disabled people) to cross. It is built, at least partially, of ignorance and embarrassment. Able-bodied people may find Peter interesting and wish to pursue the friendship, but are uncomfortable with questions they are too polite to ask and are unsure of what limits might be necessary. Peter may wish to pursue the relationship, but does not want to place anyone in an awkward position of having to assist and may be embarrassed at the need to seek help. With people who are familiar with disability, these barriers do not exist.

Peter's home is a first-floor, two-bedroom apartment shared with a disabled fellow student. It is located within a few blocks of campus and is close to a neighborhood shopping center that provides most supplies and services. The unit itself is easily accessible as there are no steps from the street. The entry door is generally propped open. The door into the apartment itself is also usually ajar, but is rigged with lengths of cord and a lever handle to facilitate operating it when closed.

The interior of the apartment is "Berkeley standard": a tiny, inaccessible kitchen with a dining area at one end, a medium-size living room looking onto a planted courtyard, two bedrooms, and a bath down a rather narrow hall and through doorways obstructed by closets. There are few pieces of regular furniture in the apartment; a dining table and two rickety straight chairs in the dining area are used by attendants. The table is too low for either Peter or his roommate to use comfortably. The living area originally contained only three out-of-service wheelchairs for various purposes and a high, hospital-type table at which his roommate works, along with overflowing bookshelves. Recently a couch was added, which is often occupied by lounging attendants. The bathroom is not directly used by either person and is carefully arranged with the various items their attendants must find available for expedient care.

The rooms with character are the sleeping spaces of both occupants. The most interesting is Peter's. It is a space about 10 by 12 feet (3 by 3.6 meters). The hospital-type bed dominates the space, along with the high-back custom-made power chair arranged alongside. When lying in bed, where he may spend several days a week recuperating or getting his strength Peter faces the door and sees everyone who enters. If he turns his head to the right, he has a full view of the street through floor-to-ceiling sliding glass doors. This is a good arrangement as there is less of a feeling of isolation during the day when he is alone.

The space, which has no particular character as an architectural design, has been embellished with an array of posters, prints, and drawings. Many of these are over-life-size posters of favorite personages—Paul Goodman, Einstein, Thoreau, Socrates, Christopher Isherwood, Bertrand Russell, Murray Rothbard, and two basketball players. There is also a painting of Peter by a friend and drawings by various children. The impact is personal and lively. The portion of Peter's room not filled by the bed is occupied by piles of books and papers, references, and portions of work in progress that he keeps easily visible so that he can direct attendants who place current materials within reach. Peter's life and his apartment in Berkeley have been carefully tailored to meet his needs.

When Peter now makes visits to his parent's home, many of the situations that existed as he grew up are still in effect. Peter's mother is very reluctant to permit him to have attendants or use outside help when he is in her home; she is insulted at the implication that she cannot provide for his needs. Realistically, as she ages, it becomes increasingly difficult for her to lift and otherwise assist him. It is also true that his needs and expectations have changed. The relatively independent life he is able to lead in Berkeley is based on a support system of attendants, drivers, friends, and roommates who meet his regular needs. Peter also has an extensive list of helpers for special needs or emergencies. All the people forming this service network are paid in some sense and always have the option of refusing a job they do not want. The arrangement is clearly reciprocal, whether as an exchange of funds or services, and Peter is able to use the system with no residual guilt or obligation. This is not true when his mother is meeting most of his needs. When Peter is home, therefore, he spends a great deal of time in bed reading and sleeping. "It's fine for two or three weeks. I usually need a vacation after Berkeley, but I could never live like that again."

Peter's life since coming to Berkeley has been constantly changing and evolving. "I've had four roommates and I'm now moving into a house with some able-bodied people for the first time. I've had more than sixty attendants and I'll be living in my third place. I've gradually become involved in several disabled rights groups, both locally and state-wide. I've become a vegetarian and my hair has gotten longer. I'm well on my way to a doctorate. What I expect is a future of continuing change and growth."

Mary Ann Hiserman

Mary Ann Hiserman is thirty years old. She was born in Salinas, California. Until five years ago, when she came to Berkeley as an undergraduate student, she had lived with her parents. Mary Ann is confined to a wheelchair. At four years of age she contracted arthritis, and at six years of age she contracted polio. In many ways her disability stems from having had these illnesses in childhood. Their effects marked her physical development. She has partial use of her arms and hands and can walk with braces, but with great difficulty. She prefers to use her power wheelchair both in and outside the home. With some assistance she can transfer between her chair and a full-sized automobile. This gives her a certain mobility that more-severely disabled people do not have.

Mary Ann is entering her second year of the three-year professional degree program in architecture. She lives off campus with a female friend, who is also disabled. Mary Ann has a part-time volunteer job with the Berkeley Housing Office. She also does volunteer work in the disabled community and works on the university campus in disabled affairs. She has no difficulty in fulfilling these many commitments, moving freely with the aid of a power chair to school, job, and meetings around city and campus.

Mary Ann has been in Berkeley for almost five years. During this period her self-awareness and the development of her potential for an independent life have been most remarkable. Until Mary Ann was twenty-two, she had not left the company of her parents, especially that of her mother, who served as her only attendant every day of Mary Ann's life. The overprotectiveness of her home environment led Mary Ann to see herself as severely disabled because she could not develop the ability to look after herself. Today she speaks somewhat resentfully of that period. "Parents have a lot to do with encouraging or discouraging independence in their disabled child. I was not allowed to be independent. My mother went with me wherever I went, even to school and back. And so I grew to need her for everything: to take me places, buy things for me, wash my face."

At twenty-two Mary Ann felt strongly that she wanted to live under other circumstances, even though she was fully aware of her need for the kind of security that home and parents provided. She spent three months at Rancho Los Amigos in Downey, California, a well-known rehabilitation center 350 miles (563 kilometers) from her home. The purpose of being there was to train for a more independent life. Nevertheless she reported, "When I returned home none of my training was of any use. Nothing at home was as accessible as it was at Rancho." She found herself in the same situation she had left. A year later, Mary Ann made a second trip to the center, this time ostensibly to find out about corrective surgery on her elbows. Actually, she was more interested in finding a way to leave home. She remained only two weeks; it was determined that surgery was not practical. Again, she returned to Salinas.

Looking back, Mary Ann feels that two important things occurred while at Rancho Los Amigos. It was the first time she met other disabled people her own age and "had a good time" with them. This was helpful in modifying her fear and disdain of other disabled individuals. Also on the second trip, she learned of the program at the University of California at Berkeley that brought disabled students to the campus. She resolved to join it herself. With the help of interested neighbors at home, she persuaded her parents that she should go. In the spring of 1972, Mary Ann entered the Cowell program. She was then twenty-five years old.

The first few weeks were emotionally difficult for Mary Ann, and though she was soon to adjust, the process of adjusting told her much about herself. At that time "my mental outlook toward independence was pure fright. When I lived at home with my

parents, my mother instilled in me a fear of being alone. When my parents went out or my father was at work and my mother had just gone to the corner store, I had to have someone babysit me. Even when I was twenty-four years old! She would leave me with a neighbor child, four or five years old. I would have to fight her sometimes to let me stay alone for five minutes."

When Mary Ann entered the program, she was the only woman of eleven students living in the program's residence, which was situated on the fourth floor of the student health services building. The setting was reassuring for her. "I probably never would have left home if I'd thought that the Cowell program was anything but a medical program. I wouldn't have felt secure." However, her fear of being alone remained. "I didn't even want to go to classes by myself. I didn't know why I was afraid to be alone, but I was!"

The first week she didn't go out on campus. But within a short time, she made friends with others in the program; friends introduced her to their friends, and as her circle of acquaintances expanded, so did her social and spatial mobility. "Once in Berkeley I had my first truly ongoing contact with other disabled people my own age. I had my first relationships with men. I learned from others and was encouraged to help myself do things."

It was through role models and not through counseling that she and others she knows were eventually able to use their own potential for development of independent lifestyles. "If someone, at that point, had tried to offer me any kind of counseling, I would have freaked out and refused. There are those who want counseling for the attention it gets them, but it never really helps them. You can't talk a disabled child or adult into moving away from home or out of his rest home or hospital before he is ready. Some will succeed in leaving, but they have to be ready themselves. It took me twenty-five years and my friends Gwinn, twenty-seven years, and Alice, twenty-five years, to get up the courage to get out."

After a year and a half in the Cowell residence facility, Mary Ann and a disabled male friend, Lennis Jones (another key informant; see pages 37–40), whom she had met there, took an apartment off campus. Two weeks before she and Lennis were to leave, Mary Ann says she suddenly became aware of how little she could actually do for herself, such as using the toilet during the night, which required

Mary Ann Hiserman.

getting herself out of bed, turning her bedlight on and off, or getting a drink of water for herself. "When I lived at home I had no adaptive aids to help me do things for myself. When I went down to the rehabilitation center I was trained in the use of a raised toilet seat, a bathtub bench, and sticks with hooks on them to help me reach things and pick things up. But when I went home, I was not encouraged to use them. Most of them sat around until I moved to Berkeley."

There were people in the community who had similar needs and who were acquainted with Mary Ann and Lennis. Mary Ann went to them for advice and prepared to move. She and Lennis moved six blocks from the campus into a ground-floor apartment. They took with them the attendants they had engaged while living in the Cowell residence. A memorable experience was waking during the night to find the apartment being burglarized. It was Mary Ann's initiation into one of the meaner realities of independent life. She and Lennis quickly investigated how this had taken place and then took precautions so that it would not happen again.

A year and a half later, marking three years in Berkeley, Mary Ann moved again, this time into an apartment with a woman roommate, also physically disabled. Now, three years later, she is still there. "My apartment is now adapted, though not totally. As I think of how to do things, a new adaptation is added. I can use my stereo, get into my front door, close my door, use the telephone, get water at night, answer the phone at night, turn lights off and on, and so on. These things can all be done with the aid of adaptations. But I also want my apartment to look nice, and not necessarily be in the same building with other disabled people. I like to associate with other people besides the disabled."

Mary Ann's apartment is frequented by others every day. Together, she and her roommate Linda have nine to ten different attendants who come in to help weekly. Linda has a close friend, Ann, who lives part time in the apartment. Both Mary Ann and Linda have friends who come to meals, to spend the night, or to crash for several weeks running. To one familiar with student life, this apartment hardly seems different from any other on the periphery of the campus; but there are important differences. It is a setting in which two disabled women with limited mobility can meet others whose apartments are likely to be inaccessible. Here, a range of social interactions from which they would otherwise be excluded are available to them. Mary Ann's daily routine must be geared to the scheduled comings and goings of at least three different attendants. This places her at home with a certain regularity of which friends and acquaintances can take advantage. They come to visit Mary Ann or to avail themselves of her hospitality even when she is not at home. The same is true of the social activity that centers around Linda. Their apartment is, in a sense, a crossroads with both women at its center.

Of importance is the role played by their attendants, each of whom enters the apartment for a period of an hour or two, three to five times a week. Then each fans out into the community, entering into a second or even a third household in the same day. Their contacts with other disabled people and other attendants make them an invaluable source of information and contact beyond what would be possible for either one of the women. Mary Ann, for example, finds she solves many of her small problems by consulting with her own or Linda's attendants, who very likely have seen a similar problem elsewhere in the community.

Mary Ann's relationship with her attendants seems typical of the disabled person who has lived in Berkeley for several years and who "knows the ropes." She, like the others, has come to have definite opinions about what makes a good attendant. She is outspoken about not wanting attendants with formal medical training who typically appear dressed in white hospital clothes and call her a patient. "No one wants them. They make you feel like you're sick, really disabled. They remind you of hospitals and institutions." According to Mary Ann, those with a medical background enter into their work with a certain set of assumptions of what should and should not be done and of what they will and will not do as professionals. Mary Ann feels that this attitude objectifies the disabled person as a medical problem and limits the kind of social interaction with the attendant that might be desired by the disabled person. She likes to regard her attendants as possible friends. They spend time together inside and outside the apartment. Mary Ann feels that she can call on them in an emergency.

Currently, Mary Ann is very much involved as an architecture student. She is the first with her physical limitations to enter the program. After one year she has demonstrated that, though she might have to be assisted with some of the manual tasks, she reaches the same goal as everyone. She hopes, one day, to become self-supporting and to be able to give up her state and county financial benefits. At this time, like other disabled individuals in California, she is caught in the bind of losing benefits if outside income exceeds an amount permitted by the state and county. She feels this seriously jeopardizes her chances for on-the-job training while a student because employers "don't take me seriously when I offer to work for free." Besides, holding a regular job often requires additional expenses, because of her disability, that cannot be met without a salary.

Mary Ann is not sure what her future will offer when she finishes. It may include living in Berkeley, but not until after she has seen other places. She, like others who have benefited by living in Berkeley, speaks of its limitations and her own need to move on now that she feels she has accomplished something.

John McLaughlin

John McLaughlin, twenty-four years old, has hemophilia (factor nine deficiency). In childhood he had bleeding problems which, from time to time, caused temporary disability. Since his illness was not yet identified as hemophilia, he was urged to remain active, to "outgrow the problem." His intermittent experience with disability made him determined to be active and to overcome his "weakness." At age fifteen, 6 feet tall, and an avid tennis player, he had a severe hemorrhage that leaked blood into his spinal canal, leaving him paraplegic and confined to a wheelchair.

At the time of this life crisis, John lived in Glendale, California, with his parents, three brothers—now seventeen, eighteen, and twenty-one years old—and two sisters—now twelve and twenty-eight. His father, an air force officer, was frequently transferred, and the family went along. The experience of having to adjust over and over again to new environments and people is a factor of early life that John cites as important in his development of strong self-confidence. After his injury, which occurred while playing tennis, he left school but then returned to finish. He went on to the University of California at Los Angeles on a Merit Scholarship. He remained there for one year, but found it difficult to manage the multiplicity of problems that confronted him every day.

Leaving college, he remained in Los Angeles, moved in with a married couple, and went to work for the Salvation Army. When neither arrangement worked out, he reluctantly moved into a convales-

John McLaughlin.

cent home. While there, he was visited regularly by a young woman whom he had known in high school. Three months after he entered the convalescent home, she assisted John in moving out. She became his attendant and together they took an apartment. This first experiment in independent living was made possible through state and county benefits and the presence of his friend.

John was then nineteen years old, and pairing-up was an important step in his life. Previously, muscle spasms induced bleeding, which prevented him from having a sex life. During the nine months he lived with his friend, the hemorrhaging problem stabilized and John discovered he could have sexual relationships and that he was not asexual, which had been a major fear. This was a period of major expansion, during which he went to work part-time for a crisis-intervention switchboard in Los Angeles.

When this period ended, John and two male friends took a long camping trip, driving through the Pacific Northwest to investigate places where John might settle down and finish college. While in the Bay Area, he visited Stanford, where he felt he could not fit in, and Berkeley, where he felt he could.

> When I got to Sproul Plaza on the Berkeley campus, I knew this was it. I'd come from Glendale, a middle-class community where things were very tight and conservative. In Sproul Plaza I was turned on by all the color, everybody smiling. People came up to ask me about myself. I already felt comfortable so it was easy to respond. Everyone seemed to know one another. Later, in a restaurant, I tipped a waitress I found attractive and wrote her a note. She responded. It was small things like that, feeling much less self-conscious than ever before, being accepted, that I liked.

John was a student on the Berkeley campus for one year. He left, temporarily, to become a full-time crisis counselor at the Berkeley Free Clinic. It was in this role that his self-confidence in being a disabled person in society-at-large matured and vaulted him into an independent life. "Before I came to Berkeley I knew I had a career potential and now I've been able to realize it. But I was not too confident with my sexual potential. Work and sex are associated in the public mind with some 'ideal stereotype'—'the best sex comes from the best-looking people.' People see my kind least of all as an ideal member of society. It is only recently that I have come to see myself as an important person in society." Self-esteem developed while working at the Free Clinic with individuals "worse off" than he

felt himself to be. John's self-confidence led to a realization that his experience as a disabled person provided him with a perspective on life that could help form others' lives and that able-bodied people, too, could be disabled.

In this period John met Ed Roberts and John Hessler, two disabled men who were strongly connected with the rise and success of the disabled student movement in Berkeley. He cites these individuals and others as role models for being socially and politically effective in the community: "I was quite bitter about my disability when it occurred and the bitterness hung on. I still found that I wouldn't hang around anyone who was disabled. At Berkeley I came into contact with the Physically Disabled Students Program and with Ed and John. These disabled people seem to accept their disabilities." Subsequently, he went to work as a peer counselor at the Center for Independent Living.

As a peer counselor at CIL, John now serves as a sort of ombudsperson for his clients. He watches over them in their relationships with services at CIL (housing, attendant care, wheelchair repair, medical counseling) and in their confrontations with such government agencies as the Department of Vocational Rehabilitation and Alameda County Welfare.

> We [peer counselors] consider ourselves successful when our clients become a lot more independent than they were when they came to us. This may mean that they've learned to handle available transportation, or to get into school or into a job, or to do volunteer work. It may also mean having better sexual relationships, improved mental and physical health, an improved self-image, and motivation to do things for themselves.
>
> When a person goes through a traumatic injury or they've had a developmental disability and they've been institutionalized for a while, self-respect is taken away. That person doesn't feel he has any power. You're on your feet and then suddenly you're on your back and all these people are doing things for you and you're not sure why. Or you've been in an institution for twenty years because after you turned eight years old your parents couldn't handle all the work that it took just to keep you going. So you don't develop what most of us take for granted: power over your environment and the ability to control the direction of your life. Most people become fatalistic and very bitter. Some of our clients are still going through the grief of having lost the ability to walk or they are just beginning to recognize the anger stored up over the years from being shoved into a bedroom or into an institution. So we work through these things with the client and help him find that people out there can change in relation to him if he can change, that you

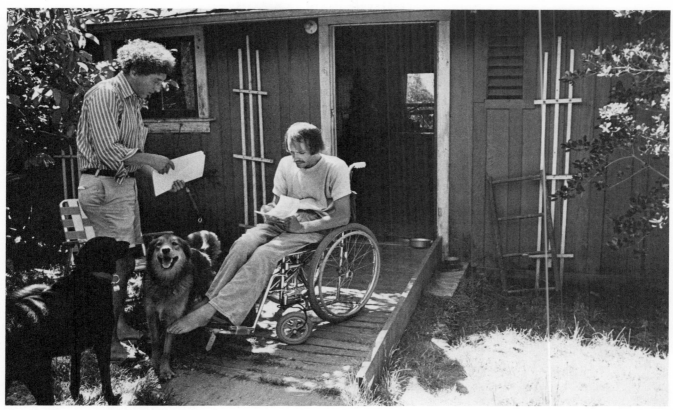

John McLaughlin and his cottage.

can notice how they change as you change.

Sometimes a person will come out of an institution and we'll help place him in an independent living situation and they get ripped off, pushed around, hooked up with the wrong people, have trouble training an attendant. You see, there's a predictable, naive phase at first, and all this stuff has to be worked through. It's all a matter of building up a lot of self-confidence, a lot of assertiveness. Just sticking with the client can help him realize his potential, can help him rediscover himself in a new light. But all the time you know he is combating a negative social process on the street: "You look different, you shouldn't be out here." "What are you doing out on the street?" "Let me help you with everything!" Or people stare at you when you go into a bar as if you have no reason to be there. But we say, "Stick to what you're doing," and pretty soon he finds that people change their attitudes toward him.

We got one guy who came from Bakersfield who had been stuck at home and had never gotten out. His mom didn't think he could. He had an electric wheelchair with a total distance of ten blocks! Now this guy's in Berkeley. He's getting around; he's living independently. Every time we talk he says, "Oh, I got to go here. I went there!" Now he's trying to get on the Board of Directors of the Regional Center for the East Bay. Suddenly, it's a whole new experience. For some others it's going to the grocery store and having people load their groceries up and take the money out of their wallet and put the change back in it and then send them home. That's where the lifestyle begins to change. Some who have never had a sexual experience with a woman, or with anybody else, will suddenly say, "I have a girl friend now and we went to bed and it was great!" It's hearing these kinds of things that keeps me in the business.

As part of his work at CIL, John runs a men's group that is a companion to a women's group. Delicate issues come up.

Like, in order for me to urinate I wear a legbag, and I have a catheter that comes out and goes into the legbag. If I'm on a date or whatever, the girl would say, "What the hell is that? Am I gonna get anything on me?" Of course I would be blown away, totally embarrassed by a scene like that. So we would try and deal with this in the group. The group tells people they have got to be open about themselves or else there can be no communication with anyone. A CP [cerebral palsied person] will say, "I can't keep the saliva from coming out of my mouth. How do I take care of that? When she feels saliva looks yukky, what am I supposed to say?" And I go, "Well, you say, 'I'll clean it off or you clean it off.' " In other words, counseling can help people become aware of their problems before they encounter them so that when they arise, they are not so problematic.

John, like other disabled people on government subsidies, is permitted to work and earn more than his benefits, keeping his subsidies for a trial period of eighteen months. The requirement is that he reinvest at least half of his earnings in ways that will make him more employable. But he does not foresee a time when he could earn enough money to live without government subsidies. "I have medical expenses that are very high due to blood costs, for example." He does foresee a time when he will move partially away from the disabled community in whatever work role he decides upon. He feels this will be necessary to keep a balanced view of society and for him to continue to develop as a well-rounded person.

John now lives in a small cottage behind a streetfront house in west Berkeley. The cottage is typical of many built as an extension of the main house, but is also conveniently located. It has a private garden facing south. John and his companion, a young woman who keeps house, acts as his attendant, and with whom he is emotionally involved, have modified the cottage and the garden to meet John's needs: access ramps, lowered countertops, an accessible shower and clothes closet, raised bins in the garden for planting vegetables. The cottage is a good setting for someone in a wheelchair because it is accessible and provides outdoor space.

Inside the cottage, one does not detect from the furnishings that a disabled person occupies the spaces. John says that he does not try to hide his disabilities, but he does not see any reason to confront others with them. "I appreciate the environment more when it's not obvious that I'm disabled. I don't feel particularly easy seeing others' medical equipment—their commode chair, for example. So I try to keep my medical aids out of the way." He speaks of the cottage and the modifications they have made as having a special meaning. "The modifications represent my ability to have control over my life. Making the modifications has added to my self-esteem. Putting in ramps which allow me to minimize my disability was an important act. When you're paralyzed, you lose control over one-half of your life—your body. In a similar way, I've come to gain control over my body by the foods I select to eat to keep my bowels regular. I've learned to identify with nature and to regulate my own systems through taking charge of my body and my house."

Gary Peterson

Gary Peterson is twenty-five years old. Blind and disabled with cerebral palsy since birth, Gary lived with his deaf twin brother, his partially deaf older brother (who is twenty-seven), and his parents for the better part of his life in a suburban community on the Peninsula near San Francisco before coming to Berkeley in October 1974. The type of independence Gary has found since moving to Berkeley is different from the type of independence he knew living at home with his parents. There, though his home was more physically accessible than his apartment at Berkeley, he felt isolated from the "real world" and hampered by notions handed down from counselors and schools that the most significant way to achieve independence was to learn to dress and to cook for himself. Since coming to Berkeley, however, Gary has gained freedom and support to explore emotional and career options. As his priorities have shifted, Gary has found that "It's a matter of do I want to do it [work] to prove that I don't have to be dependent on anybody, or do I want to eat, and nine times out of ten I want to eat."

Gary moved to Berkeley with Laird, a friend disabled by muscular dystrophy. Acting upon their decision to move to Berkeley was quite difficult because both Gary and Laird met with resistance from their respective families. For Gary, the decision came after he had left a local junior college, feeling that he was going nowhere. He then began to sense the insulation of the Peninsula community of Woodside. "I hated the whole area because I realized what I had been missing, and I realized how unthinking and unfeeling most of those people were."

As a child, Gary spent more time with his mother than with his father; he often refers to her as a very strong influence, positive and negative, in his life. Her objection to his move, which for the most part was silent, made an already difficult time even more trying. "The move was one of the hardest things I've ever done in my life, but it was one of the most challenging things too. I met with a lot of resistance from my parents, who had raised me to be as independent as I could be. I never really felt babied or sheltered, but when it came to 'Gary moving out on his own,' that was a heavy number."

Since both his parents worked, Gary spent a good deal of time alone in the house where he learned "how to make use of existing objects for other purposes, like grabbing onto a drawer to pull up to get something, or using the coffee table to lean on," and how to manage basic functions by himself. "The whole trip of just going to the toilet, for example—and the reason I elaborate on that is because like

Gary Peterson

most people who are disabled with parents at work, what was I going to do when I had to do a number?" Shortly after they moved to the house in Woodside, his parents did some remodeling to make the house more accessible for Gary. Thus leaving there to come to Berkeley was coming "from a place that was set up for me into sort of a more cramped environment, but I learned a lot about that too; I learned that despite everything you learn to get around. Sometimes I can't really tell you how I learned to do it, coming into an environment that a few years ago I wasn't even supposed to be able to live in because of what was physically involved." The trade-off of home environment for a more accessible social environment was a decision Gary has never regretted.

An attitude that pervaded much of Gary's youth was something that can be loosely termed "social acceptability: the determination on the part of school and, to a lesser degree, parents to teach me to be a good little crip, to appear as nondisabled as possible, and to effect the image of a studious, asexual, physically normal kid who happened to be sitting in a wheelchair." As a result, Gary had more than enough lessons in manners, in how to eat, and in controlling spasms, but none in ways of dealing with developing sexual feelings or emotions such as anger and frustration. Confused and curious about the physical and emotional feelings he experienced around women as he grew up, Gary was never given particular support or assurance that these feelings were normal or could be handled, often growing into gratifying relationships. As a result, he is still working on his emotional self. "A big problem when I was in school was that it was really important for me not to spasm in front of women because I had a certain image that I wanted to convey. And I would feel a spasm start coming. The spasm was sort of a whole other character who was, in effect, saying, 'I've got you right where I want you. I've got control over you.' And yet I knew that that didn't really matter. If a woman didn't like me because she saw a spasm, well, chances are that I wouldn't want to have anything to do with her anyway, but I still go through that."

Since coming to Berkeley, Gary has received support from friends, both men and women, with whom he has been able to discuss these feelings, and he is learning to accept such feelings as his personal and sexual self, "for example, just the idea that people have been turning me on to that it's okay to be angry, and that you can be angry without being destructive, and that anger is perfectly fine."

The recognition, acceptance, and understanding of these emotions has enabled Gary to become more effective and confident in various types of interactions in his life.

In their first apartment, Gary and Laird shared a live-in attendant. Having one attendant to put them both to bed was difficult for Gary. He sometimes required much less assistance than Laird and had to wait too long for a little help. Later, though he and Laird still shared attendants, each of them had an attendant whom they did not share. This enabled them to pursue different interests and to enjoy the independence that comes with privacy and flexibility. Since Laird's death, Gary has chosen to live alone. He enjoys the independence, the feeling of not having to answer to anyone, the freedom to plan his schedule as he chooses.

Gary considers his present apartment quite accessible, more accessible than the others he has lived in. He is able to wheel his nonelectric wheelchair around and has altered the kitchen and bathroom so that he can take care of necessities when he is alone. The shavings of paint and plaster on the floor at all the doorways attest to the fact that he exerts effort in living there. "I can remember times when I would use my head to help myself get out of a doorway if I had to put some extra push on the chair. When you're in a cramped environment, you learn to use everything you've got, and that can be anything from one extra finger that you didn't think you'd have to use to using your leg to kick something."

Gary makes no attempt to arrange his environment so that it looks as if he is not disabled. At the end of the hallway, there is a 90°-turn into the bathroom. The hallway also leads to his bedroom. The door of the bathroom has been removed to make sufficient room for his chair to negotiate the turn. Gary says the reduced privacy makes no difference to him; however, he has had one or two guests who were embarrassed by it. Elsewhere, the minimal amount of furniture is arranged so as not to hamper his freedom of movement. "The situation where I feel most independent is in my home. That's where I can be, say, 90 to 100 percent on my own and be sure I can take care of pretty much everything."

Being blind, Gary is in a pushchair rather than an electric chair. He has tried an electric wheelchair, but it was not particularly successful; instead, he speculates about the day when guide dogs will be trained to work with such chairs. As a result, he currently needs someone, usually a paid attendant, to push his chair every time he wants to venture out into the streets. This reduces his freedom to travel outside the home for unexpected events. "I guess where I feel most dependent is on the streets when I go out, when I have to have people push me, and in order to do that you have to trust whomever is pushing you, because they're the ones that are looking at the cars and the oncoming traffic and what not."

Gary describes himself as being a "media freak" since he was quite young. One reason for his decision to leave college was that he felt it was not the place to learn about his field. In spite of constant counseling to the contrary, Gary persisted in his desire to work in radio. He now has his own show, once a week, on KALX, the university radio station. He also does specials and some news work, such as covering the San Francisco HEW sit-in of 1977. His first attempts to work at the station were very discouraging for him. It was not until the station changed management that he was given a chance. "I put a lot of energy into my radio shows and I'm a perfectionist when it comes to that, and that's something that I really feel is valuable to me. It's something I really feel good about because I've broken a boundary, even though I have been discouraged an awful lot. I only wish that half the people who were telling me not to do it could see me doing it." The station is relatively accessible, and Gary can work some of the equipment alone. However, he is unable to plan and run an entire show alone. As a result, he has an attendant who works with him. The attendant assists him before the show in the library in choosing record selections and during the show by helping to run the equipment. Legally, however, Gary is responsible for anything that happens while the two of them are working.

In addition to the radio work, Gary has had experience in peer counseling, some of which he found quite discouraging because of what he felt were poor results. "There were a lot of people where I was peer counseling at that convalescent hospital who wanted to get out of there. But when it came down to really doing it, there was a lot of holding back. They had a lot of attachment to that place. If that's where people want to be, that's fine. I don't necessarily think it promotes growth or is all that healthy, but I guess what I'm saying is I know people who are happy there. For the life of me, I don't know how." Nevertheless, he feels that he has some aptitude in counseling and would consider returning to that type of work if it were possible for him to do it without returning to school.

Without doubt, radio is Gary's preferred option. He feels he is lucky to be doing as much in radio as he is now doing, and he is willing to take on other fields in order to support the time he spends in radio. "Right now I'm doing radio, and I'm not getting paid, and there's no chance I will get a paying job right now. I haven't ruled radio out as a paid career, but for now, I'm just dealing with what I have. I believe in things such as temporary options where maybe you do something else for a while until maybe you can see your way clear to explore. We, as disabled people, are just like any other minority."

Lennis Jones

Lennis Jones is thirty-two years old. He was born in Hayward, California, which is near Berkeley, but grew up in Corcoran, a small town farther south. He has one brother, twenty-four, and a sister, twenty-six. An older sister, with whom he was very close and who was supportive in his search for an independent life, died last year of cancer. Lennis was severely disabled at age eighteen in a diving accident; he is a quadriplegic. This year he completed his undergraduate education in psychology on the Berkeley campus. It took him seven years.

In childhood, at ages three, six, and eight, he suffered a mysterious ailment—something like arthritis—which partially crippled him for periods of time. At age eight, this disability lasted for a year and ended as mysteriously as it began. Regaining full mobility, Lennis matured into a healthy, active person. In high school he was athletic, playing both football and running track events. At seventeen, he injured his ankle by repeatedly knocking it against hurdles while practicing. As a result, he developed traumatic arthritis in his ankle. At eighteen, while swimming in a natural setting, he dove into uncharted waters and broke his neck when he struck underwater rocks. His injury was complicated by the prolonged period of time he was under water before being rescued.

The six years following the accident were spent between hospitals, rehabilitation centers, and his parents' home. During his first stay in a center, he was fitted with an electric wheelchair.

The controls were placed on my left side and I don't have wrist action there. So when I first returned home I was immobilized. When I was up, I used to just sit in the den of our house with a blanket over my head all day. I wanted to cut myself off. I had nothing whatsoever to do. My parents worked and I was alone most of the time. A high-school friend came in and assisted me, but no one in that town had any concept of what an attendant might do, no concept of electric wheelchairs. After about six

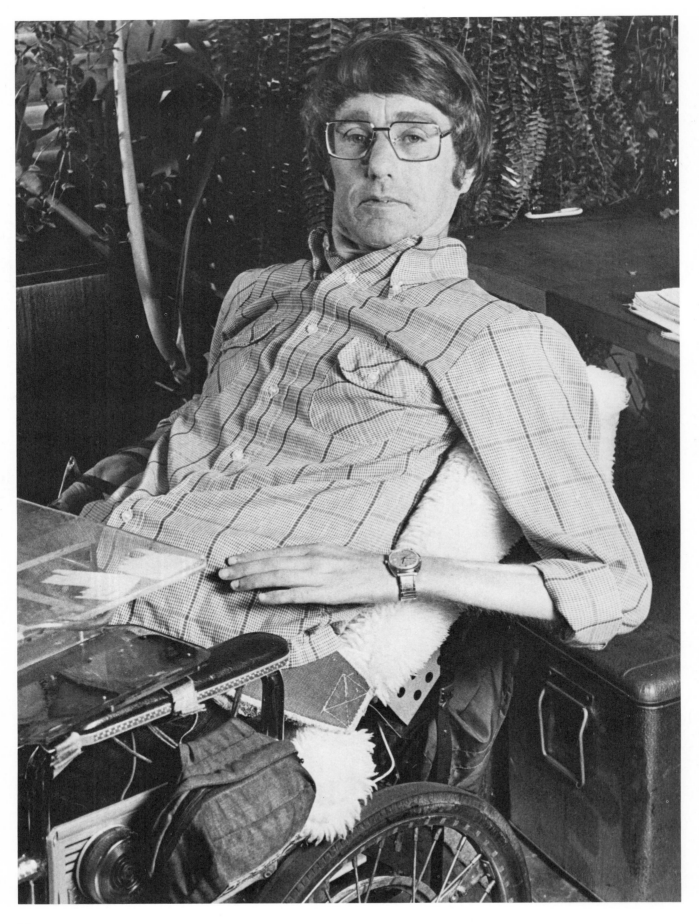

months at home I developed very bad bedsores and had to return to the hospital.

This situation continued for two to three years. Lennis was moved back and forth between home and institutions. "Then, it seems, everyone just gave up and I went into a rest home where I knew I'd probably spend the rest of my life. A year later I looked about the room I had been living in and realized that of the six people who occupied it when I first arrived, I was the only one who had not died. That's the kind of place it was. I was twenty-one at the time." His sister and he decided that Lennis should go back into an acute hospital to treat his bedsores and to have rehabilitative physical therapy.

> I had contractions in my arms like now, but the function was a lot less because I had hardly used them. I had probably not even been up in a wheelchair more than two or three times during the entire year. Actually, there was nothing to get up for. There was nothing I couldn't do in bed that could be done around that rest home.
> At the hospital my bedsores required skin grafts. A tendon transfer to improve the use of my arm was also attempted, but that failed. I was in that hospital for two years. It was there, however, that my life took a new turn. One morning the doctors came around as usual. I heard them commenting to various patients about their progress, but when they passed me they only said "Hi" and continued on. I realized suddenly that they had nothing to say to me because I was not exactly ill; I could not get any better. It was clear the hospital was another dead end and that I had to get out.
> With the help of my sister and a very reluctant social worker I was moved out, first into my sister's garage—the only part of her house that was accessible—and then into an apartment of my own. This was in Fresno. This first attempt at independent living lasted about a year. In Fresno County, welfare payments for attendant service are paid only for a live-in attendant. But there were none around who were really suited for the job. I had several. One was a little old lady, dressed in her whites, who sat all day by my bedside like a lump of vanilla pudding. Another was a disturbed young man who carried a sheath knife in his hip pocket and who used to pace up and down in my room. There was a couple in their midthirties who fought and argued continuously and finally moved out. It was during this year, while in the community hospital with a bedsore, that I picked up an article about the Cowell program for disabled students at the university. I decided to go and check it out.

Lennis came to live in the Cowell residence program in the summer of 1970. He was then twenty-

five years old. He asked a friend to drive him to Berkeley to look the situation over. He decided to remain. Someone at the Physically Disabled Students' Program office on campus put him up for a couple of days until space could be found for him at Cowell. He could not be admitted into the program immediately, but money was found to keep him there temporarily. Lennis started taking classes in the university, and by the winter quarter of 1971 he was officially admitted as a student into the university and into the Cowell program as well.

About a year later, when a group of the Cowell residents decided to move out, Lennis decided to move as well. "At that time there was no requirement as to how long you could stay, but we just got sick of living there and made plans to get into our own apartments and take our attendants with us. We had come to know one another pretty well and we broke up into pairs. Mary Ann and I took an apartment together." This move toward a more independent life cannot be credited, according to Lennis, to any single act or "awakening." On the contrary, he believes that the "mind-set" to live independently is slow to develop, built up by small increments of experience that increase one's confidence to take the step. This process of building self-confidence took place while living in the Cowell residence. The residents had developed among themselves a trust that allowed them to take the risk of moving out together.

> It worked out nicely moving into an apartment with Mary Ann. We each had several attendants, and as their schedules did not necessarily coincide, there were always people about. Yet, we got a sample of living alone as individuals.
> What was significant about that first year on our own was the things that didn't happen, like not getting sick and having no emergencies. It built our confidence. People tend to think too much in terms of dramatic events as clear-cut changing points. Maybe that's true with some things, but I think the most significant things are the small things as well as the things you might worry about that never happen.

Recently Lennis moved into another apartment. He lives alone and prefers it. The only modification he has made in each place is to replace door locks for more secure ones. Since he must rely on attendants for housework, cooking, and all personal needs, he is not particularly concerned with how accessible his entire apartment is. "If I ever get a home of my own I'll make it accessible. I'd like to have a shower and a balcony facing the sun. But these are hard to find in a Berkeley rental that is also accessible."

Lennis Jones.

His attendants play a major role in Lennis's life. He is especially attentive to their availability in Berkeley and appreciative of Alameda County's system for paying them, having struggled with these problems elsewhere. He believes the system here is best, permitting an individual to have complete control over his attendants, choosing the number one wishes to employ, deciding upon the means of their payment, with the privilege of self-determination. This places the disabled person in the role of employer.

Officials here have a much more realistic view of what we should be permitted to decide for ourselves. I think this has come about because of the early pioneering efforts of people like Ed Roberts, John Hessler, and Herb Willsmore. [These disabled men were among the first leaders in the disabled movement in Berkeley.] In Fresno County, where they insist that to have full welfare benefits you have to have a live-in attendant, they are simply making the work easier for themselves. The social worker has fewer forms to fill out. In Alameda County the social workers don't have to cover us so closely because the county doesn't see itself as our guardian. Maybe it's the existence of CIL that reinforces our image of living independently. They know that we have support services. But I think it's also because many of us are college graduates, and they know they can't con us into something or another. Anyone who has put up with a university bureaucracy for four years is already one step ahead.

In addition to studying psychology, Lennis is also active on campus in the affairs of disabled students, serving as a peer counselor and interviewing disabled individuals who would like to enter the university's program. Last year he also assisted in the preparation of the campus accessibility study, in which the buildings and grounds were surveyed by teams of able and disabled students. And he continues to serve on the campus committee that watches over the progress of the university in making the campus and its programs accessible. He has effectively assisted as a consultant in several architectural design studios in the College of Environmental Design for students engaged in design problems that focus on accessibility. More recently, he has taken on the role of leading an encounter group of those, like himself, who have been disabled for a number of years and who are seeking emotional maturity. Lennis's obvious qualifications for doing this are his own life, his work as a peer counselor, and his background in psychology, but he claims that his motivation is to help himself as much as it is to help others.

I think that for every year you spend in a hospital you mature emotionally only one month. In my case, in six years I probably matured only six months. When I left those hospitals I was twenty-five years old, but emotionally I was only nineteen or twenty. Now I'm trying to relate to people again, to recognize my sexual needs. I suppressed my interpersonal relationships while in the hospital and even while at school. My total energy was devoted to just survival and then to getting through school. Some people always concentrate on their "social needs" and never achieve an independent life because they haven't prepared themselves to take care of themselves. Relationships can become too much of a dependency situation, and this diminishes the potential for independent living. Now I have time and energy to become more considerate of my interpersonal life.

Lennis plans to enter a master's program in psychology, perhaps through CIL and Antioch College West. He hopes to become a counselor and thinks that when he does, he will leave Berkeley for some other place. Perhaps he will stay in the Bay Area. He says that Berkeley is becoming "too much of a 'crip' community, and though the support services here are great, it's up to us who have lived here and have had the Berkeley experience to move out and spread the word."

Carmen Anderson

Carmen Anderson, forty, became a quadriplegic in an automobile accident at the age of thirty-four. The accident, which took the life of her husband, left Carmen completely paralyzed below the shoulders and left her with only limited motion of her arms and hands. For Carmen, a woman of great spirit and beauty, the accident was both a tragedy and a turning point.

Carmen, born in New York City, was raised in Europe and Puerto Rico. Her family was wealthy and extensive; she and ten siblings spent their childhood in boarding schools and in the care of servants. Carmen was beautiful and always beautifully dressed. She became a model for high-fashion magazines and built up an extensive social life with her home as the center. At the time of her accident she was married, had three small children, and was living in Santa Fe, New Mexico. She also owned three import stores, one in Santa Fe, one in Guadalajara, and another in Puerto Vallarta, Mexico, with homes near each. The accident occurred

Carmen Anderson

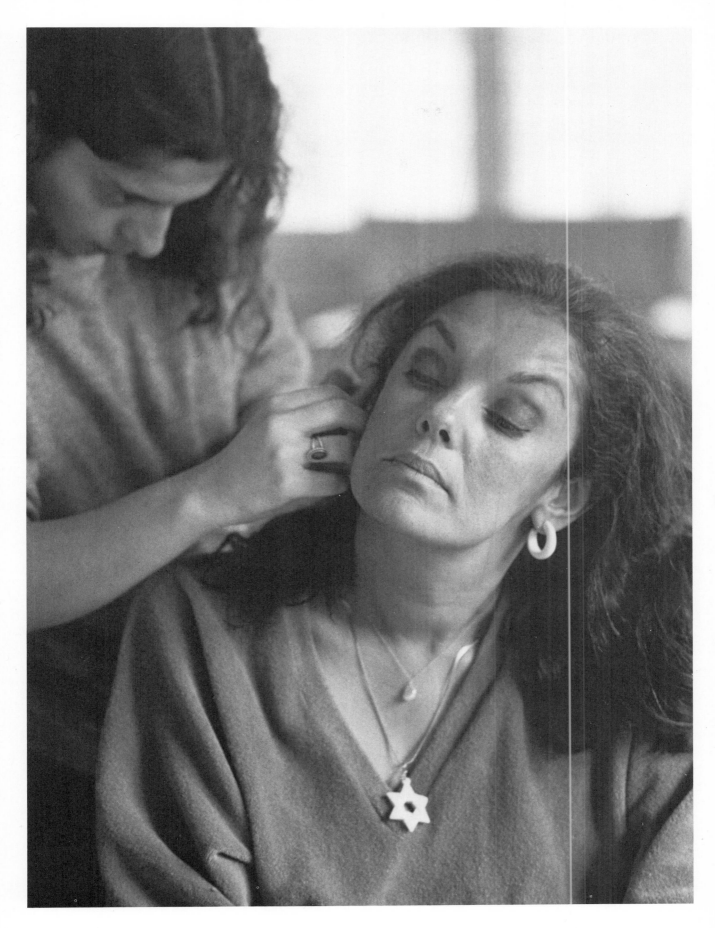

on a buying trip in Mexico, and her medical care and rehabilitation took place there.

For Carmen the rehabilitation experience offered a "survival kit in the emotional sense." Shortly after admission into the rehabilitation center she found herself sitting in bed, laughing at the absurdity of her situation. She was thinking, "Well, look at you, Carmen. You said you'd never be involved in any kind of mediocrity. Just how do you plan to rise above this one?" The approach to rehabilitation in Mexico was one of protection. She was cared for as she had been all her life. For a time she simply accepted the continued care, the fact of having everything done for her. Ultimately, however, she grasped at each chance for increased independence. The electric wheelchair offered her the first opportunity for privacy and self-directed exploration, and she grabbed it eagerly, spending her first day in the chair exploring the hospital on her own. Full realization of the extent of her disability and its effect on her life was delayed until her return to her home in Santa Fe. During rehabilitation she credited herself with no realistic sense of life: "It was as if I were caught in a time warp."

At home, Carmen became, again, the center of attention, a "queen crip" whose friends came to her for advice and guidance. She remained socially active and entertained regularly with the help of servants, but found it "very hard not to be looked at and admired." Her role changed from object of admiration to counselor-confidant for her old friends. In Santa Fe she was the only disabled person for miles around. The community was totally inaccessible and medically unprepared to deal with the problems of disability. Moreover, New Mexico offered little financial support. The expenses for medical care and attendants were high. It became apparent that she was not to continue as she had in the past.

Friends who had lived in Berkeley told her that it was "the world capital of crips," that it was ramped, activist, and supportive. While some friends warned her of dangers and felt that they needed her in New Mexico, others encouraged her to go and make a new life. Her mind made up, she packed her three children, a cook, a chauffeur, a secretary, and herself, and they all flew to Berkeley, staying at the Claremont Hotel for the first two months. Initially she was very uncomfortable in Berkeley. There were "too many cripples and chairs," and she was required to face it all too directly.

Her meetings over a period of years with "the pointer," a man with cerebral palsy who uses a pointed stick, attached to his headband, for all his manual functions (intellectually he is unimpaired, but he has no use of his hands or legs and his speech is impeded), illustrate Carmen's changing attitude. "At our first meeting, I was able-bodied and appalled. I ran away and was very obvious about avoiding him. After my disability, I met him again and I was still discriminating. His obvious spitting and his inability to talk offended my sense of aesthetics." After several meetings, however, she overcame her prejudices and began to appreciate his wisdom and skill in aiding others and in campaigning for fair treatment. Her change in attitude toward others with disabilities was paralleled by changes in her personal development. "I began to see myself in a real context, not as a queen crip. I had to match up to everyone else."

Carmen has moved in and out of the disabled community in the last two years. She is somewhat older than the majority of actively involved people, who are all in their twenties or early thirties, and lives a rather different lifestyle. She now owns a large home in a comfortable residential area of Berkeley. Her three children and tenants share her home with a continual flow of guests from her previous life. Currently, she is actively involved in establishing a small business, a bed and bath shop, and is interested in applying the holistic health movement to the needs of disabled people. "Now that there are so many of us here, we have to examine what there is medically. After gratitude comes an awareness that if there is this much, there should be more. The holistic medicine program was one attempt, but the only available money was for the aged. Another big problem was CIL; they are not prepared to take on a concept like this—too much administration." She feels more effective operating independently from the organized disabled community. She feels CIL functions well as an image but no longer sees it as a focus for her; she is working in her own direction.

Carmen has a strong desire to improve the lot of disabled people, which is expressed in a variety of ways. She opens her home for meetings of numerous groups working for various causes and entertains to support them. Carmen recognizes this need for an informal place to gather and talk, and her home functions as a salon for a group of both able-bodied and disabled individuals. She is planning a hot tub and massage area for her yard to supply noninstitutional bathing facilities for the disabled community. Carmen has always found strength in groups. When her friends experience difficulties, she offers them the same brand of support she has enjoyed. At times of need they share the home with Carmen's three children and an assortment of tenants.

Carmen's life in Berkeley is distinctive in two ways. First, as an older woman and the mother of three children, she is in a rather different position socially than the many young, single people who form the majority of the disabled community. Carmen's children are now seven, ten, and thirteen. As they grow up and become more independent, she is facing new problems of child care from a wheelchair. Dealing with a disagreement among the children prompted Carmen to say, "It was much easier when they were younger. At these ages it's really hard from a wheelchair or my bed. You hear someone yelling or an argument and you can't just go see what's going on. If you're talking to a child and he walks away, you can't bring him back. You can't count on attendants to react the same way you would. It just isn't easy."

Carmen's environment is tailored to permit her to be in visual contact with the children much of the time. From the two places she uses most often—the bed and the sun room adjoining the kitchen—she can see the backyard in which the children play. The interior of the house is open and voices carry from place to place, enabling her to "keep tabs" on all activities. The fact that Carmen is only one of several adults in the house (tenants, a live-in attendant, a housekeeper, and a disabled man all share the home) means that there is always supervision and that the children can find an adult to meet most needs.

The second aspect of Carmen's life which is distinctive is that she is among the first disabled people to start her own business. Still excited about being granted a Small Business Administration (SBA) loan to finance the opening of her bed and bath shop, Carmen said, "I've really pulled a coup. When I went in for the loan, they weren't faced with a crip with a piece of paper and a tin cup; they were faced with a person and a program that were totally together, and they came through." Carmen had both the experience and the connections to prepare a very carefully organized plan. She attended SBA seminars on "Women in Business," selected an available location, and investigated the market for her product. She planned renovation and decoration for the building, selected an inventory, and prepared all the legal materials with the help of a

Carmen Anderson and her boys: Rafael, Damian, Justin, and Jeremy.

business lawyer she met at the seminars. When her first application was turned down, she appealed, and the decision was reversed. She has now opened the shop. Carmen once stated her goal as "I want to become a capitalist model for the disabled community."

Carmen's home in the residential south campus area is the only house for two blocks that a person in a wheelchair can enter without assistance. The clues to its accessibility are visible, but not really apparent unless you look carefully. To the casual observer there is no evidence of differentness, which is just the appearance Carmen desires. The ramps are hidden in the backyard. Along the former driveway another ramp is fitted tightly between raised flower beds. A wheelchair has just room to roll between the low walls on either side—the ramp is steep, and this tight arrangement assures that the driver will not skid far if she loses control. The closeness also permits wheelchair gardening, since the plants are close and within easy reaching and smelling distance. Flower beds and vegetable gardens line the yard, which differs slightly from other gardens in Berkeley. Beds are raised and the vegetables are arranged along wide paths, which permit wheelchairs to enter all parts of the garden.

Inside the house, rooms are large and sunny; the walls are hung with bright and colorful Indian paintings and Mexican prints. The floors are polished hardwood. Only one large rug interferes with their expanse; more would pose problems for the wheelchairs that constantly move through the house. Although many people live in the house, it is rather sparingly furnished. There are no major rooms on the first floor that will not comfortably fit several wheelchairs. When the group is meeting outside the more typically furnished living room, the able-bodied visitor sits on the floor or the beds.

The second floor is a mystery to its owner who cannot reach it. Downstairs, the house is much as it was before it became accessible. The kitchen is older-home-hopeless: counters are high, drawers stick, cupboards are above the heads of all but the tallest, the stove is huge, old, and slightly unreliable. Carmen does not use it herself. The kitchen belongs, principally, to tenants and attendants. A second refrigerator in the center of the side room permits wheelchair access to food, but there is no workable arrangement for food preparation by disabled people. Eating takes place at a small, round table with two chairs or in people's rooms. Everyone eats independently, and snacks are more common than meals. The kitchen does adjoin a large

sun-porch and dining area with room for many to sit. On sunny days the whole group gathers there.

Carmen's first-floor room shows little evidence of disability. Her independence is based on the help of attendants and friends. The large wall calendar is filled. Each date shows several activities, written in a large variety of hands. The telephone sits on the bed or close beside it; its pushbutton connection to a special operator is a primary link to the world. Here there are no open closets or drawers; everything is neatly put away so the variety of attendants can locate things. The television—also linked to the bed by a pushbutton—serves as clock, entertainment, news source. One wall is lined with uncurtained windows. Open, they are another link to the world. Children, helpers, friends lean in the window to talk. Flowers bloom just outside. The telephone sits on the sill when Carmen does not occupy the bed—it serves the indoors and the out. Although this room is small, it is extremely busy. Carmen spends a great deal of time in bed, for long periods in the wheelchair are uncomfortable for her. Consequently, her friends come to her room, and she seems always available to whatever the world brings her.

Tom Dempsey

Tom Dempsey, thirty-two, has been a quadriplegic for thirteen years. He was injured at nineteen while "horsing around" with his fraternity brothers at a midwestern university. It was a freak accident; in a moment of vigorous camaraderie, he was jumped on and his neck was broken. This changed his life. Tom had been a high-school letterman and an excellent student. While he describes himself as a "country boy," his ambitions were to become an oceanographer, and he was preparing for this field with an undergraduate major in biological studies.

Although Tom's spinal lesion is only partial and he is a "strong quad," he has lost the small-muscle control and finger dexterity required for laboratory work. He does have considerable strength in his shoulders and upper arms and uses a push rather than an electric chair. Tom is extremely independent in the areas of personal care. He does not use attendants, managing his own care with dogged and sometimes exhausting determination. He does have help with major cleaning tasks, but though he eats out occasionally, he frequently cooks for himself. For the most part, he manages by being extremely

Tom Dempsey.

well organized and by advance planning so that he has appropriate equipment for whatever task is to be completed.

By utilizing both a slideboard and an overbed frame, Tom transfers in and out of bed without assistance. He drives a van equipped with hand controls and an electrically operated lift. Bathing and bladder and bowel care are also carefully arranged so that he can manage without aid. Tom is now a would-be novelist and freelance journalist who works in his room. With the aid of typing sticks and an electric typewriter he can produce thirty-five words per minute. A great deal of his research takes place over the telephone or by correspondence, but his van gives him the freedom to travel as needed.

To a casual observer, Tom appears to manage his complex life with relative ease. Less apparent is the amount of energy and time consumed by his daily tasks. Tom accomplishes a great deal by living within a well-regulated schedule. "Spontaneity is a thing of the past," and his energy is not limitless. An uphill push to buy groceries or meet a friend for dinner sometimes seems an enormous effort. Tom's relative independence is a source of amazement to some members of the disabled community. "When John (a paraplegic friend who traveled to Berkeley with Tom) and I came here, they didn't know what to do with us. We each had two or three degrees, we drove cars, we took care of ourselves. We didn't look very disabled. We were so strange that for a while there was a rumor that we were fakes—spies from HEW trying to find out what was going on at CIL." He feels that in Berkeley "there are all these people who need a lot of help, and the result is that everyone in a wheelchair is assumed to be helpless."

For Tom, self-care is natural and preferable. He thinks of himself as always having been fiercely independent. After going through a rehabilitation process that taught him to "live with an unfamiliar body" and having spent a year at home with his parents, he returned to college at a school with a program for disabled students. The focus of that program was on full independence, and Tom was one of the "most disabled" of the group. He was expected to manage without help and at first he did. But while Tom did a great deal for himself, the circumstances of his life effectively reduced the amount that he was required to do. Tom had married his high-school sweetheart before returning to college. Thus, he went from the full care of rehabilitation to parental care to marriage with a wife who assumed many of the domestic responsibilities. Tom feels now that both he and his wife contributed to a gradually increasing dependence—he because it made life easier, she because "the less I could do, the less I found out how dependent I was on her."

The marriage was successful for a time, but dependence and the disability took their toll. The changing directions of Tom's interests imposed an additional strain. After taking an undergraduate degree in philosophy, Tom received a master's in history and worked four years toward a doctorate. He taught at the college and was engaged in dissertation research but became increasingly disenchanted. His dissertation topic came to have greater appeal for his adviser than for himself. He was discovering, instead, an interest in writing. When his marriage suddenly ended, he dropped work in history and turned to relearning independent living.

After a difficult period of adjustment, Tom met and fell in love with a friend from his undergraduate days. Before long he was living with Lynn and her two children in a home that for two years was a romantic idyll. Tom had always enjoyed writing as an avocation. During this period he began to work seriously on two novels about disability and continued to write poetry as he had for years. He had considerable "true life experience" for his work and a real need to sort out his own feelings about the experience of disability. Writing, for him, is both therapeutic and rewarding. He is a skilled author whose images are powerful and moving; he hopes to influence attitudes toward disability with his work.

Journalism offered an opportunity for his writing to have an immediate impact. Tom feels that the experience of disability creates empathy with the wide range of people in pain and with those limited in any sphere of their existence. While he worked on his novels, he took courses in journalism. He now holds a master's in journalism and has published several pieces. Making a living as a freelance writer is still a far-off dream, but he is working in a field he likes. He is his own master.

The decision to come to Berkeley was made just prior to Tom's sad but necessary separation from Lynn. With no ties and a fresh degree in journalism, he was free to leave. As he says, Berkeley was the "gimp capital." He was soon on his way, driving across the country with a caravan of able-bodied and disabled friends who were also moving on. In Berkeley, he is finding his way, writing, making new friends and contacts, and living on his own for the first time in his life.

For Tom to be able to feel comfortable, operate at the level of independence he prefers, and write, he must have predictable and fairly permanent living arrangements. He first moved into an accessible motel that offered relatively little in the way of comfort or convenience. He immediately began to search for more-suitable living accommodations but found, as do most disabled apartment seekers, that the supply of acceptable apartments falls well below the demand. Housing referral services at CIL were helpful, but did not find him housing because of an overloaded market.

As he grew increasingly uncomfortable in the motel, Tom widened the range of living accommodations he was considering. He soon found a space in an apartment with another disabled man and moved in on a temporary basis. When this living arrangement ended, he found housing in a lovely old Berkeley home more suitable to his physical, emotional, and creative needs. The big, brown, shingle home looks like many others on the streets of Berkeley; the yard is a tangle of plants and flowers, overgrown but exuberant. The windows are large, open; one or two small panes are broken and covered with paper while they await repairs.

Tom rents a room on the first floor; when he located the house, it was basically inaccessible. In order to live there he spent $750 to have a ramp built and make other necessary accommodations. As in many Berkeley rooming houses, use of the kitchen and bathrooms is shared by all tenants. Before Tom moved in, the bathroom was totally inaccessible. Removal of the door made the room usable, but, as most bathrooms used by the disabled, it is only semiprivate, screened from the hall by a curtain.

The kitchen was not planned with a wheelchair in mind. Frustrated by the difficulty of cooking for himself, Tom says, "It couldn't be worse. The oven and broiler are too low. The kitchen sink has cabinets below it, which make it hard to use, the kitchen table provides no footroom for people in wheelchairs, there is no work surface at the right height. Moreover, things get put away out of my reach—a hazard of living with others."

The house, however, compensates for its physical inadequacies by offering a stimulating living environment.

This is a rooming house that exposes me to a constant flow of a wide variety of people. Some of them are vestigial remnants of Berkeley's hippie era—what remains of the flower children, maturing but not quite grownup, hippies gone to seed. There's a cross section of types: college students and older people, long-term residents who are neighbors and have become friends. The net result is a constant ebb and flow of various types of humanity through the place I live. Some have become friends and are supportive. Almost all are food for thought for a writer, suggesting further written explorations. Because they are a part of my house, they have become a part of my subject: the disabled existence.

Tom's room, by design, is quiet in atmosphere and decor. There is little visible evidence of disability. Tom says, "I try to keep everything out of sight; it is all put away in cabinets or drawers. I want my room to reflect a man who happens to be disabled, not a disabled man." The frame above the bed is the only testimony to his physical condition, and even it is painted so as to blend into the room's color scheme. The fireplace, often in use, the stereo, the typewriter waiting at his desk, the array of books and papers ready as references all speak of a "normal" life. The conveniences—clothes hung on low hooks, unobtrusive open shelves for storage, a hospital table tucked beside the bed—are not readily distinguishable from accommodations made in rooms everywhere. However, they make an independent life possible and are not merely convenient but essential.

The overall impact of the room is that of a quiet haven. Its muted, warm, peaceful quality invites those who are seeking quiet, one-on-one conversations. The same quality creates the working atmosphere that Tom requires to work comfortably; it is a direct contrast with the active, noisy atmosphere often found in the rest of the house. "When I am feeling extroverted, I force myself out of my haven and seek out whatever is flowing through the house. There's always a place where something is happening, people are gathered, and I can go with the flow."

When there is no one to be found in the house, Tom seeks contact in his neighborhood. He is the type of writer who, in order to write, must feel comfortable and secure in his immediate environment.

I've attempted, successfully I think, to design these qualities into my room, my hideaway. A feeling of comfort and ease can't exist through me without an accompanying feeling of freedom of physical mobility. This sense of freedom is nourished by the ramps and the general accessibility of the sidewalks of this area of Berkeley. I can leave my room, go down my ramp, push several blocks without detours around architectural barriers. I can find almost anything I want: hospitals, medical care, libraries, stores, theaters, restaurants, movies. This sense of being able to get where I want to go under my own power without needing to use my van, of having all the necessities within easy pushing distance, contributes to my feeling of freedom and to my emotional satisfaction with my existence in Berkeley.

The Berkeley scene.

Part 3
Networks

Both Berkeley and early America can be thought of as meccas. If one considers as immigrants people who traveled to this country seeking religious and political freedom, steady employment to provide the basic necessities of food, clothing, and shelter, and the opportunity to acknowledge and have acknowledged human rights, then the disabled people who have come to Berkeley are also immigrants. Berkeley is popularly considered a place to achieve personal freedom; what is different between past immigrations and this one is the type and form of freedom to be achieved.

One notable difference is that the procuring of basic needs, from medical care to food, was not an issue for the disabled people who chose to make the journey to Berkeley. Such needs were easily obtained where they were. Religious and political freedom too, as far as they are guaranteed to anyone, were guaranteed to disabled people in other locations. Disabled people, whether in the Midwest or in Southern California, have the right to pursue happiness, to own property, to be personally free. What is at issue is *how* the necessities are obtained and *how* one is free.

What the profiles show is that it was not a question of the quantity, but of the quality of care received that led to the move. Likewise, it was not a question of sufficient nourishment; it was a question of how the nourishment is obtained, prepared, and when it is served. That is, who is in control: the time schedules and staff of institutions or the person for whom the institution supposedly exists? Do you eat a balanced breakfast prescribed by someone else at planned times, or do you oversee and consume that meal when you want it? Do you submit to an overprotective household, or do you choose and govern your world for your own sake and for the sake of others? The key informants came to Berkeley to do it on their own.

The type of freedom sought by disabled people is somewhat different from that sought by early Americans who were subjected, at times, to intentional persecution. Disabled people did not migrate because they were deliberately maltreated. The profiles point out that they came to Berkeley to be liberated from unyielding and confining milieus,

physical and social. The restrictions of disability and the limited mobility of the chair had placed unfair restrictions and limitations on their lives. Many saw themselves being treated as either helpless or useless, and it was very easy to accept being defined as such since every interaction served to reinforce this denotation. By coming to Berkeley physically disabled people found an environment in which they could avoid being singled out or treated in such a manner.[1]

Liberation is an admirable goal; however, it is not easy to achieve. Journeying to Berkeley meant that the disabled individual had to liberate himself from a cocoon of protection or from a self-image of worthlessness or simply had to find a new image by being liberated from an old life. At the same time, the disabled individual had to go through the process of realizing his or her potential as a human being in this new social and physical milieu. To realize a human potential for a disabled person is to realize that which has not been previously acknowledged or emphasized. Because it is difficult to do this alone, what has evolved in Berkeley is a reinforcing system of informal human contacts and organizations and services generated by disabled people themselves that form a social and physical environment to support the act of becoming liberated. "Disabled-generated" means those associations that have developed through the disabled community, who created them out of nothing. In this way, too, the disabled people who have come to Berkeley are similar to immigrants who must form their own social processes, social organizations, and sociophysical environments in a new country. Disabled people have had to do this without the benefit of established traditions or customs.

Of concern here is not the evolution of organizations, social processes, or sociophysical environments as independent social phenomena, or the detailed development and functioning of disabled organizations and communities. What is central is the relationship between the evolved social systems, the physical environment, and the everyday life of the disabled person. Within this context, the focus is physical environments and the people who construct them.

The Formal Network

The disabled community of Berkeley is served by a pair of networks, the formal and the informal, which, working together, provide each individual with a diversity of systems, services, and other people.[2] The formal network is composed of organizations that operate within the community, but did not originate within it; for the most part they are governmental or charitable in nature. Government services include the county welfare office, the state Department of Vocational Rehabilitation, and the federal Social Security Program; some of the range of charities available are the Lighthouse for the Blind, the Cerebral Palsy Association, and the March of Dimes. The network of formal organizations is well known, available to disabled people throughout the country, and subject to regulation from without. These formal networks form the basis upon which the less formal structure of the disabled community rests; they provide funding for both individuals and organizations, offer technical expertise, and provide access to a variety of services, such as vocational rehabilitation and medical facilities, without which the community could not exist.

What is atypical in Berkeley is the manner in which the formal system is manipulated by the informal network to respond to the real needs of the population it serves. ("Real" needs are those designated as such by the population itself.) Without initiative exerted at the informal level, the formal level would be ineffectual. It might take care of necessities, but no more. As the informal web develops to meet the needs of those it serves, the formal network becomes more "humanly" useful. Thus, the significance of the formal network is determined by the acts of people in the informal system.

The active political involvement of disabled groups at both the local and the state level has had a noticeable effect on the responsiveness and understanding of the social services and rehabilitation programs. A major thrust of the political effort has been toward a greater involvement of disabled people in defining programs and philosophies. The traditional hiring emphasis in the formal programs had been on a knowledge of skills, such as Braille or sign language, and a familiarity with relevant programs and prostheses. Peter stresses the fact that "There are very few professionals who know anything about disability. Often the experts who are called in to run or teach in programs know a lot less about disability than the people using the program. There may not be any degree attached to the knowl-

edge, but there is a lot of expertise in this community." The now-preferred emphasis is on hiring employees with such experience. The ability to develop empathic relationships with clients is valued over learned skills. One approach is an Orientation to Disability Program conducted by disabled people themselves.

The Informal Network

In Berkeley the network most important for an enriching life is the informal. It is composed of individuals who are friends or acquaintances; attendants who relate on both a friendship and a contractual basis; casual organizations that arise out of friendships (such as drama groups, support groups, consciousness-raising groups) and exist on a temporary basis to meet current needs; and grassroots organizations which arise from within the disabled group to meet a shared need and gradually acquire a more formal and permanent character. Such grassroots organizations often secure funding and technical support from the official organizations of the formal network, yet they maintain their independence. Both the incentive to form the organization and its staff come from the disabled community, which maintains effective control of it.

At the most intimate scale, the informal network is composed of relationships between individuals—acquaintances, friends, and lovers who share a variety of common concerns, attitudes, assumptions, and values. This network is reinforced by the heightened visibility of its members; while not all members of the community of the severely disabled population have formally met one another, visual recognition and casual greetings are shared by everyone. The situation in Berkeley is unique in that the population of disabled individuals and their close associates (attendants, families, roommates, lovers) is quite large—a few thousand in number—and thus contains within itself a microcosmic version of the entire population.

The existence of common problems and the use of common facilities like the Center for Independent Living, the Physically Disabled Students Program, and the Disabled Students Union create links among all community members. Shared political concerns, shared use of the limited amount of available recreational facilities, and a grapevine knowledge of most major activities and emergencies provide another link. The effect is the establishment of a loose network of personal contacts among the entire disabled community without regard for social differences. This broad range of contacts within the group tends to facilitate information sharing and referral; knowledge of available apartments, sources of drugs, funding possibilities, and new approaches to problems of disability are examples of information spread informally. Within the limits of the disabled community, the system functions much like the "old boy" network, which is used in the outside world to spread information on job or housing availability.

An important difference is that its boundary is that of the disabled community. Disability can be so powerful in its impact that it tends to become a focal point that excludes outside involvements. The disabled population of Berkeley ties into the larger community, but its relationship is often peripheral; the primary ties for most of the disabled community appear to be with the networks that specifically relate to their needs. Consequently, the greater Berkeley community, while sharing many ideologies with the disabled community and overlapping in many aspects, tends to exist as a separate entity. Contacts across the boundaries are not easily made or maintained.

The reasons for this situation are varied. The effort, both emotional and physical, needed to penetrate the boundaries is great. In the outside world it is common for disabled people to feel pressured to adapt to the norms of the greater community. To appear as similar as possible to everyone else, a disabled individual may simply neglect his own needs: if eating is awkward or messy, he may refuse food; if assistance in using the bathroom is required, he may delay going; if he is concerned about a disability-related problem, he will avoid discussing it. Relationships that are formed under these circumstances tend to be self-limiting; they take place in the public arena where references to disability are few and not threatening. The effort required to maintain this "normal" front in outside contacts and the fear of rejection associated with not maintaining it are strong emotional barriers to the formation of significant contacts outside the informal network.

Equally important are the physical barriers. Accessibility is a primary characteristic of any link; some form of contact must be possible and not prohibitively difficult if associations are to be made. For disabled people to form contacts beyond the boundary, there must not be environmental barriers.

In contrast, attitudes toward disability by the disabled community are predominantly under-standing, relaxed, and accepting. Shared problems with bowel and bladder control, shared values regarding modesty or dependence, and shared experience permit a relaxed, humorous atmosphere in which the disabled person is seem "as he is." For example, it is recognized that only among other members of the community does one feel comfortable enough to publicly take a lighthearted and ironic view of one's physical situation. Crip humor is common and provides tension-releasing opportunities for laughter, but only among the initiated. There is no need to maintain a "normal" front—help can be sought as it is needed, and atypical modes of behavior are understood.[3]

Given both the positive incentives to develop relationships within the disabled community and the problems associated with making significant contacts outside it, it is not surprising that a rather closed network of informal ties exists. Considering the problems that disabled people have come to Berkeley to face and overcome, such a closed system seems to be the most supportive for them. Its supportive nature is manifested in social events stressing shared experiences. For example, "re-birthdays" or anniversaries of the disabling accident are observed by some.

Political goals that are shared, such as sit-ins, offer another point of contact. While only a percentage of the disabled community actively participates in sit-ins, the entire population is emotionally involved in the event. During the 1977 sit-in, conversations for the entire month focused on the activity in San Francisco, and the victory, when it was achieved, was shared by all. There are also numerous points of contact on a more practical level. The severely disabled population often shares medical, economic, and legal problems; both the information available from those who have had similar problems and the understanding available from those who have "been through it" serve as reasons for relating to others within the network.

Perhaps the most important ties are those of shared histories—often in terms of common childhood experiences and of Berkeley's disabled community—and shared futures based on their ability to influence new policy and the implementation of governmental regulations.

Informal Organizations

The organized components of the informal network are probably the most important element in making Berkeley a viable community for disabled individ-

Neil Jacobson, instructor (at center), presents his first graduating class in computer science.

uals. These organizations are physically located in the community or on campus, and they are administratively structured to perform specialized services. Most importantly, they have been initiated and developed by people who are disabled themselves, and each has a presence in the community that gives status to those who are associated with it. The involvement of the disabled members of the community in the administration and operation of these organizations makes the organizations more sensitive to the requirements of individuals and permits them to respond in imaginative and unconventional ways when it is required.

These indigenous organizations occupy an intermediate service position between formal networks, such as government agencies which tend to be cumbersome, physically difficult to reach, bureaucratic, and unable to respond to the immediate needs of individuals, and the networks of everyday contacts which are somewhat unpredictable. The effective utilization of this network is related to the amount of time spent in Berkeley and the number of contacts an individual has made. For the newcomer, access to the informal network is gradual. Initial contacts are frequently made through the network's most visible and organized aspects. Then gradually,

by word of mouth and by seeking to take care of needs, the more subtle nature of the network is negotiated.

One of the most striking and interesting aspects of this situation is the role of the informal organization in helping the disabled person receive financial and other benefits potentially available in the formal network, but not always immediately visible or accessible through regularly prescribed channels. "How to work the system" is a major benefit of the grassroots network and is made known through a wide range of disparate contacts—from medical professionals who are responsive to the disabled population to disabled individuals themselves who have learned through trial and error. Both the Center for Independent Living and the Physically Disabled Students Program are prepared to help the new arrival make contact with others in the community; they also assist in preparing applications for Supplemental Security Income or Social Security Disability Insurance; they make referrals to the Department of Vocational Rehabilitation, and they

The heart of the informal network: intersecting lines of communication at the Center for Independent Living.

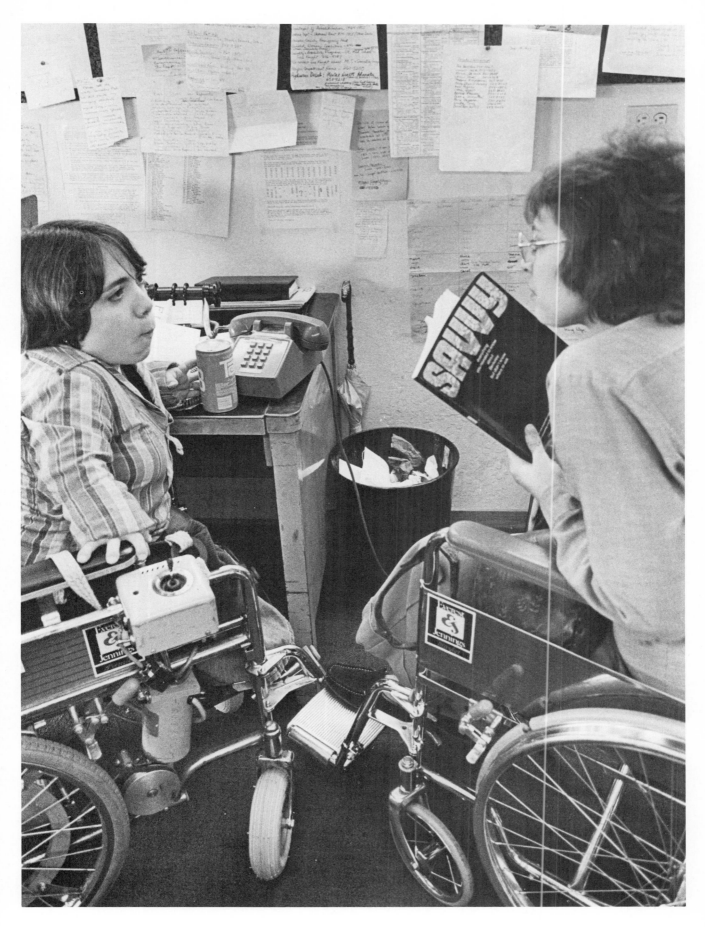

aid in attendant-referral counseling, advocacy counseling, job development, counseling in independent living skills, peer counseling, health-maintenance programs, outreach counseling (contacting hospitals, service organizations, rehabilitation agencies, and community groups to provide information about CIL), housing searches, deaf or blind services, transportation services, wheelchair repair shop services, automotive and machine shop services, and community affairs.

How an informal organization emerges can be traced in the development of an emergency attendants' referral service. During the early years when severely disabled individuals lived in Cowell Hospital, the hospital staff was available to respond in any emergency. As self-confidence and independence increased, a small number of people left the hospital to live in their own homes, and an informal solution to the need for emergency attendants was reached by providing each disabled person with a list of phone numbers of three key people who worked with the Physically Disabled Students Pro-

gram. When they received a call, this group, in turn, would attempt to locate an attendant or, if necessary, provide aid themselves.

No formal arrangement had been worked out with emergency rescue services or the fire department, and each situation was approached on an individual basis. Inevitably, as the number of disabled people living independently grew, the system became less workable and a great burden upon those whose names were on the list. When Peter became very ill late one night and could not reach his own attendants, he found that the emergency system was too burdened to help him effectively; the available trained attendants were already helping others and the available lift-equipped vans were in use. An awkward trip to the hospital in an unadapted car, without skilled attendant help, convinced him that better emergency-attendant services were essential.

A group of concerned people formed, and attendants were contacted; a list was drawn up, and an attempt was made to distribute it through exist-

Friendship.

ing organizations. Although the attempt initially failed and informal distribution was necessary, it soon became apparent that the service was too essential to continue on a purely volunteer basis. A full-time employee was needed to screen attendants, update the list, and manage distribution. The university recognized the need, and a paid employee at the Physically Disabled Students Program handled the job. Another program soon began to function at the Center for Independent Living. Special funding for the program has been made available on a yearly basis, and the service continues to be a part of the grass-roots network.

Over time, a wide variety of organizations and groups to serve the disabled have emerged and are still emerging as needs become clarified. They range from the all-encompassing Center for Independent Living to such specific groups as a gay rap session for disabled men. The significance of the informal network and its grass-roots components lies not only in the services offered, but also in the ability of the network to expand and contract to accommodate the wide variety of individuals who do or will depend upon it. Currently, the web seems to meet the needs of the community as it develops and as its members develop their wants and needs.

Attendants

In the disabled community, there are people who are not disabled but who play important parts in the everyday lives of the disabled people. One group is the attendants who take care of functional needs but who also, because of their presence, take on other relationships with those they serve. They are important, both in the intimate environment, in which they function as friends, confidants, or sources of information, and as intermediaries with the physical environment, in which they perform the critical activities that make independent living possible. Perhaps their more critical role of linking the individual with both grassroots and formal organizations serves as the foundation for many other activities. As one attendant has stated:

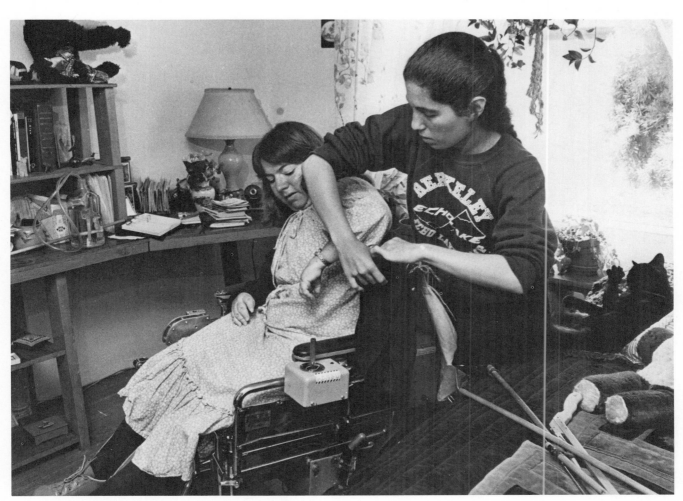

An attendant assists with preparation for the day.

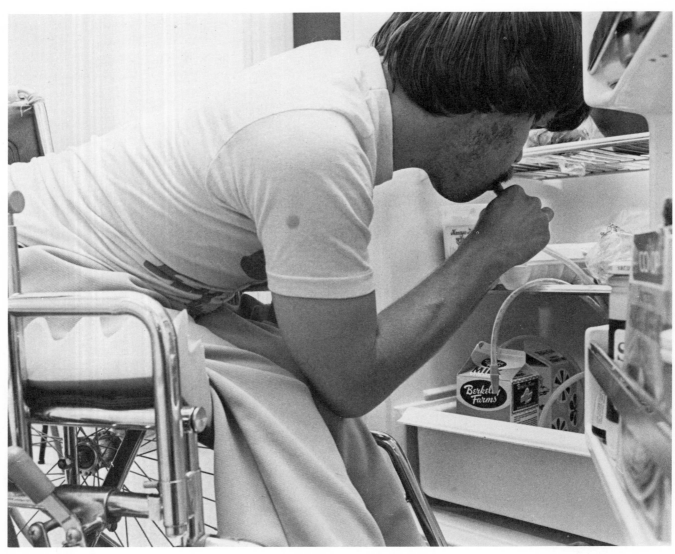

An attendant has arranged the kitchen so this blind person can manage alone.

The disabled in this county are very organized in their relationship to the county and state offices. Even though Alameda County is notoriously difficult to deal with, there is a very large disabled population and the money is always forthcoming. There is a very sub-rosa training program vis-à-vis the state. It's very organized here, and there is an established support system for the individual who is just entering the system. For instance, there are doctors here who are very familiar with the problems, and it's easy to have a prescription written for a new wheelchair. In another county, the doctors would not recognize the need and would not prescribe. There is a real question whether that is due to the county or to the population having developed a network for their own support. I would say it's the population. There are all these resources and groups to do advocacy. My role as an attendant is to make sure the client knows the ropes in order to have a proper working relationship. If someone new comes to town, I will need to know what they should do right away if I want to get paid. A new person will often ask for an experienced attendant because they know the ropes through the bureaucracy as well as how to handle the needs of the person.[4]

Attendants are drawn from a variety of sources. The most formal are the homemaking agencies: for example, Homemaker's Upjohn provides homemakers or attendants on request. However, the grassroots system of contacts and organizations generated by disabled people are the most popular sources. They provide a pool of young, able-bodied individuals who are rarely professionally trained for the job. After a short period of service, many of these individuals develop into technically, socially, and psychologically skillful workers. Whereas the county-provided homemaker/chore person is considered only a "fetch-and-carry" employee, the Berkeley attendant, unfettered by agency rules blossoms as confidant/counselor; learns to spot symptoms of various illnesses typical of the population; becomes skillful at handling the client's prostheses; and can often assist someone through the problems related to bladder care, dysreflexia, bedsores, among others. In addition, the multiplicity of their contacts within the subculture provides information and contacts valuable to their disabled client.

Once a disabled newcomer has made initial contacts in the informal acquaintance network, a great deal of activity revolves around locating, hiring, using, relating to, and discussing attendants. The type of services and the degree of regularity with which they are performed tend to make relationships with attendants intimate. That many attendants serve two or more people regularly results in a subrole for attendants as information distributors and as links in secondary relationships, in which clients know each other indirectly through the attendant.

Often, such contacts are not merely social, but really essential for a person who is attempting to establish an independent lifestyle. An attendant, commenting upon her role in this process, said:

It is especially important for a person new to the community or newly disabled to know how to make connections with others because the initial feeling is one of extreme isolation and being cut off. Especially in the case of a quadriplegic, where there is a lack of direct feeling, the impulse is to get in touch as quickly as possible. To achieve this you have to rely upon visible signals, upon a lot of devices which compensate for the lack of feeling. You must try to use concepts to replace feelings, use these concepts to carry someone over and into a sense of being a moving, dynamic, integrated member of the community. This requires a great deal of care in every gesture, in every kind of move you make within the setting into which you come; a misapprehension can be very severe.

While the role of the attendant as a social link is important, it is only one of several roles that are equally essential. For example, the role of the attendant within the dwelling is critical, because for most severely disabled people independence in their own dwelling is impossible without the aid of attendants. Finding an effective balance between the two roles the attendant assumes—social connector and extension of the disabled person in the physical environment—is a major chore for him or her. The desire to be helpful, to make things easier, which springs from friendship, may be countered by the desire to promote independence and the necessity to insist that the disabled person "do it himself."

The role of mediator with the environment is often described as "no more than a very concentrated version of general life. Everything I do with people generally is very concentrated in a situation with a disabled person." The attendant may serve as the hands or arms of a disabled person, merely a physical extension, or may assume a role in which he or she controls and makes decisions about many aspects of the environment. The type of interaction is determined by the personalities and needs of the individuals involved. An experienced attendant says:

Part of the job for me is helping the disabled person to articulate his or her own identity after the body has been broken and arranged into another form. What has to be done, especially for new quads, is that a sense of identity has to be translated into what is virtually an alien form. There is a lot of tension in this because invariably the person wants to go back. So, you have to keep pulling, affirming the value in the present form, which seems ungainly and unattractive from many points of view. You have to keep providing connections, affirmations; keep providing support that this body is fine, that it is just different.

An important element in facilitating a successful adjustment is the approach in handling the environment; a major portion of the adjustment to disability lies in learning to get a variety of physical tasks accomplished, either directly or indirectly. The attendant attempts to make his hands and arms available without directly influencing the choice of how or when to use them.

An example is given by one attendant who focuses on a semi-accessible kitchen. Rather than making the potentially threatening suggestion, "You could do this if I set it all up," the attendant does what he can to create a potentially usable space and waits for an opportunity such as "I would like to learn to cook" to make any direct suggestion. "You may come into the environment and think this person is capable of doing more, but you must keep in mind that this is not your space."

What both the formal and the informal networks represent in Berkeley and what they represent for disabled people and for society is the importance in human life of individual and group determination to realize needs and wants. Without interactions that give new and relevant meanings to one's life and to the world in which one wants to live, to its objects and social processes, to its organizations and social structures, there would be no Berkeley experience for the disabled community. As a place that is in a state of becoming, Berkeley has formed and is forming a community and a community of services for disabled people through disabled people.

The annual Fantasy Day parade in Berkeley: a band of warriors.

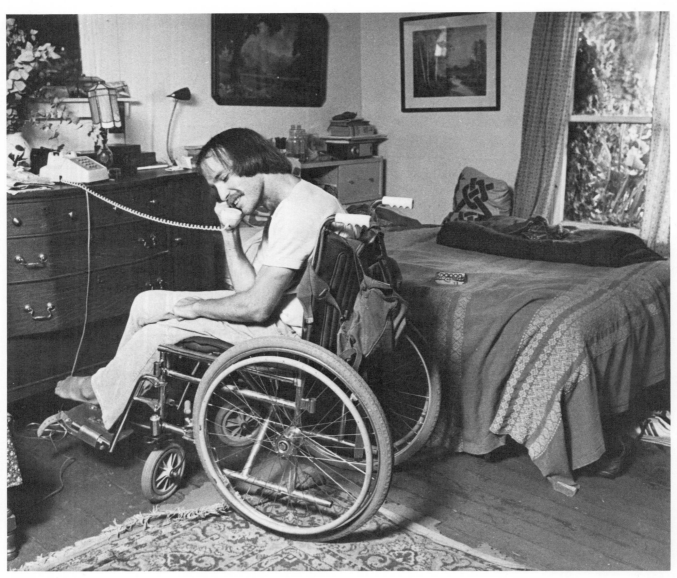

The bed–sitting room in John McLaughlin's cottage.

Part 4
Places

The behavioral counterpart of archetypal place, what people do in these settings, constitutes the "meaning" in our environment. It is what makes a *place* out of a space. Living overlong in an environment composed of too few or improperly organized archetypal possibilities drains from our lives the social and psychological contexts and opportunities to act in meaningful ways.[1]

For a whole and healthful life, each individual needs to express a range of emotions each day. Of course, it would be impossible to make a list encompassing this range because of the infinite length of such a list, on the one hand, and the interrelated nature of the emotions and the acts that express them, on the other. For example, as humans we eat not only for nourishment, but also for energy to participate and be productive as well as for pleasure. We groom not only for the cultivation of our own image, but for the enjoyment we believe it gives others. We work not simply out of necessity and because it is a societal ethic to work, but also because through work we express our inner needs and come to terms with our authenticity.

Too often able-bodied people think of disabled people as having a limited emotional life—as having a limited need for the expression of self, as being, in more than one sense, less than whole people. When we began this study we felt we had no such biases; yet we came to see that limited personal experience and societal values played havoc with our ability to perceive, to confront, to interpret. We found ourselves repeating interviews over and over again because each time we were amazed and troubled that unconscious assumptions and attitudes subtly interfered with our desired empathetic stance.

During this process we encountered Mayer Spivack's concept of *archetypal places*, which links together the human experience with the environment of that experience:

> When . . . people live in environments restricted to a severely limited range of settings in which to carry out all the behavior that constitutes the human repertoire, their ability to function as individuals and family groups, and the integrity and quality of their society, may be impaired. People fail to maintain deep, lasting interpersonal relationships, they may suffer in their ability to work, provide or eat food, to sleep in deep renewing comfort, play, raise children, explore and protect territory, to meet with their peers, and make decisions which control the shape and quality of life. Each of the foregoing functions, and others, are associated with thirteen characteristic settings in the physical environment, with the rooms and furniture which focus and support behavior patterns in specific and appropriate ways. Such settings, taken together, in their smallest irreducible group, are archetypal places.[2]

We found Spivack's view useful in assuring that there would be breadth to our inquiry that was compatible with our search. Therefore we chose the concept of archetypal places as an organizing schema.

Spivack's schema (see page 62) permits a great number of environmental needs to be organized under a relatively small number of basic human requirements, so that the former can be seen as nuances of the latter. Thus, for example, the need for security, in its many forms, can be discussed under the more general rubric of "shelter"; in this way the breadth of requirements the residential environment must meet in order to adequately satisfy this basic need can be indicated.

To Spivack's concept we added the dimension of environmental scale. Thus, the environment is considered as existing at three levels: the intimate, the dwelling, and the community. This framework allowed us to draw some distinctions between the types of supports disabled people require at each level and to better understand the kinds of interactions that occur there. The intimate environment might include the disabled person and his bed or wheelchair or the disabled person in some of his interactions with his attendants. The dwelling environment might include the actual place of residence or places within the community that serve residential functions—the place of work, education, or ongoing contacts for social, or political, or recreation activities. The community environment includes both the physical environment of the community— the extent to which it is accessible, for example— and the services and supports it provides to the disabled population. This third scale is especially noted as the environment in which the disabled person is least likely to effect permanent changes suitable to personal needs.

Archetypal Places

GENERALLY RELATED LIFE CYCLE STAGES

TASKS	A — INFANCY: Reflex control; orientation; communicate with siblings and parents.	B — CHILDHOOD: Gain motor, social, verbal, intellectual, emotional competence.	C — ADOLESCENCE: Forge identity; establish peer group regulations; social/sexual exploration.	D — COURTING-MATING: Group with peers; pair-bond; obtain sexual privacy.	E — REPRODUCTION, CHILD CARE: Nesting/nurturing: symbiosis; socialization.	F — MIDDLE LIFE: Care of aging parents: re-emphasis on worldly affairs; redefine indentity.	G — AGING MATURITY: Maintain identity, contact, health; accent care by others, mortality.
1 SHELTER	Elemental protection; protection for nesting activities; retreat from stimulation, aggression, threat, social contact; emotional recuperation.						
2 SLEEP	Neurophysiological processes; recuperation, rest; reduced stimulation; labor and birth, postnatal care of mother and child; death.						
3 MATE	Courting rituals; pair-bonding; copulation; affectionate behavior; communication.						
4 GROOM	Washing; mutual grooming.						
5 FEED	Eating, slaking thirst; communication; social gathering; feeding others.						
6 EXCRETE	Excreting; territorial marking.						
7 STORE	Hiding of food and other property; storage; hoarding.						
8 TERRITORY	Spying; contemplation; meditating; planning; waiting; territorial sentry; defending; observing.						
9 PLAY	Motor satisfactions; role testing; rule breaking; fantasy, exercise; creation; discovery; dominance testing; synthesis.						
10 ROUTE	Perimeter checking; territorial confirmation; motor satisfactions; social and community control.						
11 MEET	Communication; dominance testing; governing; education, worship socialization; meditation; cosmic awe; moral concerns.						
12 COMPETE	Agonistic ritual; dominance testing; ecological competition; inter-species defense; intra-species defense and aggression; mating; chauvinistic conflict.						
13 WORK	Hunting; gathering; earning; building; making.						

THE TOTAL SET OF BEHAVIORALLY DEFINED ARCHETYPAL PLACES

A 1 Protection from elemental extremes; explore dwelling. A:2 Recognize bed; learn daily rhythms. A:3 XX A:4 Lose fear of wet face, sudden temperature change; regular grooming as primary contact ritual. A:5 Regulate feeding satisfactions. A:6 Discover excretion as separate from self; associate with setting and time. A:7 Acquire confidence in food abundance. A:8 Identify bed as primary secure place. A:9 Explore close environment; develop manipulative, cognitive skills. A:10 Route connects parts of shelter structures, provides orientation & change; motor satisfaction. A:11 XX A:12 Master frustration in competition w/siblings for attention & toys. A:13 (See A:9).

B 1 Differentiate subsettings; retreat from overstimulation, threat; emotional recuperation. B:2 Associate bed w/fatigue; learn volitional control of sleep; illness and recuperation. B:3 XX B:4 Learn to bathe, dress oneself. B:5 Coordinate feeding tools; communication; differentiate food from symbiotic source in mother. B:6 Autonomously control excretion. B:7 Learn to prepare food. B:8 Establish play "turfs"; orient to neighborhood; play protect territory from lookout; plan, wait. B:9 Role modeling; interact w/peers; fantasy, exercise, exorcism, creation, discovery, dominance testing. B:10 Enlarge route maps; differentiate settings; provide social encounters; learn safe wandering limits. B:11 Regular play/meeting rituals & places; elaborate functions; dominance testing. B:12 Games; fight; agonistic ritual; dominance testing. B:13 Acquire intellectual, motor skills.

C 1 Find alternate private shelter: auto, attic, stairwell. C:2 XX C:3 Meet w/opposite sex in private, public settings; obtain sexual privacy anywhere: autos, barns, etc. C:4 Groom for mating encounters. C:5 Communicate w/peers over food & drink. C:6 Privacy in excretion. C:7 XX C:8 Expand territory into intellectual domains, job. C:9 Learn autonomous hobbies. C:10 Provides social contact w/opposite sex. C:11 Meet w/peers, both sexes; establish new rituals. C:12 Sexual display: cars, sports, clothes (see C:3). C:13 Refine work skills.

D 1 Find new shelter. D:2 Share bed w/mate. D:3 Select mate; achieve couple privacy. D:4 XX D:5 Share food w/mate; increase food abundance. D:6 XX D:7 Enlarge larder for family. D:8 Expand territory to include mate. D:9 (see D:12). D:10 Maintain community of contacts. D:11 Meet w/couples. D:12 Personal display; ecological, mating competition. D:13 Apply skills toward life support.

E 1 Expand shelter for offspring (see E:5). E:2 Maintain sexual privacy against invasion by new young family. E:3 XX E:4 XX E:5 Increase abundance; feed family; gather, communicate w/family. E:6 XX E:7 Increase capacity & variety of food. E:8 Expand territory to include young & check frequently. E:9 XX E:10 XX E:11 Expand functions, contacts; governing, educating, mystical awe. E:12 Display in common values; conspicuous consumption. E:13 Improve capacities, performance.

F 1 Shelter contracts as young leave. F:2 through F:7 XX F:8 Territorial needs contract as young leave shelter. F:9 through F:13 XX

G 1 Maintain location or adjust to imposed change; adapt surroundings to needs. G:2 More time in bed, sleep less; possible confinement, compression of world to bedside. G:3 Adjust sexuality to changing libido; possible illness or loss of mate (see G:2). G:4 Possible inability to care for self. G:5 Arrange special diet; reduction of taste, smell spectra. G:6 Possibly require aid and equipment; lowered mobility may reduce functional dependability. G:7 Possibly require assistance gathering & preparing food. G:8 Passive observation of archetypal activities performed by others. G:9 New leisure activities to fit changing capacities. G:10 Reduction in home range scale; fear of exposure to attack. G:11 Need for contact w/& support from peers. G:12 Probable withdrawal from competition/defeat by young; defensive, evasive postures. G:13 Less active roles w/in former context; fend off retirement.

Reprinted with permission of Mayer Spivack; reproduced from *Architectural Forum*, October 1973.

Shelter

Shelter can be broadly viewed as a place of retreat; a place to escape from aggression, stimulation, threat, social contact, and the elements; a place for nesting activities. The behavioral needs that are met by shelter are for physical comfort and for security. These needs exist on a continuum from the intimate to the community level and must be satisfied on each level.

The Developmental Implications

An important aspect of growing up and developing a full set of environmental expectations is the evolution of a concept of personal shelter. From infancy children begin to seek a "shelter," first by crawling into and under things, hiding in small places, and selecting a small corner rather than a whole room as the setting for their play. As they grow older, this need is expressed by building forts and treehouses, digging caves, and fiercely protecting "my property." Adolescents express their developing independence by seeking an alternative shelter; the car or van, the attic or basement room, the distant city to which one runs away in fantasy or reality are substitutes for the rejected shelter offered by and tied to the family. Ultimately, leaving the family home to live alone or with a mate is a cultural signal of independence—moving out is a sign of finally being "grown up" and assuming all the rights and responsibilities of adulthood.

Each of these maturational experiences is laden with symbolism. Both in the mind of the maturing child and in the eyes of the world, the gradual development of independence is tied to the expression of a separate shelter. Confidence in the ability to "do it myself" is built by gradual successes in the effort to make a place of one's own; personal as well as geographic boundaries are developed by the possession of a space whose access can be controlled by the individual.

Those who are disabled from early childhood often miss or only partially experience these activities. They may be so "sheltered" by concerned parents that there is no need or opportunity for them to develop a concept of shelters of their own. Playing outdoors without attendance is almost impossible in a wheelchair. Those classic childmade environments—forts—are generally inaccessible, and treehouses are hopelessly out of reach. The severely disabled child, under the best of circumstances, may be excluded from the play with others which creates shelters. Alone, the effort required, the difficulty of handling materials, and the need for assistance are enough to overwhelm most efforts.

Shelter is often viewed by the disabled child as the protection and comfort that is provided by others. He is likely to view himself as having little influence on his surroundings; adaptations and changes are made by others. Because the spaces he occupies are rarely his own, the disabled child often lacks privacy. There are no places in which to hide, no retreats from everyone. Mary Ann recalls her childhood as a time of *always* being protected and sheltered, looked in on and cared for. Confined to a wheelchair that she could not move herself, Mary Ann could never retreat. The expressions of distress so common to the escaping child—slamming the door, hiding behind the furniture, locking yourself in your room—were not available to Mary Ann.

Gary also grew up in an environment adapted and controlled by others for him:

> When I lived with my folks, they did a remodeling job on the house. About six or eight years after they moved into the house they put a new addition on, and they put another bathroom in and the bathroom was designed for me. It had an overly large shower and a double showerhead because I couldn't turn myself around. One thing interesting about having something adapted to me is that I got kind of lazy, in the sense that it was always there, and I knew if I went in the bathroom I was always going to be able to get up to the sink. One bad thing about that is you go in bathrooms sometimes and maybe somebody would leave something right in the way of the sink, so I couldn't get up there. I'd have to move something and I'd get really angry; but looking back on it, it was because I had it so good. It was all there; I didn't have the challenge, and in one sense that's what apartment life around Berkeley has taught me: it is a pain in the ass, but it's challenging and it's good for me because it keeps me sort of on my toes as far as my own abilities.

Adolescence is usually a time of testing. Many small separations are undertaken in preparation for the larger separation to come. Among able-bodied people, resolution of the endless and inevitable conflicts of this age is often reached by separation. The adolescent finds alternate places to seek shelter, places with an identity that belongs to him and perhaps his peers. The room is only one alternative among many. Teenagers frequently choose to be absent from the home to find alternative environments. For some disabled teenagers their room may begin to serve this function. One young disabled woman describes her room as her "home base." She spends all her time there surrounded by her own things, maintaining her privacy by escaping into continuous schoolwork—an escape acceptable to both herself and her parents. However, there are inevitable difficulties in changing the image of a room that has functioned as a symbol of unity with the family into one that symbolizes independence. These problems are heightened if the room must also serve as the scene for family assistance in moving about, transferring, bathing, and so on.

As adults, most people have the experience of selecting, acquiring, modifying, and occupying a home or shelter of some form. This home is important not only for all the practical functions of shelter that it serves but also as a symbol of self in Clare Cooper's terms,[3] an image of its occupant that is constant in his own eyes and in those of the community. For the disabled individual there has been little opportunity historically to create this symbol. Houses or institutions were selected, built, and adapted to meet the needs of caretakers. With increasing numbers of independent disabled people, however, the situation is changing.

Numerous severely disabled Berkeley residents own or occupy homes alone or with others and find it rewarding. John takes an active role in planning and controlling his personal environment and relates this to good health, building self-confidence, and discovering himself.

> By getting in touch with my environment [his house], a harmony is created. When you work with your environment you also learn to depend on nature and on other people just because the harmony is there. It's a healthy reciprocity. Like a social phenomenon in traffic. If you let someone go ahead, later on they pay that back to someone else. I think I have developed unusual compensations for understanding the environment that may be useful to others. Being forced to deal with the environment so closely has caused more awareness of how to deal with it better. I know by now whom I can ask for help, by the way they look or don't look at me, avoid me. This makes me more aware of the potential things have. Being able to spot the potential in a thing or person builds resourcefulness.

Conflicts sometimes arise from the necessity for environmental "appendages," which assure access to a home but also declare the disability of the occupant to the world. Carmen's house has two large and essential ramps to permit wheelchairs to travel from the house to the garden and from the garden to the street; both ramps are disguised as part of the garden itself, invisible from the street. The reasons are both practical—the police recommend locating ramps where they will not call attention to the in-

creased vulnerability of the occupants—and psychological: Carmen wants the house to look as normal as other houses in the neighborhood. Ramps do not fit the image of normalcy.

The problem of selecting, adapting, and occupying a house of one's own is further complicated for the individual who has been disabled from birth or early childhood. Lack of experience in controlling the surroundings, either directly or by directing assistants, presents major difficulties for home seekers who are newly independent individuals armed only with a brief experience at a rehabilitation center or with no experience outside of the family home or convalescent hospital. They must deal with an unfamiliar and complex set of realities in their search for shelter. Housing must be found that is accessible. Too often a lack of understanding of all aspects of accessibility, such as room and door sizes, counter heights, or turning radiuses, prevent even essential needs from being met.

Finding and adapting acceptable housing that integrates with the network of community associations and services and that provides security and elemental protection can offer psychologically rewarding experiences on both the personal and interpersonal levels. Gary stated:

> I had all these big ideas of what I was going to do when I got over here and how I was going to approach things, and I think it's really important to just cool it for a couple of months, until you really get an idea of what your environment is like; what's out there, what's available. Make sure stuff in your house is accessible so you can get to it, make sure you've got a phone, cause I think that's really important. My attitude since I've gotten here has really changed. One of the things from an architectural standpoint was that I had come out of a house that my parents had done a remodeling job on, and they made some modifications on the house that made it easier for me to get around. Then, as far as physically being able to get around, I had it made. I had all the conveniences. I had grab bars all over the place. And I was coming from a place that was set up for me into sort of a more cramped environment, but I learned a lot about that too. I learned that despite everything you learn to get around. Sometimes I can't really tell you how I learned to do it; I just can catch onto things fairly fast anyway, coming into an environment that a few years ago I was not even supposed to be able to live in because of what was physically involved. This place that I'm in now I love, despite the fact that it is a little hard to manage. It reminds me a lot in some ways of the house that I had because even though it is an apartment, it has sort of a homey feeling. I don't feel like I'm in one of those plastic, fantastic highrises.

The Intimate Environment

The most intimate forms of shelter occur within the personal-space bubble. Clothing and protective devices, such as umbrellas or sunglasses, offer both elemental protection and some shelter from psychological invasion. For disabled people, these devices are supplemented by prosthetic devices and equipment. The wheelchair is so closely related to its occupant that it extends both the physical and psychological space occupied by the individual. While it provides a protective metal shell in the material sense, it also makes the occupant more visibly distinct and psychologically accessible to those who do not see disabled persons as people with the same rights to privacy as others.

The basic needs at a personal scale are related to physical and emotional security. The immediate surroundings of most disabled individuals include a variety of devices—manual, mechanical, and electrical—that enable the person to meet his basic needs. Varying in nature from catheters and legbags through wheelchairs and mechanical beds to electric door openers and voice-responsive phones, these devices cooperate with the person's existing abilities and furnish the assistance he requires to make possible an independent life. If these devices fail, many disabled people are literally helpless. Late-night wheelchair breakdowns have left many stranded on the street, immobile and vulnerable.

Electrical failures can both immobilize electric wheelchairs and deactivate voice-responsive telephones. The most minor accident, such as dropping the slideboard used for transferring, can isolate a disabled person in a situation that he is unable to leave. Physical security at the personal scale implies the need for back-up systems for any electric or mechanical device that can fail. This need is frequently met by the presence of other people who can assist in emergencies. The preference for living in close proximity to others, particularly other able-bodied individuals, is one response to this need. Being dependent on attendants or machinery and being helpless for those hours of the night when there is no one around to help decreases feelings of security. A fear of Mary Ann, who has a disabled roommate, is: "You think about being alone at night; thinking that if something happens at night, you can't get yourself out of bed, like in a fire or something."

Physical security for the disabled person can mean more dependence on elemental control than it does for the able-bodied person. Spinal-cord injury frequently affects the metabolism; the body is less able to adjust to temperature change and may be unable to sweat. The usual responses of exercising to warmup and of sweating to cool down are not available, so comfort is possible only when the temperature is within a restricted range. Tom's room is always kept in the upper seventies (20–30° C); his windows are not open on even the hottest days, due partially to the great difficulty of opening the windows without assistance. Lennis can frequently be found sitting in the full sun, often wearing a sweater and with a slight sunburn. For him, a concern in choosing a place to live is that the windows should face south or west so that he can sit in the sunshine. For individuals with metabolic dysfunction, it is essential to provide a heating system that permits each individual to control the temperature and ventilation of the space he occupies.

Other disorders, such as multiple sclerosis, tend to reduce the body tolerance for heat; comfort may be possible only in spaces that are cool and breezy. Two male informants, both afflicted with multiple sclerosis, have chosen apartments with large windows that can be fully opened. They prefer natural air currents to the chill of air conditioning.

For all individuals with temperature sensitivity, a major requirement is flexibility and the opportunity to personally control comfort. Responses to this need vary from being prepared with extra sweaters and jackets kept within easy reach and carried on all excursions, to keeping the body constantly supplied with liquids (a water bottle or glass and straw are permanently affixed to many wheelchairs), to restricting the selection of spaces in which to live and work to those with accessible and flexible temperature-control systems.

The need for elemental protection is often increased by various factors related to disability. Asked about how she deals with the elements, Mary Ann responded, "I hate them all. Rain makes your wheels and brakes slip, and it's hard for cars to see you. Cold makes your circulation poor." In Berkeley, the weather is usually mild, there is never snow, temperatures are moderate, and rains are confined to a few months of the year. A common approach to elemental protection here tends to be passivity. When the weather is inclement, activities that necessitate going outdoors are simply postponed.

Lennis, who describes himself as a "flexible survivalist," says, "I deal with the problem by 'contingency planning.' For instance, if I need to miss a class, I make sure I have all the books and there is someone there who will take notes for me. I just have to switch gears, not let the situation bring me to a grinding halt."

Other souls can be seen in the midst of rainstorms in a wide assortment of protective coverings. Hoods, capes that cover the back of the chair and keep the seat as well as the driver dry, and umbrellas that are fitted into special slots on the back of the chair are common. During the rainy season, two of our informants described "devices I would most like to see invented" as a hood similar to that on a baby carriage, which would fold away but was always there when needed, and a "golf cart-type cover, a canopy which would keep the whole chair dry."

John finds the elements a pleasing aspect of the environment. "Berkeley is an accepting place. It has places of power.[4] The bay is like open arms to fog, ocean, the elements. I see more people enjoying the rain here than in other places."

Security from the threat of physical harm by others is a constant concern for many wheelchair occupants. They feel that the chair itself is an advertisement of their vulnerability and inability to resist attack, and many regard themselves as "moving targets" for purse snatchers and muggers. A less obvious threat is posed by the unconscious fears and hostilities many people have toward disabled people. While typical street violence may be avoidable by careful selection of times and routes, the danger of unpredictable violent assault by an individual who feels threatened by disabled people can inhibit making potentially rewarding contacts.

Peter stresses that while security is an important consideration, and one that he is constantly aware of, "Danger is just a part of it all; part of being disabled is accepting that a lot of things are going to be harder, more time consuming, less safe. Most of us are very accustomed to being in some form of danger. We are susceptible to infections, injury, and so on; but you can't let that get in the way of leading your life. So, you just accept the danger, and if you want to do something enough, you do it."

One can never be certain about security from attack. Most disabled people are extremely careful in their planning to avoid areas that have a dangerous reputation, time periods during which streets are likely to be deserted, situations in which they are likely to be isolated with an unknown individual. The desire to avoid difficult situations, however, may result in spending more time at home than is actually desired.

The Dwelling Environment
The dwelling provides the primary shelter; it offers a retreat from all hostile forces and provides com-

fort. For most disabled individuals the dwelling is the only environment in which a real sense of both physical and emotional security is possible. The importance of direct control of the surroundings is a critical element in this feeling. The home of the disabled person is generally more specifically adapted to the needs of the individual than that of an able-bodied person.

The dwelling must serve as a sure "escape route" from threatening situations. This implies ramps to entries that are easily maneuvered, no barriers like curbs at streetside, and door hardware that is workable. Handles with lever-type action, keys on extenders, adequate space for wheelchair manipulation to open and close the door, good lighting, and accessible doorbells are some common adaptations. Special devices such as intercom locking devices controlled from the bed are also in use.

Once indoors, the dwelling must offer security from invasion. Locks must be effective and easily operated. Many of the best locks in terms of security are dependent upon small-muscle control for their operation; large-scale versions, which are more manageable, or different designs are preferable. One informant noted:

> When I go out, I lock everything—every window. When I come back it's really hot, but it's better than being ripped off. I'm not as worried about being ripped off in this place, cause while this place is accessible, I really go to great pains to see that it doesn't happen; and after I've done all I can, if it happens, it happens, and, well, I am insured and I do have my stuff marked with my name. I am usually out with someone, but if I'm around at home, I will keep my doors locked if I'm not expecting anybody. And the whole thing behind that is that I have taken a self-defense course, and I would give somebody a pretty good battle. I'm most vulnerable when I'm down in bed. If someone were to come in and I were to be in bed, I'm not as physically capable as if I were up. I can move around in bed, but when I am laying down, it's sort of like someone pulled the plug on me. But it's not one of those things that I can just sit around worrying about all the time.

Windows that permit the occupant to see the visitor before admitting him are important. They must be low enough to be used from a wheelchair and located so that the chair can be moved into an effective viewing position. For those who are restricted to a single room, a voice-activated entry communications and access system may be desirable.

To find an effective balance between security and social isolation is a problem for those who need to spend long periods of time in bed and cannot leave the bed without assistance. Admitting visitors personally is impossible. Various approaches are taken. Peter often leaves his door open; visitors and attendants come and go freely, and he counts on the constant flow of a number of people through his home to provide security. His apartment is located in a building in which neighbors can hear any disturbance, which supports this approach, as does his decision to share his apartment with another active disabled man, who also brings a steady stream of visitors into the space.

Carmen handles this issue by sharing the space with a number of able-bodied people who can respond to visitors. Regular callers are given keys, and the doors are open during active hours. Mary Ann and her roommate solve the problem by giving keys to attendants and other frequent visitors. They schedule all other visits in advance so they are prepared to greet the guest. Due to the high attendant turnover and the dangers inherent in having distributed many keys, this approach requires periodic lock changes.

The security problems posed by the necessity of hiring attendants and providing them with access before their reliability has been proven is a constant worry for disabled people. Attendants are often hired from among the "street people." Most are conscientious, reliable, concerned, and value working with people. However, others are untrained, irresponsible, or simply out to take advantage of an easy victim. Stories are told about homes robbed after attendants were hired, given keys, and then never seen again. Screening programs and referral systems attempt to control this problem, but the undeniable vulnerability of those who are dependent on assistance is a continuing problem that even the security of the dwelling cannot overcome.

A sense of security is sometimes enhanced by the presence of a telephone, another means of communicating with people. This link with help, however, is not always reliable, particularly when it cannot be easily or quietly employed. Lennis described an uncomfortable situation in which he heard someone in the next room at about three o'clock in the morning. It turned out to be his attendant, but Lennis had some uneasy moments; he hesitated to use his phone line to call for help because when it is activated, anyone in the next room can hear the operator come on the line. When asked if he would feel more secure if there were a lock on the door between the bedroom and living room and on the door between the bedroom and bath, he answered that if he started putting so much hardware on the

doors, there was the danger of being locked in. He felt security was, to a large extent, within his own head.

Too often such concerns as effective security or adequate protection from the elements while entering or departing a dwelling must be relegated to the status of "luxury items." Merely finding a building with an accessible entrance and adequate space in the interior poses monumental problems. Gary has experienced many difficulties simply finding minimally acceptable housing.

Most apartments, particularly in the newer buildings, are cramped. There's just not enough room to move around. The biggest hassle has been hallways and making turns in hallways. This place that I'm living in now, the hallways are relatively wide in comparison to the other two places that I lived in. I guess that's the first thing; basically, if you can find an apartment that is in an older building, like this, you've got half a chance. If you're going to be moving in with another crip, you'd best get two bedrooms, particularly if there are two electrics; otherwise it's just going to get too cramped. As far as closet space and stuff like that, this is the first apartment where I could even get near the closets.

I moved in this apartment and I said, this place is sort of cramped. When I first moved in, we knew that it wasn't really what we wanted or what we were looking for. But we had other priorities at the time and it was the lesser of two evils. The other places that we looked at were just totally out of the question. We'd looked at three or four places, and we said, well, okay, this place is still cramped, but we can do it. For almost a year we did it. And for me, I guess, I'm in a better position to try out things like that, because I'm not, say, a quad or someone who has limited use of their hands. I have good use of my hands and my arms, and considering that you develop all kinds of weird-ass ways to get in and out of doorways. I mean, I can remember times when I would use my head to help myself get out of a doorway if I had to put some extra push on the chair. I would get myself up against the chair and try to push myself out of the door, and maybe one end would go and the other end would get stuck, so maybe I would have to use another portion of my body to either open the door or something like that. When you're in a cramped environment, you learn to use everything you've got, and that can be anything from one extra finger that you didn't think you'd have to use to using your leg to kick something.

Shelter has strong psychological overtones. As well as offering security and access, it must provide the symbols of comfort. Returning to the hearth is more than a literary cliché; the presence of a visible heat source like a fireplace or a sunny, protected patio is an important element in the concept of dwelling.

Heating systems that offer even and controlled temperatures are important for the maintenance of physical comfort. Heat sources that offer varying degrees of warmth and the opportunity to adjust to the source are emotionally important. Any heating system to be used in the homes of the disabled should be designed to be easily operated with minimal muscle control. In addition surfaces that can become hot and cause burns must carry visual warnings as some disabilities destroy those sensations that warn of burns or other injury.

In extreme climates, metabolic problems may tend to confine some people to the home unless temperature-controlled access to transportation is available. Sheltered access to the garage or a heated garage may be a necessity rather than a luxury. A sheltered front entry is important for those who require time to operate locks and opening devices, and nonskid surfaces on outdoor paving may be necessary for those who do go out in rainstorms.

The Community Environment

At the community level, one of the most important aspects of shelter is its environmental messages. A town like Berkeley, which has demonstrated its concern for the welfare of the disabled population with visible acts such as curb cuts, timed stop lights, and ramps, sends a message to disabled inhabitants and visitors that clearly says, "You are welcome here; this place offers shelter and concern." The physical environment was frequently the first subject mentioned by the informants in discussing Berkeley. It induced an immediate sense of security for many upon their arrival. "If they care enough to make things physically accessible, which was never true anywhere else I lived, then probably they will also be more accepting of me personally."

Berkeley also offers shelter for a wide range of public and semipublic activities. Most restaurants are accessible and have come to function as common gathering places in which one can find shelter from the elements and social companionship. While the private homes of the vast majority of the population cannot be entered, such public facilities play a particularly important role in social interactions among able-bodied and disabled people. They provide both an area in which to meet and a ground upon which the two populations can participate equally.

Sleep

The need for sleep is physiological; the body demands periods of rest and recuperation or reduced stimulation alternating with periods of activity. Certain periods during life have an unusually high rest requirement: infancy, pregnancy, illness, old age. Frequently, special accommodations are necessary to meet such excess needs for seclusion.

The Developmental Implications

The typical life cycle includes a variety of sleep patterns. The newborn sleeps almost continuously, waking only to eat. The need for sleep diminishes gradually through childhood and adolescence to a minimum requirement during the prime years, after which the need for rest again increases with age. The daily sleep cycle is associated with physiological variations in need based on activity and maturity level; even in infancy, however, the need for sleep is also affected by emotional needs. The child who resists sleep—afraid to miss anything—and the adult who sleeps constantly—attempting to avoid something—are symptomatic of the emotionally charged values associated with sleeping.

For the disabled individual, who has a greater physiological need for sleep or for bed rest, the values held by the culture may conflict with his real needs. Time spent in bed may be viewed as laziness or as a form of escape. Children who have been told for years that "the early bird gets the worm" may find staying abed difficult or threatening to their concept of self. Uninformed critics frequently assert that "if he would just get up and around, he'd be much better off." Generally, the American culture favors an activist approach to problems rather than passive acceptance of them. Developing a positive self-image in the face of conflicts, either with training or through the perceptions of others, is an important aspect of adjusting to disability; the issues around sleeping are just one of its many manifestations. Peter says, "An important goal of the 'Crip Lib' movement is conscious acceptance of the fact that sleep and rest patterns will be different; that attempting to fit into normal patterns is not necessary."

The Intimate Environment

The bed is the most common setting for sleep. While an able-bodied person may find it possible to nap on miscellaneous pieces of furniture or the grass, a strategically placed and equipped bed is the only place in which most disabled individuals can sleep. Getting into the bed itself presents a major problem—a great many people require the help of an attendant to manage the transfer from chair to bed or from bed to chair.

Those who can accomplish this without an attendant's aid often use special equipment. Tom uses both a sliding board and a rigid overbed frame with a suspended rope loop above his bed to manage the transfer. After making sure that everything is properly placed (phone on the bed, light switch within reach, tissues and medications on the hospital table suspended above the bed, doors locked, wheelchair in position), he removes the left arm of the chair, places it within easy reach, places the slideboard (which he has previously set conveniently on the bed) between his seat and the bed (they are almost exactly the same height so transfers can be made easily in both directions), and levers himself from chair to bed using the chair arm and then the loop as supports. His legs must be lifted into position, and he must slide up to a comfortable spot before releasing the loop. To get out of bed, the procedure is reversed. It is not a decision easily taken, so advance preparation is essential.

Peter, who requires assistance, goes through a similar bedtime routine with much of the actual physical work done by his attendant. The ritual of placing and checking each item that might be required in the night is also followed by Peter. Much of his studying is done in bed, so his books are set in order with the other required materials. Peter sleeps on a water mattress on a hospital-bed frame. He is prone to bedsores, so the attendant carefully adjusts the covers and the sheepskin pad, which provides additional protection for the skin. The bed height is planned to require as little lifting as possible by the attendant who places him in the bed. Because Peter cannot turn himself, he essentially stays in one position throughout the night. If he has a lover, a foam mattress lies alongside his bed at the same height, offering additional space.

The bed must be perfectly adapted to the needs of the individual. Such beds may vary from those with the adaptations previously described to beds that electrically or manually change positions, to beds that can be raised or lowered, to beds with sides to prevent falling due to spasming, to beds with emergency call systems built into the headboards. While it is essential that the bed meet the physical needs of the individual, it is also important that it projects an acceptable image to the person who may spend a great deal of time in it.

Hospital beds are often seen, by the informants, as too institutional in appearance. Mary Ann said, "They remind me too much of all that time in rehab centers and of the awful Stryker Frame" (a rotating bed used in hospitals to prevent the development of bedsores; it is often used in combination with traction devices and associated with pain). Many who did not voice their dislike of the institutional appearance silently tolerated the hospital bed by disguising it with bright bedcovers, pillows to hide the head, and other design touches. However, the hospital bed offers flexibility not available in standard beds and is used, in a disguised form, by most of those interviewed. Peter, who makes no attempt to disguise his hospital bed, says, "If people are stupid enough to think I'm sick because I'm in a hospital bed, let them think it."

For many, it is necessary to spend a great deal of time in bed. Thus, the bed may be used for many necessary functions other than sleep: eating, socializing, working, even bathing may take place there, as well as the traditional playing and mating. The atmosphere of the bed must support all these activities. Lennis says, "I spend most of my time in a sleep setting. I think a lot of quads do. I expand from my bedroom. The bedroom is my own personal space. I can control the heat and light and the fan and the noise all from this bed." Another quadriplegic man states, "I'm not good at resting and I feel really helpless when I have to spend time in bed. I don't like laying my trip on someone by asking them to do things for me. It has an effect on relationships with people. I try to keep things around me, so that people don't have to get them for me. I do business from my bed—a lot of phone calling and things."

The Dwelling Environment
For the able-bodied individual, time spent in the bedroom may be primarily devoted to sleeping, and since the most of the hours spent there are times of darkness, sunlight and view are of little importance. The common practice of placing bedrooms in the rear of the house, with poor views, no concern for orientation, and no contact with the street may be acceptable in a room designed primarily for evening use, but for the disabled user who spends a lot of time confined to the bed by illness or by a schedule that requires an attendant's presence for movement, this arrangement is not satisfactory. A brief look at the type of room that several people have chosen and planned for their own use demonstrates some of the considerations.

Peter selected a room that opens toward a small deck and the street. His bed is placed so that he can see the plants on the deck and watch the continual parade of passersby on his busy street. His room is at ground level so that he is in contact with sounds as well as sights and can speak with acquaintances through the open doors.

Carmen chose a room looking out on the garden through large, usually fully opened windows. She likes the sunny western orientation and the smell of plants in the room. Her bed is located so that she is aware of the garden. On sunny days, she gets closer by moving to "Cleopatra's barge," a canopied, colorful bed in the garden arranged by her attendants or friends.

For John, the bed space occupies one of the two large rooms of the cottage. The space is used for both bedroom and living room. Claudia, the woman with whom John lives, has a place to paint and write in one part of the room, and in another part, John has his desk and typewriter. The bed provides John with the opportunity for periods of rest, a day or two or more, while remaining a part of the activity of the living room.

The bed is placed in a corner diagonally across from the entrance door. With its brightly covered spread and bunches of colorful pillows, it appears more of an oversize couch or Turkish divan than a bed. It is visually a comfortable element within the space and does not call attention to itself as a bed in the living room.

The Community Environment
Sleeping away from home is a problem for most disabled people. Planning ahead is essential. A bathroom that cannot be entered or a doorway that bars a wheelchair cannot be overcome by even the best attendant. So motel chains that make a practice of accessibility must be chosen or each visit must be scheduled. A skilled assistant is almost mandatory for even the most independent, severely disabled person—the adaptations and devices which enable the individual to function without help at home are not available in hotels, and hotel employees with the necessary experience are rare. Tom, departing for a vacation, planned to drive through the night whenever possible. "Each time we stop it's a big hassle. You have to make sure there's an accessible motel, call ahead, move all the equipment in. You're never sure if the bathroom will work, and you don't know how people will react. It's easier to just keep on driving, but them, if you do get tired, you can't stop just anywhere."

Mate

The rituals of mating include courting, pair bonding, expressions of affection, communication, sex-

ual expression, and child care. The formation of intimate relationships and the expression of the feelings generated in these relationships is an important dimension in the lives of disabled people.

The Developmental Implications
Children pattern their play and their plans for the future after the behavior of the adults around them. One of the most important aspects of this patterning is the concept of the family, of ultimate marriage and possibly having children, as an expression of adulthood. This process is as important in the development of most disabled children as it is in the lives of their able-bodied peers. They grow up as part of a family, and their expectations for the future may include the development of "their own" family. While this may be accepted within the families of disabled people, who see them as whole persons, it is frequently a difficult idea for others to grasp. For some disabled children, there is a false expectation that they will remain a "child," cared for by the same family group through adulthood. A few anticipate institutionalization.

Major problems for many disabled people occur as a result of society's unwillingness to view them as sexual beings and potential mates. Institutions traditionally treat them as children, separating the sexes and regarding expressions of affection as a perversion or inappropriate behavior that must be discouraged. Troubled by this negative image, the disabled person must also deal with the cultural images that associate sexuality with physical perfection and beauty. As Tom says: "I see myself as having sexual potential, as having marriage potential, but if you took twelve women off the street and lined them up to look at me, I wonder what they would see?"

One effect of this prejudice can be seen in the continuing efforts of the informants to change attitudes. As Peter says, "If there's a little kid on the street and he asks, 'What's wrong with you?' there is a certain responsibility to educate him in disability. The answer must be calm and direct and honest. You are always sort of a representative, and you can influence his attitudes in later life."

In Berkeley, some change in attitudes can already be seen. John says:

Before I came to Berkeley I had career potential and I've realized it. Berkeley told me I had sexual potential as well, which means that in some way the community must recognize it. Career potential is

June wedding.

always there, but before coming here I was confronted by an attitude toward me of my being asexual. It goes along with the stereotype. The best sex comes from the best looking people! Righteous turn-on! Rehabilitation center turn-on! People see a disabled person least of all as an ideal society member. It is only since coming to Berkeley that I can see myself as a person important to society.

Developing reasonable expectations of the self and finding potential lovers are difficult tasks for all adolescents. The teenager who has been disabled from birth must throw off a lifetime of societal assumptions as well as battle the physical difficulties of making contact. Newly disabled people must reassess their own value system, which had awarded points for beauty and athletic prowess. Peter uses the term *physicalism* to describe the value structure that must be overcome; like racism and sexism, it is often particularly important in relationships between the sexes.

The Intimate Environment
Privacy is essential for the development of close, open relationships and for sexual expression. The problem of working things out so that it is possible for a relationship to begin, develop, and possibly become intimate are particularly difficult when environmental barriers close other doors to you. Tom describes his frustration in pursuing relationships that seem to show promise. "I used to live in a first-floor apartment with David. The woman upstairs and I were very close. We spent a lot of time together, but there was no elevator so I never saw her apartment, and I had a roommate so we were never alone. There was just nowhere to go. Maybe it wouldn't have worked out anyway, but it never had a chance."

The adolescent years for disabled people can be particularly difficult in this respect. Most teenagers are in pushchairs and are dependent upon the aid of parents or friends to move around. Making acquaintances under these conditions is difficult, pursuing them impossible. The acquisition of an electric wheelchair can radically change the life of a person who has rarely had any real privacy; it offers the opportunity to go somewhere alone, to make one's own choices, to control one's mobility. Once involved in a relationship, it can permit a relatively equal status among partners for even the severely disabled. When both partners can move about independently "taking care of themselves," there is less necessity for the more able-bodied partner to assume a caretaker role. One Berkeley woman who is slightly disabled herself recently returned from a vacation with a more severely disabled friend. From her unique viewpoint on "both sides of the fence," she expressed her understanding of the difficulties of sustaining a relationship complicated by disability: "If you're the person causing the problem, you feel responsible. It can complicate relationships. In some ways, our vacation was a hassle just keeping from becoming upset or making him feel like a burden; yet I had one of the better times of my life just because of who I was with."

The issue of dependency in a marital or romantic involvement is a serious problem for many disabled people; even in situations in which the disabled partner has led a fairly independent life prior to involvement there is a constant danger of falling into patterns that lead to dependency. Tom, divorced after eight years of marriage, is now amazed by the extent to which he had become dependent with no understanding of the destructive effects it was having on his relationship with his wife. A "strong quad," Tom now does everything for himself; he cleans, cooks, drives, works, bathes, and writes without assistance. When he needs help with tasks requiring special dexterity, he hires someone to perform them. Yet, during his marriage, his ability to "take care of himself" was so eroded that his wife's most serious concern when she left was that he would be completely incapable of managing the simplest tasks alone.

The major factor in the development of this dependence was a failure to adapt the environment to his needs. "It just didn't seem necessary. She drove the car, and as long as I was a passenger and had some help we managed. She did most of the cooking and so forth. It was easier for her and we couldn't change things easily. If she helped me get dressed and pushed me to the bus stop, we could both sleep longer."

The importance of organizing the environment so that each disabled person can meet his needs without burdening a relationship cannot be stressed enough. Attendants who have become emotionally involved with their employers universally emphasize the importance of terminating the professional relationship if they wish to maintain the emotional one. The intensity of physically caring for someone has a dual character; it leads to the development of attractions and closeness and then destroys the same closeness when the caretaking is a necessity—neither a free choice made from love, nor a job which can be completed and left, both physically and emotionally.

Carmen says, "You should never make a lover

out of an attendant. It's true about the mystery—familiarity does breed contempt. On the other hand, it is good to have as a lover someone who has been an attendant to someone else. They understand." When an attendant does become a lover, however, the role must be redefined.

Perhaps the most important aspect of mating or courtship is the validation it offers of a person's worth and the meaning it often appears to impart to life. A male paraplegic says, "Being disabled, I feel alienated. I want to be—I like to feel I'm still sexually attractive, seductive. How can I be appealing if I'm still in a chair? I've come to realize life has to offer something more than sex. I'm now searching for that meaning. I want to feel alive."

The Dwelling Environment

The homes of disabled people are often the homes of a family—houses containing children, friends, pets, and mates, in addition to the disabled individual. There has been a prevailing tendency for designers to view disabled people as isolated from social contacts and associations. When disabled people *are* regarded as members of a family, a tendency remains to treat them as a special case, providing them with a specially equipped sick room. A space is provided near the kitchen so the homemaker can also function as a caretaker. The rest of the family lives upstairs and lives apart.

While this pattern is not appropriate for anyone who is truly regarded as a family member, it is still a spatial necessity in many homes. Two-story houses make up a large part of the residential stock of this country, and the upper half is usually inaccessible to the disabled person. When a family member becomes disabled, and the existing home has no accessible private space, arrangements are often made that are difficult for everyone. In one case, the dining room is the only possible place for a disabled young man. His room functions, however, as a corridor to the kitchen, denying him any real privacy. Furthermore, it cannot be closed off completely from the living room and lacks a full bathroom. He is in the unfortunate position of both feeling guilty

The new baby.

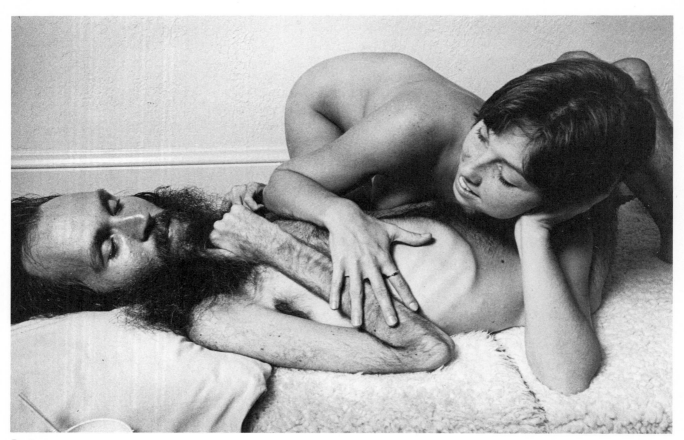

Intimacy.

for the inconvenience of his presence and resenting the lack of any real comfort. The likelihood of a member of any family suffering a temporary or permanent disability is high, and should be considered in planning any home.

For the many disabled individuals who do lead active sex lives, both the environment and the personal support system must be arranged to make lovemaking comfortable and convenient. Often, there are complications of prosthetic devices and transferring, which require the aid of a skilled attendant. Carmen, describing the problems she finds in lovemaking, says, "Most men don't know how to get past the wheelchair, and I don't know how to get past the iron maiden myself. Making love with me is a real trapeze act—the first time is uncomfortable, a little frightening. A lot has to do with bladder problems and my catheter. And there's the time thing: you can't just jump up, take a shower and douche, and be done. You need all those other hands. By the time you've taken care of one night, you're into the next."

Mary Ann commented on the added complications when the relationship involves two disabled people in wheelchairs. Like many other facets of life for the disabled, lovemaking cannot be totally spontaneous. "You have your plan when you want to go to bed; it can be worked out. It can be any kind of situation when two people become interested in each other. It might be two disabled people with an attendant." Arranging a bedroom space so that it permits sexual relationships to take place with whatever assistance is required, and with privacy as well, is essential.

The Community Environment
The tendency to view disabled people as leading rather isolated existences, or at least relating primarily to other disabled individuals, is reflected at the community level in seating arrangements for disabled people that ignore the presence of a partner. One young woman, frustrated by attending numerous movies and concerts separated from her date, proposes a folding seat for the side of her wheelchair, which would permit her date to sit close at hand. "As it is," she says, "when I go out with someone, we are so separated by the chair that he never even gets to put his arm around me. There is no easy sort of progression."

When a couple who are both in wheelchairs are on the sidewalks, a different spatial problem occurs. Two chairs are frequently too wide to travel side by side, and when they follow each other, communi-cation is impossible. The most comfortable position for talking appears to be side by side, but facing in opposite directions—an arrangement that also tends to block sidewalks unless a widened area is provided.

The community also tends to express its reluctance to accept disabled people as sexual individuals in the design and operation of hospitals and care facilities. Rooms are rarely provided that have space for a mate to visit for even temporary stays. Beds tend to be single, and privacy is often limited. "For the patients' protection," bedrooms can rarely be locked from within. Such "don't touch" messages sent by the environment are reinforced by policy.

Groom

Grooming is a daily activity for most mature individuals. It is very closely related to self-image; the term *well groomed* implies a well-being beyond the basics of cleanliness. Grooming is also very directly tied to caring or caretaking: the appearance of being well cared for implies a relationship with someone who is deeply concerned with another's well-being. The classic example of the unloved husband with missing cuff buttons and unmatched socks, while sexist, expresses accurately a societal attitude toward grooming.

The basic elements of grooming are cleanliness, mutual grooming, caretaking, usually child care, and also the care of ill, disabled, or elderly people. Good grooming is an important element in maintaining a healthy body and an attractive, cared-for appearance. The appearance of being unkempt, uncared for, unconcerned is a classic symptom of mental illness, of a loss of awareness or concern for one's effect on others.

The Developmental Implications
In infancy, grooming is intricately related to caring, holding, feeding, and eliminating. The infant is constantly being groomed during its waking hours. Unable to care for itself, a baby is totally dependent on others for its survival. The baby who is simply fed and changed in a mechanical way may not have a healthy psychological development—the caring expressed by holding and lovingly caretaking is essential for survival. Our earliest sensations of being loved are often related to grooming; the gentle washing of a face and brushing of hair often retain their power as an expression of intimate concern into adulthood. The implications of trust and acceptance in grooming are retained throughout life.

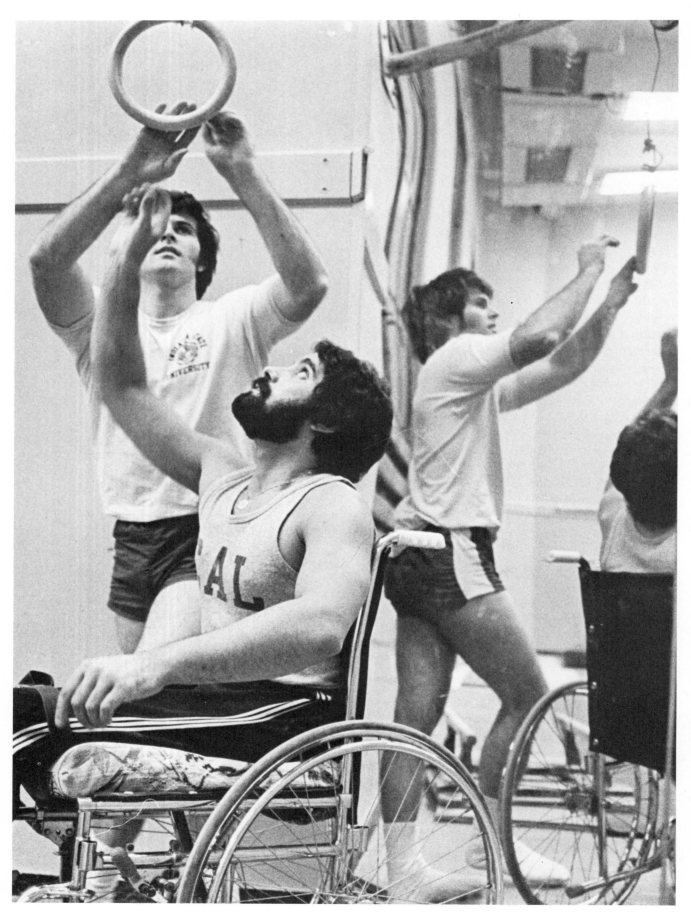

During early childhood, grooming often becomes the focal point of parent-child conflicts. The Dennis-the-Menace image of dirty, squirming children who regard a washcloth as potentially dangerous is as accurate as the image of sweet-smelling, pajamaed children fresh from the bath. Grooming is frequently the focus of the first moves toward independence. Children want to control their own cleanliness. They see the way they are groomed in terms of their own or their peers' values rather than as an extension of their parents' self-image. Simultaneously, the need for the warmth and the feeling of being cared for that has been expressed in grooming begins to find other outlets.

Disabled children may not experience this rebellion toward being groomed or may have less control over the extent to which their grooming is managed by others. In a society that is often said to equate cleanliness with godliness, few mothers are inclined to permit a child who is disabled and wants to play to be as dirty as the child might like. Disabled adults recall numerous childhood experiences that focused on cleanliness. One young woman expressed regrets at never having been permitted to play in the mud or puddles that other children enjoyed; confined to a wheelchair, she needed assistance to leave it, and her mother, horrified by the prospect of all that dirt, would not assist her.

The reasons for an emphasis on cleanliness vary in tone and legitimacy. Some parents have a valid concern about their child's ability to resist disease or to cope with being damp and cold. Other parents feel that their disabled child should suffer no further "reductions" in the acceptability of his appearance in front of others, than already exists. Too, the simple fact that someone else, often the parent, must handle all or most of the child's grooming needs presents a practical argument for staying clean. The mother of an able-bodied child who has been making mud pies can send him to wash himself; mothers of disabled children often do not have this option unless the child can be taught to meet his own grooming needs. One young man said,

> I think one of the reasons that dressing and cooking for myself was sort of one of my priorities when I was younger was that it was pushed on me, in the sense that a lot of people that I went to school with and had to deal with—teachers and administrators and so on—felt that the basic way that you raise a disabled kid or that you teach a disabled kid is to make him as much like his normal brothers and sis-

A sense of self invested in one's body: working out in the gym.

ters as possible. In other words, the idea was, "don't show your disability," so that was pushed on me a lot—the idea that, gee, someday you're going to be able to dress all by yourself and then you'll be a big boy—as if because I couldn't dress myself at such and such an age, there was something wrong with that. Learning to dress was sort of a standard for all disabled people. For instance, I remember putting a shirt on and buttoning it, and that was a really big deal, and I hated the ordeal. I really did, cause, you know, in the back of my mind I knew that I wasn't doing this for me. I can't really say for sure now whether that whole syndrome is the reason why they aren't priorities now.

During the teenage years, grooming becomes socially important. It is necessary not only to look attractive, but also to look like one's peers. Fads in dress, hairstyles, makeup are all typical of teenagers; resistance to these fads on the part of parents is almost as typical. From a resistance to bathing and hair care, adolescents make a radical change to a monopolization of the bathroom and mirror. Experimentation with appearance is typical. For those who depend on others to manage their grooming, this period is potentially very frustrating. Even the most attentive assistant is likely to be influenced by his own personal taste in the type of appearance he creates. Those who do their own grooming but have difficulty owing to limited small-motor control or limited reach may also be frustrated by the difficulty of achieving the picture they have in their minds.

In adolescence there are rapid advances in one's social and sexual development. Perhaps at no other time in life is one as concerned with the changes taking place in peers and oneself as during this age. The school locker room, where dressing and undressing, bathing and grooming take place, is traditionally an environment in which the adolescent observes and compares himself or herself with peers. The disabled person who does not take part is excluded from this experience with peers and consequently does not have the benefit of shared knowledge and possible peer-group support.

During courtship and marriage, mutual grooming becomes important. The intimacy of caring for a lover and being cared for in return is one of the many elements that help form a strong bond. When disability limits the possibility for reciprocity, caretaking may become an obligation or a burden for one partner. Both attendants and disabled people have emphasized the importance of regarding grooming as a voluntary expression of feeling. When assistance is regularly required, it should be planned as an attendant service, rather than as an extension of the love relationship. Expressions of affection through physical care can be rewarding, but they may also be a physical or an emotional strain; this is avoidable if services that are or become a burden are handled by attendants.

Child grooming, from the point of view of the parent, is an important aspect of being a parent. It is a form of personal contact which establishes a direct and intimate involvement with the child that is maintained, at least symbolically, through adolescence. Parents handicapped in their ability to personally offer this nurturant care may find it necessary to create effective substitutes for both the physical services the child requires and the emotional contacts the parent misses. It is important to develop an understanding of what the real needs are and how they can be met, without being unduly influenced by standard social roles.

The Intimate Environment

At the most personal level, grooming is generally considered a private activity that is essential in maintaining an attractive, well-kept appearance. The activities, devices, and techniques associated with grooming have traditionally been surrounded by an aura of mystery—the secrets used to produce the desired image are hidden, sometimes even denied. The "natural look" that is sometimes created by careful application of makeup loses its allure when the truth is revealed; the societal ideal, at times, seems to be the creation of an illusion of continuous, effortless perfection. Those who are recognized as spending great amounts of time or money on grooming are often regarded as vain.

Given these social values, many disabled people prefer to be responsible for their own grooming, if at all possible. Facilities that are adaptable to the specific needs of the individual can help achieve this. Adaptations in clothing, like Velcro fasteners in place of hard-to-handle buttons, enlarged zipper pulls, stretchable waist and cuff bands, used in combination with articles of clothing selected for their ease in dressing—sweaters, T-shirts, ponchos, loose dresses—can make it possible for some severely disabled individuals to dress themselves. Mirrors that are appropriately placed, small appliances such as Water Pics, blow driers, electric toothbrushes, and so on may make some other tasks possible.

Personal grooming for disabled people may entail the use of special appliances or equipment associated with the disability. Problems related to skin breakdown, catheters, various ostomies, amputa-

tion, and such may require extra attention to cleanliness. Frequently, this equipment is viewed as "too revealing." One disabled man said, "Well, you've seen the able-bodied side of me, now you get to see the other half." Some disabled people prefer to "put it all out front" and confront visitors with the full spectrum of the disability. The message is: "This is the way I am and there's absolutely nothing I can do about it, so take it or leave it."

Those who are unable to care for themselves must rely on attendants to create their "image." This role has many parallels in everyday life. The hairdresser, manicurist, beautician, and masseuse are all traditionally engaged in grooming as a profession. Attendants who assume these roles may have a strong influence on their employer's appearance. Surroundings that make these kinds of procedures possible are essential. Front and back mirrors in a space that is well-lit and -equipped can be important in assuring a person that he looks good.

The emotions associated with caretaking are often associated with loving or sexual feelings; attendants who provide these services frequently find that their involvement is more intense than that of a typical employee. This closeness can be stimulating and rewarding for both parties. But both attendants and disabled employers warn that it is essential to maintain some emotional distance to sustain an effective working relationship. If the emotional tie intercedes, the two roles should be separated.

The Dwelling Environment

Personal grooming frequently takes place in the bathroom and bedroom. Bathrooms are notoriously the most inaccessible rooms in any dwelling. Western society has tended to regard the functions that take place in the bathroom as private and potentially embarrassing; thus the spaces allotted to these functions in most plans are generally small, entered by means of a narrow passage and a small door, and placed at the farthest extremes of the building. As a result of these design decisions most bathrooms are inaccessible; not only are they too small to accommodate a wheelchair and permit it to turn, but they generally do not permit it through the doorway.

Existing homes that are modified for wheelchair access are forced into rather awkward solutions. Removing the door and jamb widens the entry without making structural changes; the effect is to permit access, but eliminate modesty. The bathroom in Carmen's home is typical; built in the space that was formerly a back hallway, it is screened only by a draw curtain, which is difficult for the most able-

Grooming.

bodied person to adjust to. The simple solution was to abandon modesty as a value. While the toilet is fairly well screened, the tub is almost completely exposed; bathing is, thus, a rather public event accompanied by conversations from room to room with attendants and friends passing in and out. Carmen plans to hang a net chair from the ceiling beside her tub; it will be out of the way and will provide a seat when needed, further emphasizing the acceptance of nudity in this household.

In other two-story homes in which such extensive modifications are not possible, even less-satisfactory arrangements are common. In one man's home, the only downstairs bathroom is a minute powder room adjoining the kitchen. The doorway is so narrow that he cannot enter without bumping the sides. Yet his comment is, "I'm happy if they're just wide enough so I can get through somehow."

His bruised knuckles and the scratched furniture beside the door testify to the fact that he can and does get through "somehow," but the effort is frus-

trating and energy consuming. The powder room to which he gains such difficult admittance offers only the minimal conveniences. It contains a toilet and a sink at opposite ends of the room. Since the space is too narrow to permit turning, both fixtures cannot be used on the same trip into the room. As a result, most washing and all bathing takas place at the kitchen sink, which is so high that assistance is required to use it. While he has good use of his arms and could easily accomplish most grooming without aid in an appropriate environment, the combination of a passive attitude—"I don't want to make any more trouble than I already have"—and the expenses of making extensive modifications has enforced a dependent status that is uncomfortable for everyone, but unlikely to change.

Dressing rooms or bathrooms can be designed to encourage and support independent grooming. Mirrors can be tilted or placed low enough to permit use from a wheelchair. Mirrors, however, should never be placed without consulting the user because the reflected image of the self can be very hard to deal with for a disabled or disfigured individual. Tom has placed his mirror so that it only reflects his "normal" upper body; he simply prefers not to look at his paralyzed legs and is unwilling to see himself in a wheelchair. Gary, who had a bathroom designed to fit his needs in an earlier home, says, "I really enjoyed the fact that that bathroom was designed for me. It made it a lot easier to be more independent around the house. But since I've moved out, I've discovered, for example, that I don't need a double-headed shower since I've learned to adapt my body and use my arms to get water where I wasn't able to get it before."

While many disabled people do accept the traditional values associated with grooming in our culture, many others feel that the traditional values are false or arbitrary. They say, "Independence is not determined by who brushes your hair or cuts your toenails." The physical demands of caring for oneself simply may not be worth the energy that must be expended. Mary Ann could perform much of the daily routine with adaptive tools, but says, "I can do a lot of things with tools, but it just takes me so long I'd never get anything done." Gary puts the issue in a perspective that is common: "Sitting home as a younger kid, it was one of my fantasies that if I could learn to cook for myself or dress myself, then I'd really be on the road to independence. But for me, that's really not what independence is. For me, it's on a larger scale of knowing that I live in this apartment. It's my territory. I have a say. I don't have to ask anybody but me."

Good grooming for this group may reflect the willingness to turn over grooming tasks to attendants whose standards may vary. By growing beards and long hear, choosing a natural rather than a "made-up" appearance, the effort spent on grooming can be reduced and the time gained can be spent on preferred activities.

For all disabled people, the basic elements for cleanliness must be available. Bathroom sinks must be usable from a wheelchair. A sink with an open space below it to accommodate the legs (the pipes should be insulated to prevent burns) is more comfortable for most wheelchair occupants than a boxed-in sink that must be approached from the side. For those with limited reach the faucets and tap may need to be placed toward the front of the sink; the treatment of the side of the sink should be determined by individual abilities. In most cases, a single lever that controls both volume and temperature is the easiest hardware to use. When the sink is

to be used with assistance or by a disabled adult caring for children, an extendable spray attachment is useful.

Bathing is essential for health and for reasons of cleanliness and pleasure. Bathtubs and showers designed in the typical manner are usually inaccessible; assistance is required to enter either of them since a wheelchair cannot cross the lip and there are no grab rails for transfer. One woman does not like sliding shower doors. "They put a railing on the tub and to get in the tub I have to sit on the railings and slide over. This hurts."

Numerous aids to bathing have been developed, but they do require the modification of bathing areas. The shower chair is designed to move into the shower and to facilitate self-bathing. For those who are able to transfer without assistance, it presents an easy solution to comfortable and safe showering. To use it, however, there should be no raised edges that must be crossed. Showers can be designed to empty through a floor drain without unnecessarily soaking the rest of the bathroom. By using an open shower plan, it is possible to permit a full turning radius, which is necessary unless multiple showerheads are present.

Showers may also be equipped with fold-down seats for those disabled people with greater mobility. Effectively placed grab bars and safety rails will then permit transfer. Gary uses the following method for showering:

Once I'm in the shower, I'm pretty much on my own. I've got a wire chair that I use in the shower and a grab bar over the shower and I stand up, hanging onto the bar. I sort of walk over to the shower and sit down in the chair. I have a chair just on the edge of the shower, like on the lip, so when I sit down and get straightened around in the seat, then my attendant will sort of lift up my legs and push me all the way back against the wall. Once I'm there, the knobs for the hot and cold water are right in front of me. When I'm going to take a shower, I usually have my attendant get the towels and stuff ready before I even get my clothes off, and warm up the water a little bit. But once it gets warm enough for me to stand it, then I have the shower turned off. That way when I get in, it's at a point where I can adjust it to where I want it, rather than going in and having it just be totally cold. When I first started I had some problem because it took me a while to learn, and I came close to scalding myself. I get in the shower and I get myself wet, and then I turn off the shower and I wash myself. Usually when I turn off the shower, I make it a point to shut off the hot water first. I knew from the beginning that that was what I was going to do, but a couple of times, maybe I didn't really know where things were or was tired, and I turned off the cold water first. I'm fast enough now that if I do something like that, I can usually grab for it. When I'm in the shower, I don't want my attendants always right there at the shower with me. But what I will do is have them stay around with me, because when I turn on the shower the nozzle may not be in the right place, so I'll have them adjust that cause I can't reach it enough to adjust it easily.

He has also used a bathtub by transferring himself into a commode chair that has been preplaced in the tub. However, he found it both uncomfortable and dangerous and thus prefers the shower.

Bathtubs can be equipped with bath chairs that provide support for bathing, but grab rails are also needed. When long or frequent baths are required or when water therapy like whirlpools or jets is desirable, the installation of a hot tub that can accommodate a few people may be beneficial. Carmen is reserving a protected area of her yard for a group bath. It will eliminate the weekly trips to the hospital's therapy center for bathing. She also hopes to use it for therapy (her attendant will be able to get in and work with her) and as a relaxed gathering place for her disabled friends, most of whom benefit from water therapy but now spend that time alone. Most private or public hot tubs are not equipped with the hoists or seats needed by disabled people. The hospitals that are so equipped have an institutional atmosphere and regulations, which make bathing serious business rather than a pleasurable experience.

John and his friend Claudia made several modifications to their cottage. One was to install a full-length mirror in the combined living room and bedroom, where clothes are kept and dressing takes place. It permits John easy and complete access to a whole self-image. Another was to put a toilet and a wash-up sink in a sunny location, part of the small back porch. Within the adjacent kitchen they installed a wide, easy-access shower. An important part of their environment is the backyard, which faces south and is entered by a ramp they built from the washing-up porch. Here, there is a private place to get into the sun and tan. This is important to John and Claudia.

The Community Environment
Although many aspects of basic grooming are performed in a private setting, certain regular care procedures like haircuts, manicures or facials and periodic maintenance (hair combing, makeup reapplication) take place in public settings. Public facilities vary greatly in their usability. Bathrooms with

a reasonable turning radius and reachable sinks are rare; mirrors placed or tilted for use by those in wheelchairs are more rare. Regulations currently in effect will correct this in some buildings.

Facilities like barber shops and beauty parlors are often unprepared both physically and psychologically for disabled customers. The chairs in the shop, which are designed to adjust in height and turn for the operators' convenience, are difficult or impossible to transfer into. Since the shops were designed around these chairs, there is often little or no space for work to be done in a wheelchair. Where space is available, equipment that is needed for an efficient job and mirrors that permit the customer to observe the process are often missing.

For many disabled people, these services are essential since tasks such as trimming finger and toe nails and cutting the hair may be impossible to perform personally. Unfortunately, these services can be offered in a manner that is uncomfortable or embarrassing. Various approaches are taken to this problem. Sometimes attendants, even those unskilled in these activities, are pressed into service; or the periods between care may be lengthened.

Feed

The concept of feeding includes the biological requirement of nourishment (satisfaction of hunger and thirst), the emotional satisfaction associated with eating both as a symbol of love or nurturing and as a form of social gathering and communication, and the preparation or provision of food for the self and others. Food is often the focus of ritual activities.

The Developmental Implications
The act of feeding or of being fed is associated from infancy with warmth, love, and nurturing. One of a baby's earliest sensations is hunger and the satisfaction at its appeasement. The psychological associations of these early experiences remain with us through adulthood. Food is valued not only for its ability to satisfy hunger, but also as a reward, as a substitute for love, as a primary reason for social interaction, and as a symbol of caring.

Individuals who are disabled from birth are often unable to experience the typical progression from total dependence upon the mother, through weaning from the bottle or breast, to the gradual introduction of solid foods, to eventual self-help. Progress from one stage to the next may be delayed; for instance, bottle feeding may be continued as a convenience when the child cannot hold a glass. Some adults require help with eating throughout their lives. Food may never have the same psychological associations for these individuals. Although closely associated with being cared for, the ritual of eating in a family group may have less-positive connotations for disabled people owing to food requirements that differ from the ordinary: that is, being fed, requiring special seating or equipment, needing specially prepared food, experiencing oneself as inept or socially maladroit.

The concept of self and the images of others may both be directly associated with food rituals: "bottle baby" is a common term of derision among preschoolers, picnicking with friends is an important shared experience beginning in childhood, going out for sodas or junk food is considered typical of adolescence, and dinner dates typically characterize the courting period. In adulthood, the ability to prepare or to provide food for others is a symbol of responsibility and of caring.

At each stage of development, the setting in which food is prepared or consumed tends to assume an importance of its own. The kitchen may be seen as the center of the home, the source of warmth, good smells, and happy feelings. The soda parlor or fast-food drive-in becomes not merely a place to acquire food, but also a social center, the place to meet and to get to know people. The neighborhood bar is sought not only for drinks but for the solace, support, and contact with a subculture that it offers. Access to a full range of these settings plays a major role in defining a place for oneself in society. Disabled people experience the same needs for social settings, but the possibility of experiencing them depends upon accessibility and the acceptance of individual differences.

The Intimate Environment
The preparation and consumption of food is often viewed as a social activity—a time for gathering, talking, and sharing. For many disabled people, this assumption is not accurate. For a variety of reasons, both physical and psychological, severely disabled people often choose to eat in privacy. Awkwardness in the handling of food, both in preparation and in dining, may result in embarrassment for those who prefer to hide their handicaps. Frequently, people who effectively feed themselves in private are embarrassed into hunger in public places. Disabled people suggest several dimensions in the choice to make dining a private activity.

Many disabled people whose food is cooked for them will also need some assistance with eating. The morning and evening meals may often be taken in bed, before the attendant has assisted them in getting up or after the attendant has assisted them in retiring for the evening. Bedside feeding by the attendant is often a pleasant and socially interactive experience, a situation to which perhaps only a few close friends will be admitted.

For those who have difficulty feeding themselves, meals taken at home may be the only nourishment all day. So for those who have an active schedule the only food intake may be the morning and evening meals, because there are no intermediate environments for assisted dining in the public environment.

Carmen always eats in her bed. She chooses it for comfort and convenience and also because she requires considerable help with her food—it must be cut into bite-sized pieces or be "finger food" (placed in her hand). Food is prepared for her and her children by a cook who serves each of them in their chosen spot. The children frequently eat by the television, Carmen in her bed, and assorted visiting adults and tenants at the kitchen table or in their rooms.

The Dwelling Environment
The dwelling requires space for both the preparation and the consumption of food; owing to individual capabilities, these spaces cannot fit any given pattern. Flexibility is a major concern, not only as a way of handling the user's varied needs, but also as a consideration when the kitchen is likely to be used by attendants or other household help in addition to the disabled user. However, the significance of the kitchen is how much of the space is accessible. As John says, "The kitchen for me is unconquered territory. I rely on others to make my jeans, cook my food. The dependency doesn't change my attitude toward my own independence. It's another form of consumerism."

Special considerations should be given to features like counter heights. Most wheelchairs require a work area lower than standard height, and kneehole space below working surfaces and cooking tops or sinks should be high enough to permit protruding chair parts as well as legs to enter. The space must not contain potentially dangerous surfaces, such as unwrapped hot-water pipes. Sinks should be shallow enough to permit individuals with limited range to reach the bottom and should be equipped with hardware that can be turned on with a single, easy motion of one hand (the single-lever faucet works for most). Faucets should be placed so that they can be easily reached (the location may depend upon the individual's ability, with placement on the stronger side usually preferred).

Range tops can pose special problems for individuals who cannot sense pain; burners must have a visible or auditory warning to prevent burns. Controls placed toward the front of the range top and operable with limited muscle control may be needed. Burners that are not located at the front of the range top may be out of reach and, therefore, unused. The height of the standard range top is a problem for many; pots must be lifted onto the surface and then cannot be seen into or stirred. A lower range surface that is level with the adjoining counter solves both problems; pots can be slid into place as well as slid off and seen into while cooking.

Kitchen storage and working space are two additional areas that require special adaptation. The standard kitchen storage arrangement places food and equipment either above the countertop or in closed cabinets below it. Both places are inaccessible to anyone in a wheelchair; only the midlevel drawers are useful. Alternate arrangements, such as open shelving at accessible levels, rotating open shelves below the counters, and an accessible pantry with open shelves, help to solve the storage problem. Careful organization of all supplies and equipment and the placement of every item in an easily reached space are also important. The kitchen will probably be used by a variety of cooks; it must be sensible and easily understood.

Working space in a kitchen for physically disabled people needs to be generous. A wheelchair must have space to pivot and turn without excessive effort, as the user's hands may be full. Space for attendants or helpers in the kitchen is frequently important. A kitchen that is too small to permit the disabled individual to be present with the cook may represent the loss of control over yet another area. For the individuals who cook for themselves, working surfaces which are continuous permit foods to be slid along from one work area to another. When this is not possible, a cart that rolls about may be required to move things from place to place; the lap is fine for small items, but hot and cold dishes need a steady surface.

The adaptation of a kitchen for the spatial needs of its users is an important factor in assuring good nutrition. A kitchen that allows limited meal preparation but prevents the preparation of full and appealing meals may tend to lead to a dependence on convenience foods like TV dinners. Such convenience foods demand little preparation and utilize the more accessible parts of the average kitchen, but unfortunately, they tend to be nutritionally deficient and expensive, and they reduce the likelihood of a group feeling a communal sense of sharing.

Spaces for eating may require special adaptations. If groups of disabled people in wheelchairs are to be served, a large space is needed to accommodate them. Tables must be placed so that they can be approached from several directions without moving those already seated. The scale of the table itself, however, should be small, so that food can be easily passed by those with limited range. Those who choose to eat alone also have special needs; the space must be adaptable.

Many people have developed systems that make it possible for them to feed themselves. Gary comments:

> It used to be that around the house whenever I wanted a glass of milk or something, I would have to have somebody pour it. So I would have attendants come in and fix me a sandwich and a glass of milk and it wouldn't take them an hour to do it, but I would have to pay for that hour because that's the way attendants work, the hour minimum. So what can you do? I really got tired of that and I saw ways by which I could do it. I've got a tube on the milk carton and for my juices, and I can have stuff made ahead of time and sitting on the table so when I want to eat, I can just eat it. I also have a 5-gallon water jug fixed with a tube near the table.
>
> I'm pretty independent around the house. I have access to my icebox but I don't cook for myself. It's something that I could do, I think, but right now I'm just not into putting energy into it. I'm into other things, and so I have people come in and cook for me, but I still consider myself independent.

Other problems are posed by the difficulty many disabled individuals experience in eating their food. The lack of muscular control in the hands requires that food be precut in relatively small pieces to permit easy feeding. Some people need to be spoon- or fork-fed. The appearance of either procedure is not in keeping with the gracious mealtime image that dominates our culture. Although meals tend to be the primary ritual gathering time for most families and groups, this is not the case for many severely disabled individuals. For them, meals are most often described as "pick-up" affairs, prepared and eaten on a very individual basis.

 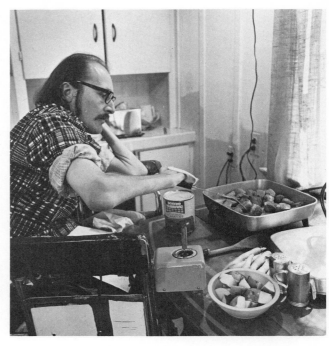

 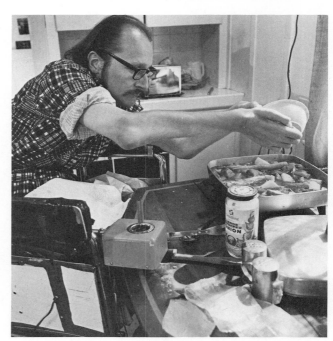

Preparing Sunday dinner.

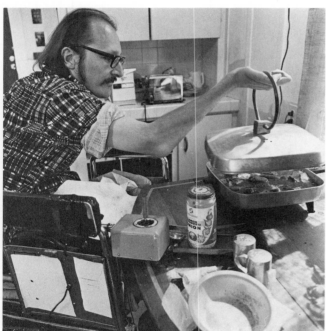

The Community Environment

Eating away from the home is a way of life for some disabled individuals, a frightening experience for others. Most, however, view it as an occasional treat—an opportunity to try new foods, see new places, and escape from the routine at home. Owing to the unpredictableness of accessibility in restaurants, visits must be either restricted to those that are known quantities or carefully planned ahead to check access, barriers in the surroundings, parking availability, and, in some cases, the menu. In Berkeley, this situation has designated certain restaurants as regular gathering places, some as simply reliable places for a meal, and others as taboo due to attitudinal or physical barriers. Word about where to go for meals spreads informally and quickly, but is so effective that interviews with dozens of people, many unacquainted, turned up not just some of the same names time and again, but the exact same comments about their acceptableness.

Characteristics of the more popular restaurants were friendly and understanding help; ease of entering, both in terms of a location within wheeling distance of the home and the absence of barriers; convenient but inconspicuous tables near the entry; good food; and good company, in that tables are shared and conversation is open. One coffeehouse, on Telegraph Avenue, popular with a wide variety of Berkeley residents, is particularly favored by the disabled population, who like the busy, conversational nature of this environment and the constant aura of something about to happen. It is also the cafe most frequented by counterculture individuals, with which Telegraph Avenue abounds.

In the Telegraph Avenue area itself, there are at least a half-dozen cafes accessible to and frequented by disabled people. These are convenient places in which to socialize with other disabled individuals who may not readily find a disabled friend's house accessible. Thus the cafe provides, in a certain sense, a metaphor of home, where food and drink can be "offered" and socializing can occur.

Many disabled individuals do eat in more public settings, but sometimes their food selection is restricted to those foods that are easily managed and are unlikely to cause digestive distress. Tom explains his situation with some dismay: "The doctor told me after the accident that I could expect to have the digestion of an old man within a few years. Unfortunately, I still have the appetite of a young man." Digestive problems are common for those with restricted activity. In addition to experiencing specific organic problems, their bodily processes are

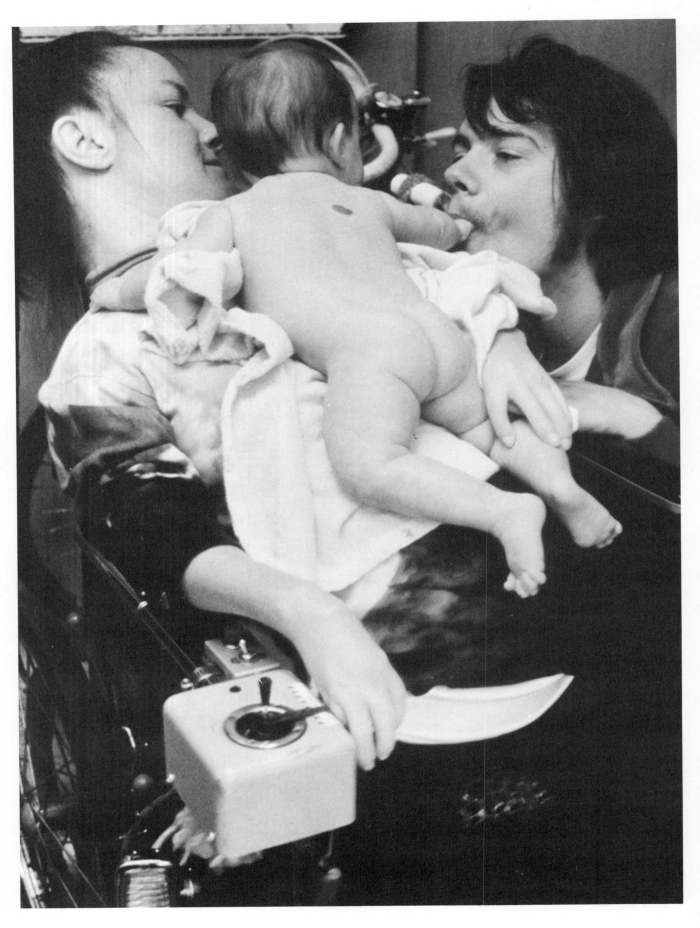

slowed by the absence of stimulation that physical exercise normally provides. While most eating patterns are fairly normal, sometimes the diet must be carefully watched. Spicy or overprocessed fast-foods, though convenient and readily available, may be indigestible.

Dining in restaurants or with friends is appealing and may appear to be a good solution to the difficulty of preparing food for oneself, but the unpredictable contents and forms of the food available make this a difficult solution for many. One man has tried many restaurants but tends to avoid those that are cafeteria-style because of the difficulty of maneuvering the trays. "Maybe it's just me; maybe if you go in there people really will want to help." He does frequent one popular, cafeteria-style coffee shop that is known among the disabled community for its helpfulness. "They really take care of you."

The wish to avoid awkward situations or potential embarrassment in using public dining facilities is common. Many of the informants say that they either call ahead to check accessibility and reserve an accessible table, or they limit their dining out to places they know or that have been screened by friends. "It's not as exciting, but at least you know what you're getting into."

One woman, a quadriplegic with very limited arm and hand motion, does not eat in any public setting because she needs a lapboard to hold her plates, special utensils, and glasses adapted with a straw attached to her hand. She feels that the lapboard causes her to appear "more disabled" than she sees herself; someone approaching her would "just see all this hardware, not me." A student, she finds it impossible to go home for lunch, and not wanting to be seen eating in an atypical fashion, she often goes hungry or snacks occasionally on bites of friends' sandwiches.

Excrete

Excretion, the process of emptying the bowels and bladder, occupies a position among humans that is unique. In the animal world, this process has a dual function of clearing the system and marking territorial limits. The excreted products have a value as identifiers and are not regarded purely as waste. Humans tend to view excretions with some embarrassment and a general sense of privacy, since the marking function is not active. Complex technological systems have been developed to dispose of them rapidly and with no trace.

Parenting.

The Developmental Implications
During infancy, excretion is an unregulated process, responsive only to bodily demands. For a period of time, the baby does not appear to distinguish the excretion from the self. Once this separation is made, the child begins to learn to control excretion autonomously; bowel and bladder training are begun, and the social expectations for continence and regularity are expressed. This period is often difficult (it is recognized as a source of neurosis in later life), and for a disabled child it may entail added problems. In some cases, effective control may be impossible. The child's attempts to gain control to please the parent will simply be frustrating. In other cases, no serious attempt will be made to establish control, but the child will be faced with the reactions of a culture in which toilet training is regarded as a prerequisite to growing up.

Adolescence brings another set of difficulties. The disabled adolescent who requires assistance in using a bathroom will not be able to indulge the need for privacy in excretion that seems typical of that age. Another aspect is that at an age when conformity in all things is important, a disabled teenager may have to use separate bathroom fixtures or use common facilities in an atypical manner, emphasizing his "differentness."

The typical bed or bathroom environment is not designed to facilitate these procedures. Most bathrooms are too small to be comfortably used by two, and few bedrooms have plumbing. A compromise arrangement is typical, but it often sacrifices privacy or convenience. The "bathroom trip," as it is often called, evokes a variety of responses. Carmen, who is irrigated regularly, says:

> I've gotten to the point where I just let it all hang out. Even if I'm being irrigated or something, and someone walks in, I figure it's just a part of the way I am and they might as well accept it because it sure isn't going to change. For a long time I was uncomfortable. I always wondered what people thought when they saw this sudden rush of yellow into the bottle. Last week a friend who went through some real illness with me came to visit and the first thing he said was, "I see you're peeing yellow again." We could both laugh about it, and I realized that no one seems uptight about it anymore. Maybe it's because I'm more comfortable.

Tom, however, is very modest and not only performs the bowel and bladder routines without assistance, but prefers to put the required apparatus out of sight, maintaining a bathroom in which none of the required medical aids are visible. While he enjoys traveling, he often cannot manage without assistance in motel bathrooms. This loss of privacy is a real deterrent to his taking trips.

Mary Ann has a bedpan setup for the night. Her toilet has a raised seat, which she feels entertains her friends. When Mary Ann herself is on the raised toilet seat, she says, "If the door's open I don't mind if people come and talk to me. Actually, I just love sitting on the toilet in the bathroom. I stay in there about an hour. I prop up my feet and read the paper with a cup of coffee in my hand."

For those who have experienced traumatic injuries, a period of retraining the bowels or learning to use a catheter and legbag may present some of the same issues as childhood toilet training. Guilt, embarrassment, and a desire to develop control coupled with difficulty in doing so can make this time a problem. Similar problems often occur in old age as the dependability of this function decreases.

The Intimate Environment

The conventional approach to excretion is to separate the waste entirely from the person. To function effectively within this system, a person must possess sufficient muscular control to restrict the flow of urine or retain the bowel movement. A great many disabled people do not have this control; as a result, they "carry their plumbing around with them" rather than use a bathroom in the usual fashion.

The most common arrangement is a catheter (either permanent or temporary), which empties directly into a legbag in the daytime or a jar at night. The bladder empties spontaneously and must flow freely into the bag or infections from backed-up urine will result. To prevent the occurrence of infections, legbags must be emptied regularly. There are various ways of accomplishing this: A clip that can be controlled by the individual is one method; other systems require assistance. In any case, a suitable location for emptying the bag is needed.

Portable urinals for men are also common. They can be used without leaving the wheelchair but may require assistance, which is difficult to secure in public places, and a suitable place for emptying. Some people find it necessary to assume postures that permit natural drainage in order to eliminate.

Bowel problems are also handled in various ways. Many people have found that a careful diet and regular habits produce predictable regularity; others require the use of laxatives, suppositories, or irrigation, each of which often necessitates assistance from others.

The Dwelling Environment

In most dwellings, the bathroom is the setting for excretory activities. The inefficiencies and inconveniences of the standard equipment have been thoroughly examined by Alexander Kira in *The Bathroom.*[5] These concerns plus others especially related to disability should be considered in the planning of this space. An important concern is the presence of a suitable drain for emptying a legbag. Standard toilets are too high to be used easily in most cases (the drain needs to be below the level of the drainage tube), and floor drains are not usually equipped to flush. Some urinals and bidets offer a good solution for specific cases.

The problems of limited bladder and bowel control are complex, both physically and psychologically. They cannot be solved simply by making existing bathrooms dimensionally accessible. Nor is catheterization an acceptable solution for everyone. One of the informants is a young man afflicted with multiple sclerosis; the problems he faces are just one example of a wide variety of difficulties. He does have limited bladder control and does not require a catheter when he can be assured of finding accessible bathrooms nearby. He lacks the muscular control for long waits and therefore is hesitant to venture beyond familiar environments unless catheterized. Catheterization, however, is a task that requires an attendant and that must be planned in advance. Caught in the middle, this young man "solved" his problem for a time by staying on familiar grounds; he attended a school that was recently built, familiar, and fully accessible, and he insisted that his acquaintances visit him in his apartment rather than running the risk of finding their bathrooms unusable. When he graduated from the small, familiar school and came to Berkeley, however, this young man had to adopt a new approach. The buildings are old and complex, bathrooms are not predictably accessible, and they are often difficult to locate. Because the distances to be traveled increased and the range of his activities widened, catheterization became essential. Psychologically, he still finds the catheter difficult to accept, abnormal. Geographically, however, he now has a wider range of activities; he can explore at will and visit without fear of an embarrassing "accident."

Individual solutions are commonly homemade when standard equipment is unsuitable. Gary has equipped his bathroom with a large jug in one cor-

An accessible bathroom.

ner. A plastic tube projects from the top with a funnel at one end; this permits him to urinate without assistance and without leaving his chair.

Commode chairs, which are commercially available, meet some needs, while careful arrangements of grab bars and lifts make it possible for others to use existing facilities. Any arrangement that reduces dependence on an attendant for bathroom functions can contribute to self-dependence. When assistance is required, the space must be arranged to permit two people and a wheelchair to maneuver comfortably. If modesty is valued, curtains or doors should be available to screen the toilet facilities.

A great deal has been written about the dimensional requirements for an accessible bathroom; while the legally required standards are an improvement over the limited space typically provided, they do not take the wide variations in capabilities of disabled people into consideration. Transferring onto a toilet requires using available strength effectively. In many cases, one side of the body is stronger than the other, or range may be limited so that a frontal approach is preferred. A flexible arrangement that allows either a side or a frontal approach and is well equipped with grab bars for varying reaches and heights can be used by a greater number of disabled people. Gary describes the arrangements he has made:

> As far as toilets go, in every apartment that I've ever lived in, the toilet has always been totally inaccessible. In one apartment, I was able to have a grab bar designed. I'd go in and the toilet would be to my left, but it would be through another door, so I had the grab bar designed so that when I got up, my feet would already partially be in the door and all I had to do was turn around. My first apartment was easy because the toilet was located right next to a wall. It wasn't through a door. All I had to do was get up, grab the bar, pivot around, and there I'd be, but this other apartment was another thing. I'd have to walk part of the way to get to the toilet. It worked a couple of times and then I hurt my leg on the way in and that was it. It was sort of a pain in the ass to start with, but I thought it was good for me—it was challenging. So what I do now is I have what they call a commode chair. It's got wheels on it, and I've got like a bucket underneath it, so I just take the thing in my room and stand up on my grab bar, they pull the chair under me, and I sit down and take care of business.
>
> I don't know how relevant this is, but I'll throw it in anyway. On every toilet that I've ever been on in my life, I have never been able to wipe myself after taking a shit, cause I just can't sit on the toilet, move around, reach back there, and try to wipe myself. It just doesn't work. It's partially my physical disability, but I don't know if toilets could be better de-

signed for me. I can't bend forward and reach back; I'll lose my balance. There have been times in my life where I've had a case of diarrhea or something and I just need help cleaning up my act. That's all there is to it. I don't like it when other people have to do it, but it's got to be done. In a way I come out a lot stronger, feeling better about myself. You discover, hey, that person did it, and they got through it.

The Community Environment
Public bathrooms have been a focal point of the drive to create a barrier-free community. It is essential that accessible toilet facilities be available so that disabled people can move about freely. While the need for more space within the bathroom, for grab bars, and for appropriately designed sinks and drinking fountains has been the subject of legislation, the simple need for more accessible and more clearly marked public bathrooms, in more locations, and with easier entry has received less publicity.

For many disabled individuals muscular weakness means limited control. Toilet facilities must be available; a long delay is simply not possible. The absence of available bathrooms in many public places is a major deterrent to exploration or extended travel.

Store

To store means to put out of the way and also to have on hand. Storage is consequently an action with differing purposes: in some cases, the object being stored is of such limited immediate value (in the sense of use) that it must be gotten out of the way—in storage. In other cases, however, the object stored is used frequently. While it must frequently be gotten out of the way (off the floor, off the bed), it may be needed several times a day or several times a month. Its location, then, becomes more an issue of immediate availability.

For disabled people, the actions of storing and retrieving objects are complicated by the physical limitations of the particular disability. That might range from an inability to use high or deep storage places to an inability to use almost any kind of storage without assistance. The strategies for providing storage, then, follow the particular limitations. A second dimension of storage is the special equipment associated with the particular disability.

The Developmental Implications
In infancy and early childhood, storage is handled by others. A parent or caretaker takes responsibility

for ordering and putting away the child's possessions, often controlling access and selection. During the early years, most children begin to assume some of these responsibilities and opportunities. They gain access to a toybox or a shelf, a kitchen cabinet or a woodpile, and begin to choose their own playthings. Often they display as much interest in returning the object to its place as in playing with it. An interest in order is seen in very small children who persistently fit objects into their correct holes, repeatedly empty and refill containers, and insist that each toy occupy its assigned position before they go to sleep.

As the environment becomes more complex, the need for storage places becomes more important. A child's natural inclination to create order is encouraged by "a place for everything." When no such place exists, chaos and stress often result. Of equal importance to children are places in which to hide things. In an adult-dominated world, simple storage tends to be accessible to and controlled by adults. An early expression of independence for many children is the creation of secret places that are theirs alone. A common experience of childhood is collecting or hoarding, either for the pleasure of doing it or in preparation for some future event (food for "running away," candy for tea parties, wood for future construction). Planning and storing these collections seems to be the primary activity; future plans merely furnish an excuse. All activities serve as preparation for the gradually increasing responsibility for and control of possessions as one grows older.

Children who are disabled at birth or during their early years may miss these opportunities to play at storage. The child who has all activities planned and his play objects brought to him, whose possessions are always arranged for him, who cannot hide private possessions or arrange his collections is inexperienced in ordering his life and possessions when he strives for independence. An adult may still require assistance in the actual placing or retrieval of objects, but if he also lacks skill at organizing and planning storage, space problems will arise. Attendants seem reluctant to take control and to organize space themselves, feeling that to do so would encourage dependence; yet, they find it difficult or impossible to work in a poorly ordered setting.

For the adolescent, storage is often used as a space for hiding personal objects. Diaries, pornographic magazines, letters from friends, and adult books are all part of the growing-up process that is regarded as secret and hidden from parents. When a disabled teenager's parents maintain tight control of their child's entire space, many of these normal explorations cannot occur due to the fear of discovery. Storage is also a frequent focus of adolescent rebellion; by refusing to conform to a parental notion of order, teenagers assert their separateness and begin to experience power over their surroundings. Maturation could be delayed if disability or parental intervention limited a developing adolescent from experiencing or expressing conflicts, sexual curiosity, and so on. All these adolescent experiences are a part of the struggle for independence when the individual leaves home.

The Intimate Environment
At the most personal level, everyone makes use of intimate storage—pockets, purse, attaché case, backpack. Within these containers are things like talismans, money, identification, credit cards, cosmetics, brushes and combs, the things that are needed to get along outside the home. Many of these things are used to underscore who one is, if that is necessary, or to help one gain entrance to outside situations. If a wallet or purse is stolen and one is suddenly without this set of objects and papers, one feels quite "naked" or "exposed," with a sense of personal injury.

What pockets of clothing or a purse are to able-bodied people, the wheelchair may be to the disabled person. Because the chair goes everywhere, is always available, and does not change from day to day, it may function as a major storage facility for its occupant. Wheelchairs in Berkeley display an ingenious assortment of storage devices adjusted to suit the needs of each user. Because these storage pockets are one of the few custom aspects of the chair, they are often individualized, a visual symbol of their owner's personality.

Most chairs have several different storage areas with varying accessibility. Side pockets, both inside and outside the armrest, are indispensible for many riders who use them as a wallet to carry identification, money, keys, and credit cards. The pocket may zip, be open, or close with Velcro strips, depending on the owner's dexterity or need for assistance. When aid is required, it is particularly important to have the space well organized so casual helpers can locate the desired item.

Rear pockets or backpacks are used for bulk storage. A sack designed to be used on the handlebars of a bicycle can be adapted to fit the handles, offering out-of-the-way storage. Extra clothing, appa-

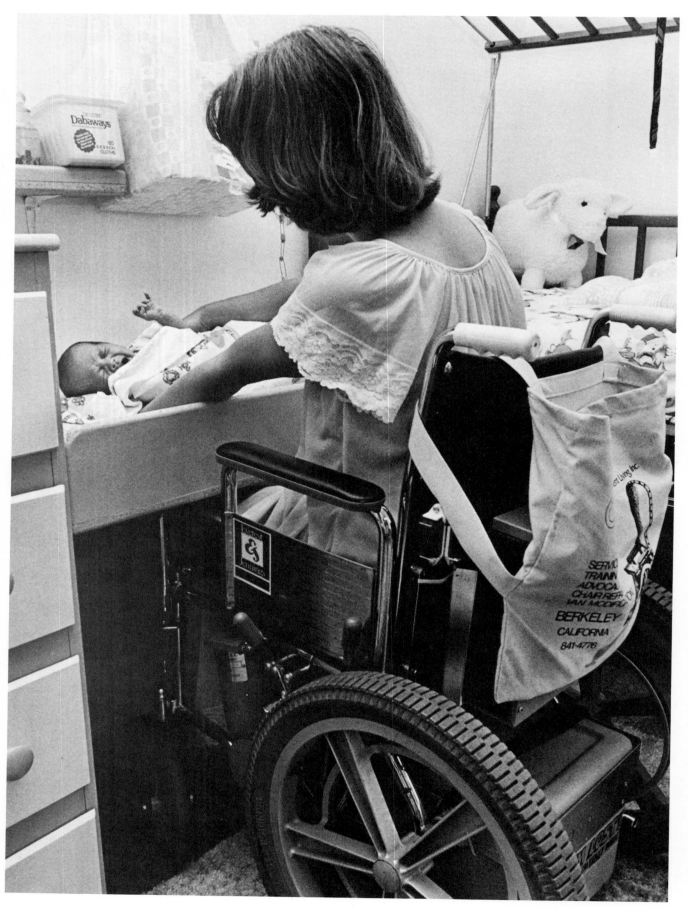

ratus, and packages fit easily into this space, but all probably require assistance for retrieval. Because these packs are large and easily seen, they are often decorated; tie-dyes, embroidery, and mottoes are common.

Special storage for adaptive sticks, keys, and specialized equipment like alphabet boards is often required and becomes an essential part of planning wheelchair storage. This may be accomplished with a variety of clips and magnets that are attached where needed, or it may be carefully organized in a custom unit, such as Lennis has. On his chair a lapboard with a compartment underneath is permanently attached across the front. The top is made of clear Plexiglas so that he sees the contents from above, and it is designed to hold a tape recorder, a juice glass, space for books, clips for papers and cards, desk-type holders for pens and pencils, and a surface for writing and eating.

At the most intimate level, the disabled person needs a means of storing his or her personal objects and papers that permits their use in the typical interactions of the day-to-day environment. Ideally, these objects and papers could be manipulated by the person alone, but many severely disabled people attach to their chairs bookbags and backpacks that can only be used by able-bodied people.

The Dwelling Environment
Within the house itself there is a need for accommodating the objects required by the disabled person in a manner that achieves two aims: getting the objects out of the way and doing this in a manner that permits their retrieval. (Retrieval can also imply access. An example is the television, which is stored or placed out of the way, but which is also made use of.)

Getting objects out of the way can be motivated by two objectives: the desire to keep the space open for movement and the desire to normalize the house by removing objects that indicate disability. The latter motivation seems to vary with the individual's attitude toward his disability. In some cases, it seems that the house can take on a totally unconventional appearance that makes it more suited to the person's disability. In other cases, there is a conscious effort to create a room like any other. In these cases, there may be a conflict between the need for special equipment and the desire for normalcy.

For the less severely disabled person, it may be appropriate to modify storage from an ergonomic

An ordered setting for a tender relationship.

viewpoint, taking into account how the disabled person actually functions in the acts of storing and retrieving in order to realize the right placement and design of storage areas. For the more severely disabled person, it may be appropriate to provide conventional storage for many of the household objects that will in fact be stored and retrieved by able-bodied attendants.

It is important to recognize that disabled people who do not have the ability to directly utilize storage facilities still need and prefer to maintain control over these spaces. This can be accomplished in various ways; open shelving that is visible from the wheelchair, coded storage that can be readily described and inventoried by an attendant, transparent storage containers, and "wheel-in" closets are a few of the possibilities.

Access to storage controls the amount of independence possible; usable items that are out of reach or demand assistance to be properly located cannot contribute to functional independence. Storage units that place items within reach are usually open and exposed. Hooks at a convenient height on the wall for clothing and open shelves and work surfaces arranged so that equipment or supplies can be easily grasped and used facilitate the number of tasks completed without assistance.

Mary Ann uses drawers, hooks on walls, tables, and any kind of counter for storage. It helps if these are at the appropriate height. She also uses tools that help her reach some things. An extra wheelchair and crutches go in a closet "so people don't have to see them." For retrieval, she puts the most-used thing at the front of a shelf or closet and the less-used things at the back.

The typical approach to storage is to put away, out of sight and reach, all the functional items of daily life and to leave on display only decorative items. This approach necessitates a preparation and clean-up period for every activity in which the materials to be used are gathered, set up, taken down, and returned. Not only does this process consume time, but for disabled people, it may demand skills that are not available. Gary describes the difficulty of using conventional storage facilities:

I haven't really tried to physically get into any of the closets around here, except the linen closet that I've gotten a few things out of sometimes. That's a pain, but it can be done. The linen closet is next to the bathroom. You go in the bathroom and it's the closet right behind you. That requires going partway into the bathroom and reaching back into the linen closet. Now, the only hassle is that if I do it and don't prepare myself ahead of time, I can get

93

caught on that damn floor as I did the other day. It took me about a half hour to work my way out, and to tell you the truth, I don't even remember how I did it.

The Community Environment

Storage is typically regarded as personal, that is, limited to the person or the dwelling rather than the community. However, a wide variety of storage forms do occur in community settings, and many of them pose special problems for disabled people. Lockers, cubbyholes, and mailboxes are frequently placed in public areas to permit the temporary storage or distribution of materials. Because the need for them is not critical or of primary importance, their location may be inconvenient or inaccessible. Lockers and mailboxes are equipped with locks that require small-muscle control, or they are too high or too low to reach from a wheelchair. Cubbyholes are located above standing eye level, where they are out of reach and the labels cannot be read. Access to this type of storage is particularly important to the disabled individuals because of their limited ability to comfortably carry things with them, or to lift them from or to storage.

Wheelchair storage in public settings also poses awkward problems. The wheelchair is a bulky and cumbersome item; even when designed to fold up, it demands considerable space in an out-of-the-way location. Many disabled individuals can and prefer to transfer into standard seating in buses, theaters, and restaurants, but this is only possible if space is available in which to accomplish the transfer and temporarily store the wheelchair.

While shopping, many disabled individuals have difficulty getting items from shelves and holding them until they reach the check-out counters. The use of carts is impossible, so items must be collected and held. Small shopping baskets, provided by either the store or the shopper, work for some; others require a storage space that is fixed to the chair to avoid spilling. The most common approach is to pile items on the lap and to hope that they do not roll or slide onto the floor. Wheelchairs, as they are now designed, place most storage out of the reach of the rider with limited motion. For many problems, the best solution might be a new type of chair or turning over the task to others.

Territory

The need to establish territory exists on both the physical and the spiritual plane. Physical territoriality is a part of such activities as spying, guarding, de-

fending, and observing—activities directly related to the control of a space. Establishing a territory on the psychological level entails planning, meditation, contemplation, and waiting.

The Developmental Implications

In infancy territory is closely related to security. The bed is identified as the primary secure space or territory, and as ventures are made beyond this space, a territorial symbol such as a stuffed animal or a piece of blanket is often carried for reassurance. Childhood brings the confidence to branch out beyond this secure space, but such ventures are often accompanied by a great deal of play security. Lookouts are established to warn of the invasions of territory, elaborate plans for protection are made, and child-sized turfs are identified. Defense is manifested early with "This is my property and you can't step foot on it." During this period, the disabled youngster may be at a distinct disadvantage. Not being in a position to readily defend his own territory, he is also limited in his ability to participate in the establishment of joint territorial ventures like forts and treehouses. To the extent that territory is used as a means of establishing a world separated from that of adults, he may be completely hampered from doing this either by peers unwilling to tolerate adult intrusion or by adults unwilling to make the effort to enable participation.

Adolescence is marked by an expansion of territorial interests into intellectual and spiritual domains. "Worlds of the mind" are discovered and personalized. Frequently, a child who is limited in the pursuit of physical territory has a headstart in this area. For many disabled youngsters, activities of the mind have been an active pursuit since early childhood. While this relative sophistication offers a rewarding personal experience, it may be a disadvantage in peer relationships. Several informants commented that they "got along better with adults than children" and had had little experience with other children.

Somewhere in the period between adolescence and adulthood, a move is made to establish a truly personal territory. Characteristically, one moves out of the parental home into "a place of one's own," thereby declaring both the establishment of a separate identity and the right to control one's own space. Disabled people frequently lack the resources and the ability to make this move on their own; it may be delayed or it may never happen for a

Peter Trier in his own territory, as his portrait shows.

94

variety of reasons. The establishment of a personal territory almost invariably precedes the sharing of a territory with a mate. For those who are unable to make a break from the parental home, this stage is almost never reached.

The Intimate Environment
At the most personal level, the body is regarded as private territory to be shared only voluntarily. This notion is reinforced in our culture by the assumption that any physical familiarity implies intimacy and accompanies an affectionate relationship. For able-bodied people, the barriers to physical contact are typically penetrated only by the family, lovers, and occasionally a medical professional. Disabled people must overcome the attitude that the body is an exclusive territory to permit a wide range of attendants, friends, and medical personnel to handle and care for their bodies. The relationship may be contractual, professional, convenient, or affectionate and does not necessarily imply intimacy.

Culturally, the impact of having to give outsiders access to one's body is a general devaluation of physical modesty. Since it is impossible for disabled people to maintain even visual privacy in many circumstances, they deny the value of doing so, and develop important intimacies in other ways. Devaluation of modesty was experienced on a grand scale during the HEW occupation in San Francisco for protest purposes. Large numbers of disabled individuals and their attendants sat in the building for twenty-six days as daily workers came and went. Sanitary, bathing, and sleeping facilities were limited and privacy was nonexistent. Although maintenance of bowel, bladder, and cleanliness programs is particularly essential to good health for disabled people, who are more susceptible to infection, the solution was to abandon modesty as a value when it was inconvenient. An attempt was made to limit exposure while government workers were present, but those who were being exercised or dressed could not easily remain covered. No extreme effort was made to do so. The effect was not to increase discomfort, but to increase closeness and solidarity.

For disabled people, as for many others, the territory of last resort—the one territory absolutely free from unwanted invasion—is that of the mind and emotions. Many of the informants set aside and value a daily period of meditation or contemplation. This territory requires no defenses that must

A family.

be established physically, and it is as accessible to disabled people as it is to anyone else. However, for various reasons, the territory of the mind may be somewhat more vulnerable in public situations. Berkeley is the scene of a great deal of religious recruiting; followers of various religions approach people on the streets seeking either donations or converts. One disabled man stated that he feels particularly vulnerable to these approaches: "They see me coming and they know that I can't get away. It's not like I can just turn around and walk off. Being in a wheelchair I'm expected to be nice and I guess I hate to spoil the image, but it always makes me uncomfortable."

The Dwelling Environment
In a situation in which access to the most personal territory—the body—cannot be controlled, the dwelling space itself may assume greater significance. It offers a retreat into total privacy, a physical area that can be controlled. Like the body, this territory may be subject to invasion by attendants or others, but they are under the verbal control of the occupant and act at his bidding to achieve his goals. Gary says, "The situation where I feel most independent is in my home. That's where I can be 95 to 100 percent on my own and be sure that I can take care of pretty much everything."

The dwelling, sometimes only a single room, may be the only territory that feels completely secure. When this area is depersonalized, as in a hospital or institutional setting, and the individual has no personal territory, a real discomfort is felt, which can be carried into all situations resembling institutions. The effect is seen in a refusal by some physically disabled people to use hospital beds or have corridor handrails installed; despite the advantages of these devices, their association with the impersonal quality of an institution rules them out.

Territorial marking is a typical means of both defining and personalizing one's space. It is accomplished in a variety of ways. Decorating—modifying the surroundings to reflect personal tastes and preferences—is common among all people. The limits to each person's sphere of influence in any group-living situation are often indicated by the limits of their decorating efforts. A stronger statement of territory is seen in the dwellings of some disabled individuals who adjust their surroundings only to the needs of disabled people, providing no accommodation for able-bodied people. Peter and Brian, both confined to wheelchairs, for years shared an apartment in which the only available seats were as-

A public mural establishes that physically disabled people have turf here.

sorted wheelchairs—an educational experience for the able-bodied visitors used to spaces adapted to their needs. Peter says, "There are now two cruddy wooden chairs, but we tend to forget about them. They have to be carried in and most people just sit on the bed."

Within the dwelling, there remains a need for assistance in establishing territorial rights. A group of attendants in discussing the problems of working for newly disabled people commented that "An attendant could move into a person's environment and loom so large as an active, dynamic force that he could overwhelm the disabled person, taking over his territory. The other side is to help the person compensate for the fact that the environment is always overwhelming in a way that is totally unperceivable to anyone who is able-bodied."

A recognition of the territorial needs of a disabled individual and the special steps that may be required to assure them are important both in working with and in designing for disabled people. Traditionally, no arrangement has been made for personal territory of residents in institutions. In some cases, this need for a defined private space may have very specific dimensions. Mary Ann, normally a very social person, emphasized the importance for her of having her own room: "I want a space that is really private. I don't necessarily want to be watched by my neighbors and I don't like to be seen

from outside at night." For others, a similar assurance of a personal territory may be based on security devices or upon the ability personally to manage all the elements of the territorial space.

The Community Environment

The notion of "territory" within the community seems directly related to familiarity with the space. A building that is geographically within one's territory—for instance, a cottage in the yard—will only be experienced as part of the available territory if it is accessible. Similarly, a community setting like a park, although shared with numerous others, will be experienced as a part of one's territory if it is familiar.

Security is a major element in establishing familiarity. If the population and the patterns of an area are understood, it is easier to predict danger and to sense potentially troublesome situations. When there is no normal frame of reference, it is difficult to predict security and to plan evasive strategies. For those in wheelchairs, familiarity is only possible in accessible settings. The nature of the environment effectively determines the areas with which familiarity is possible; second stories, raised areas, roughly textured surfaces, and narrow spaces are only some of the many areas excluded from the experience of those in wheelchairs. The result is a territory riddled with holes of unknowable space.

The presence of insecure holes in a person's territory tends to reinforce an already strong sense of vulnerability. Many disabled people lack the ability to either fight or flee and therefore see themselves as easy victims of predators. A common safety precaution is to remain within an area viewed as one's own territory, at least during nighttime hours. When this territory itself is penetrated by holes that may contain hidden dangers, the usable territory often shrinks to one's own dwelling.

Territory is frequently used as a means of social control. From the overt establishment and protection of turf by street gangs to the subtle manipulations of business executives, territorial imperatives are important in defining relationships. In relationships between able and disabled people, able-bodied people often tend to have the power, for disabled people through lack of mobility are more apt to have to take a passive role in terms of territory. Meetings occur most frequently at the home of the disabled person, owing to his difficulty in traveling and the possible barriers in his surroundings. Meetings on the other's territory must often be initiated and controlled by the disabled individual, who knows his spatial requirements. However, in order to actively engage others on his territory, the disabled person must do a great deal of strategy planning. Knowing this, the able-bodied person can often take command of how and in what circumstances meetings will take place. This imbalance, while practical and subtle, may exert pressures on developing relationships that are hard to pinpoint and discuss. The give-and-take quality is easily achieved only when access and initiation are approximately equal.

Play

The concept of play is often restricted exclusively to children's activities. Adults are assumed to have a serious purpose in all their activities, which removes them from the realm of play. In fact, play is a universal activity, engaged in by all cultures and at all ages. It is an essential part of both physical and intellectual development and includes such activities as motor satisfaction, exercise, creation, discovery, and synthesis. Emotional development partially depends on such play activities as role testing and rule breaking.

The Developmental Implications
Play is one of the most significant activities of infancy and childhood; it fills the hours between sleeping and eating and contains the early forms of many other behavior patterns. In infancy, the disabled child's play is like that of most children. It is a process of exploring, developing abilities, discovering limits, and testing rules. Babies are remarkably adaptable and, lacking past experience to tell them how infancy should be, are able to make the most of their capacities.

Toddlers are exposed to limitations as parents, out of overprotectiveness, embarrassment, fear of reactions, and practical considerations, may limit the child's contact with other children or restrict his activities. Other children, curious about differences, may be removed or prevented from natural reactions so that relationships are strained. The give and take of play may be limited, and active physical pursuits may be impossible. Even passive play, such as observing others or withdrawal, may be limited by the need for a caretaker to participate in all activities. One result may be an unchildlike approach to play. Peter's mother often said, "Oh, Peter entertains himself so well," which was true, but symptomatic of what he now sees as undue seriousness for his young age.

In *Build Your Own Playground,* Jeremy Hewes states, "I think the most important thing we can do for kids is trust them, trust them to take the chances that are appropriate for them, at the time that's best for them. I kind of suspect that if you don't give a kid the chance to take a risk on a playground when he's five, he'll do it at a time which may be—in terms of society and in terms of the child himself—less appropriate."[6] Unfortunately, many disabled children are not given the opportunity to take chances. Until very recently, even campus or recreation programs designed especially for disabled people tended to be overly cautious. In recent years, a new trend in playground development has extended into this area and new experiences are being stressed. Play structures that offer a wide variety of kinesthetic experiences are being designed, and play attendants are being trained to facilitate rather than inhibit experiences.

Many childhood explorations are spatial. In adulthood the most frequently remembered childhood experiences are associated with secret places: hideouts, forts, playhouses, treehouses, or the space under the limbs of a tree or in a mud cave. Gaston Bachelard points out that adult attitudes about space can often be traced back to these early childhood experiences and that comfort in a small nook, the need to be "up off the ground," or a preference for enclosed areas is rooted in the places built and

Sports.

played in as children.[7] For children with limited mobility, these experiences are often impossible because the spaces of their childhood may be the bed, a corner of the kitchen, or an accessible porch. A related issue is that of individuals who are disabled later in life and are confined to a wheelchair but have already developed spatial attitudes based on their abilities as children. The accommodation of psychological as well as dimensional needs in spaces occupied as an adult is essential.

In later childhood, much play revolves around association with other children. Childhood games often form the basis of shared memories for adults who have otherwise disparate backgrounds; memories of games, such as the experience of being the last selected for a softball team, are a link that transcends other differences. Participation in these activities is an important aspect of growing up and should be experienced if at all possible. Neighborhood groups sometimes adapt games to compensate for handicaps due to age or physical limitations; some summer camps also include adapted games in their programs for disabled kids.

Summer camp is in itself an important play experience for many children. The design and approach of these camps has varied over time; camps may be integrated or segregated, overprotective or extremely casual, designed primarily for safety and control or to encourage independence and exploration. They offer the opportunity to interact with other children in a protected atmosphere without parental intervention, which is a play experience some disabled children are otherwise deprived of.

Play during adolescence generally includes sexual experimentation; it is a period of testing and exploring, of coming to understand the responses of both the self and others in a playful, nonpermanent context. People who have grown up in a tightly structured situation in which few group experiences occurred, even during adolescence, often report that this lack of an opportunity to "play at sex," to develop gradually in a natural setting, was an aspect of their disability that was most disturbing and very difficult to overcome after leaving home.

Competitive play is also a common feature of adolescence. The opportunity to test oneself against others in battles of strength or wit is a traditional rite of passage marking progress toward adulthood. The need to compare the self with others and to define one's place in the crowd seems universal. This very competitive drive is one of the major causes of spinal-cord injuries to adolescents who are participating in athletic events or who are otherwise test-

ing themselves. For the person who becomes disabled during this period, a major problem lies in redefining one's place among others, for all too often, the accident victim has based much of his identity upon athletic skills or physical appearances.

Disability, then, not only removes physical skills, but actually threatens the self that existed based upon these skills. One informant, a former high-school athlete, developed multiple sclerosis shortly after graduation. He was working as a grocery clerk and playing baseball for fun. His life was totally dependent upon continued physical strength. He did not view himself as an academic, and all of his positive self-image was centered in physical competence. As his eyes and then his strength failed, he became severely depressed and entered a nursing home "feeling like nothing." A long period of grief was required before he could stop mourning his former self and begin to see potentials in his future. He also discovered that his problem was actually compounded by visits and activities with his friends from the past who were unfamiliar with his new personality. They tended to spend their visits reminiscing. This served to reinforce his fears that he was not a "person" in this new state.

The Intimate Environment
Play can be active or passive; it may require special effort or consist simply of passive appreciation. For disabled people, active play often requires specially adapted equipment or assistance, and as a result, passive or relatively passive play activities are particularly important at the personal level. A great many of these activities are not only satisfying in themselves, but also permit vicarious enjoyment of sports, places, and events.

The television undoubtedly ranks as the primary implement of passive play; it is readily available, and there are often few alternatives. It offers an infinite variety of experiences without making any real demands on its viewers. The programming of special events, sports, and adventure programs serves as a substitute for real experience and works to "fill in the blanks" in interactions with able-bodied people, broadening the base of shared understanding. The recent popularity of electronic television games has added a new dimension to the television as an entertainment device. Competition and interaction with the television or with others are now possible. For many disabled people with some muscle control, these games offer good and pleasurable exercise as well as an opportunity to compete on an equal basis with others.

Since a major function of play is to furnish social contact, the telephone is another instrument that may serve as a play object. When other people are not readily available, the phone offers this opportunity for contact. One informant is in a situation in which the phone has become the focus of his recreational time. Unable to leave the house for six months because of poor access, he began contacting organizations to see what they could do for him. This effort to solve his access problem soon became an end in itself; he would spend hours calling organizations, talking to people, following up leads. When asked what he did for fun, his response was that he made phone calls, spending hours each day on the phone. Although his use of it is extreme, the telephone serves a similar function for many who contact friends and acquaintances primarily by phone to avoid the difficulties of physically getting together. For those with no speech or hearing difficulties, the telephone permits completely "normal" contact in which their disability is not apparent and cannot be an issue.

Solitary play, however, is not dependent upon mechanical devices. Reading, watching the activities of animals or of people, playing card games and doing puzzles are also common activities for which spaces should be provided. A sunny window overlooking the street or an active place is frequently the preferred area in any setting. If a person in a wheelchair is to use the area, it must be designed to allow adequate room to maneuver, and the windows should be placed to permit easy viewing.

Play at the most personal level is private. It demands equipment and spaces that can be managed alone. In selecting television, radio, or stereo equipment, controls that can be handled or adapted are necessary. A telephone may be voice-activated, amplified, or attached to a speaker phone system. Areas within the room should offer supplies close at hand and at a convenient height. Fantasy, fed by reading, movies, and television, is often a major play activity. It permits activities of any nature and transcends the limitations of everyday life. Several of our consultants are science fiction buffs who enjoy reading for the access they gain to an imaginary world. Others seem to find fantasy worlds in their own minds.

The Dwelling Environment
The dwelling and its immediate surroundings furnish the location of most play activity for some disabled individuals. Leaving this environment may entail too much effort, be too threatening, or simply

not offer the opportunities possible in an adapted environment. Because this space has to meet many needs, it is important that it offer a variety of types of enclosure. Well-populated, active areas and quiet retreats, areas to garden or areas from which to enjoy a garden, and areas from which to observe activity or gathering spots are all important. A design that incorporates a varied selection of areas in which to play can enhance the life of the occupant; making the spaces accessible can permit full involvement for the disabled resident.

Sunlight is an important consideration in designing for disabled people. The sun has the psychological effect of putting one in touch with nature, a particularly important consideration when other contact is difficult. However, the sun must also be respected as a threat to the health of some disabled people who lack the ability to physiologically adjust to heat, who are insensitive to the pain of sunburn, or who may otherwise suffer from overexposure. Designs that permit both protection and exposure to the sun, which feel open and light, are valued. One disabled person described the sensation of sun and light as "not hiding in the shadows," an important dimension of emerging independence.

Water is another important consideration. Bathing is potentially a very playful experience. The water offers support and freedom which is not available in any other way to many with limited mobility. Yet the bathing experience is often complicated by the complex arrangements required to enter and to leave the water.

Confinement to a wheelchair does not preclude the enjoyment of motion. Mary Ann refers to wheelchair dancing as motor play. She says she has done this activity both at the Center for Independent Living in large groups and in her own apartment with a few friends. Her apartment has hardwood floors and no rugs, so it is suited to this activity. Also, there is a fairly open space in the center of the living-dining area, where there is room for two or three people to dance.

The Community Environment
A great deal of activity that might be labeled play occurs at the community level. Special settings for play are part of every community. Parks, playgrounds, schools, and recreation areas created and maintained by public agencies are important scenes of recreational activities. For disabled people, these areas may be particularly important because vacant

Wheelchair dancing.

lots and other informal play centers are usually inaccessible, and because private facilities like swim or exercise clubs can be prohibitively expensive and also inaccessible.

The development of accessible and enjoyable public facilities requires an understanding of the diversity of interests and abilities of potential disabled users. Both passive and active play are important. Passive activities include simply sitting in areas that are comfortable, easily reached, out of the way of impatient traffic, and yet within the circle of activity; observing others at play or involved in competitive activities; and being moved through an environment by another person or by a vehicle (as in amusement park rides). Designing spaces that disabled people can passively enjoy as they travel through them requires the sensitive consideration of the needs of the observer. Disability has many faces. Metabolic problems may require settings in which the heat and cold are controlled or predictable. Visual limitations may preclude seating at a great distance from an activity. Surfaces may be impossible to rest upon if they are sloped or impossible to travel across if they are too soft to offer good traction or too slippery to generate friction. Such problems are easily overlooked.

Spectator sports are enjoyed by many disabled people; stadiums often provide space for wheelchairs at some accessible level in the stands, and athletic events can be enjoyed in their normal context. Unfortunately, the adaptations made for disabled people do not always consider the logical consequences of their seating arrangements. Commenting on a recent football game he had attended in his wheelchair, one man said, "The game was fine except when it got exciting. Then everyone stood up and we couldn't see anything."

The Japanese garden typifies an approach to land use that some informants find particularly appealing. Within a relatively small area, a wide variety of scenes are set, permitting the visitor several different experiences within a limited range. The illusion of distant vistas, quiet lakes, and miniature waterfalls can be produced in a space readily accessible to a wheelchair and convenient to residential areas.

Active involvement in recreational activities may vary from swimming, through wheelchair hiking, to horseback riding. Motor satisfaction remains an important concern for those with partial disabilities; they continue to enjoy exercise and often prefer that it be combined with socializing. Wheelchair athletics have become a well-organized and highly visible sport; although competition at this scale is not for

everyone, informal wheelchair games are enjoyed by many. Space for such impromptu games should be a part of the plan for any facility. Individual activities should also be planned for. Swimming, for instance, is a pleasant and beneficial exercise for many, and the addition of a lift or ramp can make a pool usable by disabled people. Heated water and dressing rooms will prevent chills. Hiking trails can be adapted for wheelchair use, offering contact with the wilderness that is otherwise very difficult to achieve.

Some disabled people manage to turn the necessities of their disability into an advantage. The necessary exercises and bathing routines can be playful and fun. Carmen once scandalized the staff of a local hospital by bringing along a bottle of bubble bath for her weekly period in the Jacuzzi. The wheelchair itself can be a source of pleasure. A man in his midtwenties says, "I love having a hot wheelchair. This one does 4 to 5 miles [6.5 to 8 kilometers] per hour, but the new chair will do 8 to 10 miles [13 to 16 kilometers] per hour. My wheelchair is an extension of me. A lot of people are uncomfortable with it, both disabled and non."

Children's play areas are now being imaginatively designed to enhance the sensations of motion experienced in a wheelchair. Rocking bridges, suspension devices, and textured pathways can induce the physical sensations of jumping or tilting. Pathways or corridors that wind and turn offer visual surprises and variety; one informant equated this sensation with dancing. For many activities disabled people depend upon a world that is as direct and barrier free as possible; for play they may enjoy greater variety, a range of challenges, new experiences.

Route

The development of routes, both mental and physical, is a task performed from childhood; exploration, the establishment and verification of perimeters, and the development of mental maps of familiar areas are essential for defining one's personal environment. In response to this need, social and community controls have developed that both formally and informally regulate the routing process. The environment is fitted with clues or landmarks, such as street signs, curbs, and fences, that serve as concrete symbols of routing notation.

Routes are divided into those used by pedestrians, by animals, by bikes, and by cars and trucks. Each route taken, however, becomes part of the traveler's mental map of the world; as it is used repeatedly it becomes indelible, an important part of experience shared with others who also use this route. Decisions of where to go and how to get there are inevitably influenced by the existing mental map, which serves as a useful reference for future experience.

The Developmental Implications

With the first experience of mobility, the infant becomes engaged in the process of exploring and mapping. Mothers of crawling infants discover, to their dismay, that forbidden treasures are no longer safe. Small babies soon develop an image of the areas in which they live; the toys, the kitchen, and other places with which they have become familiar are returned to repeatedly. As the baby's territory expands, the routes begin to carry the baby into territories that are not safe or permissible, and so social or parental controls begin to define the perimeter of the baby's range. Distinctions develop between sidewalk and street, between "my yard" and the neighbor's, and between routes to be taken alone and those that must be taken with an adult.

Familiarity with routes is almost a universal prerequisite for the extension of independence into a new area. As children exhibit familiarity and confidence with a new route, they often gain permission to travel the route alone. Initially, route learning occurs primarily by association (trips taken with a knowledgeable person) or by exploration within a controlled area. As the child's age increases, the type of controls exerted over areas to be explored changes. Permission to explore an unfamiliar space may be based on an adult's abstract conception or image of the type of place considered. Conceptual aids like maps or route descriptions function as devices to make an unknown area familiar before actual exploration begins.

Disabled children often miss many of the developmental experiences that lead to familiarity with large areas because they are physically deterred in their ability to develop routes. Exploration is frequently limited to areas that are within reach. The adult who acts as a caretaker may take the child on walks or move him from room to room, but rarely pursues the endless exploration of every aspect of the environment that occupies so much of a child's attention. A mother of two quadriplegic children finds particularly frustrating the limitations of modern wheelchairs: "When you are dealing with children, what you really want is an all-terrain vehicle. What is available are just miniature versions of adult chairs; they're fine for sidewalks, but they don't work at all in the places children want to go."

Areas up or down steps, through narrow doorways, or across difficult terrain remain unexplored on the disabled child's mental map. Often the routes explored are primarily those of interest to the adult who controls the wheelchair. Mary Ann relates that the difficulty of traveling prevented frequent pleasure trips. Many of the outings with her mother were functional.

> It was a real chore for my mother to take me to the store. She had to get me ready, get herself ready, put my push chair in the car, put me in the car, close up the house, and leave. When we got to the store, she would then have to get me out of the car, get the chair out, then me into the chair, and lock the car. I would then get pushed around to the places she wanted to go, not to where I wanted to go. If I had lived in a city and had had my electric chair, we wouldn't have had to use the car. There were no stores in my area and most of the places I wanted to go were inaccessible. I was dependent on my mother for those reasons. The environment encouraged my dependence.

The paths of childhood are meandering and rough; they pass under bushes and over logs and lead to destinations that appeal primarily to other children. The discussions of children are filled with references to these paths and destinations; the treehouses forts, and bush caves, the streams and grassy spots form a private world of their own in which all the routes can be explored. Missing this experience may become a social barrier in later life.

A primary reason that people explore new routes is for motor satisfaction; the exercise of walking or running serves as a direct incentive. This motivation is less significant, if present at all, for disabled people. Traveling from place to place induces enough dangers and difficulties to reduce its attractiveness as a way to spend time for some. The possible difficulties and dangers tend to reduce the amount of time spent in nonfunctional route exploration. There are exceptions, however. Peter says, "I really enjoy getting out and driving around. I like the freedom." John frequently refers to pleasures associated with owning a van. For able-bodied people, to sit behind the wheel of a vehicle and drive might be considered primarily a sedentary experience, but for John, it is an active experience, akin to play. When he's behind the wheel he feels no one knows of his disability, that he is on an equal basis with everyone else.

For the disabled adult, routing may primarily be an activity directed at finding safe, direct, and accessible routes between established destinations. Those who do not control their own chairs may actually be almost totally unable to map their surroundings; like passengers in a car driven by someone else, they have no responsibility for directional decisions and simply do not notice. While Berkeley is physically modified for accessibility, many other communities are not; traveling without assistance in them is impossible. A resident of a small town described his experiences before coming to Berkeley: "I didn't have a power chair so my Mom or Dad always pushed me. Even if I had had an electric chair, I couldn't have done the curbs; someone always had to help. I would have been trapped on a block once I got there."

The Intimate Environment
At the most personal level, routes exist as mental maps or as instructions applied to space. The development of these conceptualizations requires experience and testing; notions that seem as basic as "north and south" or "left and right" are understood through the experience of applying these abstract concepts to physical situations. An informant who has been disabled from birth and cared for in a very protected environment exemplifies the confusion that can result from not having the opportunity to apply these concepts. She is now living in Berkeley, alone for the first time. Although her entire childhood was spent in an adjoining community, the local hilly terrain and her need to be pushed in her wheelchair prevented exploration. She made daily trips to school in a van, but she could not describe how to make the trip to anyone else. Nor could she have found her own way if she had had to. Before coming to Berkeley and acquiring an electric wheelchair, even the concept of finding her own way was alien.

For this informant, directional orientations in explaining locations are confusing; in her experience *left* and *right* describe the sides of an object and not directions to be followed. This confusion is natural; most of her time has been spent in a fixed location: bed, couch, or chair. Movement has taken place around her. Self-directed movement for her and for many other disabled individuals was dependent upon the acquisition of an electric wheelchair.

The power chair is undeniably one of the most important factors in developing independence. Susan O'Hara, who is disabled and serves as head of the dormitory students' program at the University of California at Berkeley, says, "Coming to Berkeley is, for many, the first experience with a power

chair. This is a big experience. It changes one's life. To have someone walk alongside of you rather than behind establishes a new relationship. When someone pushes, it's easy to forget their presence."

In addition to the social impact, traveling without aid changes one's attitude toward routing. "With the power chair you can stop and start at will. When someone pushes, you tend to think of stop and start in terms of absolute necessity. With the power chair, there is a feeling of freedom, the choice to stop and start at random. When one moves about alone, one confronts the public alone. In a push chair people tend to talk over your head about you, your needs. This is especially true in stores. When you are in a power chair, people have to confront you as an individual or avoid you. It's you and them." A young woman described her experiences shopping in a push chair: "I go into a store and the lady asks my mother what I want rather than asking me. Perhaps she thinks I can't talk. If I were more aggressive I might be able to go more places and meet more people." Now that she does have an electric chair, she has the equipment to explore places and to confront people on her own. But the process is slow; she must learn both the physical and emotional routes to independence.

Although the electric chair offers added mobility, it conveys an image that some find disturbing. Carmen has her power chairs anodized black "to keep the shiny surfaces from reminding people of its use and purposes." To her, the chrome is both institutional—"everything in hospitals is polished chrome"—and too automobilelike. Another man states that he prefers not to use his electric chair, although he has one. He has a weight problem which he controls with the added exercise afforded by the manual chair, which also "makes me look less disabled. I want to look capable." The decision to use a push or electric wheelchair is often controlled by the routes along which it will be used. One informant came from a small town in which he would "buzz down the sidewalk and people would freak and yell, 'Look!'" In Berkeley electric chairs are common, and he travels without attracting special notice.

The Dwelling Environment
Within the dwelling, routes are typically established that offer the greatest convenience and then are used repetitively. Wheelchairs demand wide passageways and hard surfaces—nonslip flooring for maximum traction. The effects of wheelchairs rubbing against walls or corners have been dealt

with in various imaginative ways. In the CIL, plywood extends up the walls above the height of footrests and bumpers. In some homes, a rough lumber baseboard provides an attractive finish for the lower wall and absorbs scratches. Ceramic tile can also be used in frequently traveled areas, but carries institutional connotations unless it is handled carefully. Tile, too, may be fragile; some people have installed 1-foot (0.3-meter) -high plastic guards along baseboards.

A major problem within the dwelling is posed by doors; these must be accessible from both sides, lockable for security, and offer the occupant the opportunity to see the visitor before admitting him. Despite the fact that her apartment was not designed for accessibility, Mary Ann has solved the problem with an impressive assortment of adaptive sticks with which she can do almost anything. With a "key stick" she can reach and unlock the door, which is then pushed open with another, longer stick. The long stick also flips the light switch, and a pullstrap attached to the doorknob permits her to pull the door shut or to open it. In entering buildings with an elevator, these or similar devices permit her to use the buttons to call the elevator and designate the floor she wants. A strap on the handle of a hinged elevator door could also be used to open it. Examples of various physical solutions to these problems are illustrated in the Catalogue.

Many people who require a power chair to travel long distances prefer to use a manual chair within the dwelling. The manual chairs are smaller, lighter, and can maneuver in smaller spaces. They are also quiet and less vehicular in appearance. The possibility of using a variety of chairs suited to particular activities has some appeal; shower chairs that are not injured by water, commode chairs, and reclining chairs are all available and may make a specific route or activity easier to pursue. The problems of storage and the difficulty in transferring from chair to chair, however, limit many disabled people to a single chair. A great many electric chairs are as personalized as a fingerprint; they are tailored precisely to the needs of the one person who occupies them and cannot be replaced by a general-use chair.

The Community Environment
At the level of the community, routes begin to include a knowledge of the world, an ability to get around, the skill to plan trips, and the capacity to take care of oneself. Moving out into the world with confidence requires learning and practice on the

part of the mover and accommodation and understanding on the part of the planners of the physical environment. Mary Ann mentioned a hierarchy of means that enable her to be mobile: wheelchair and crutches; BART (Bay Area Rapid Transit), which is limited by the location of stations and the wheeling distance of her destination from the stations; and her van, which is on order. She mentioned environmental barriers in a casual manner, citing doors that had to be opened by someone else, staircases, and the lack of elevators and curbs. When asked about social barriers, she said, "If I go someplace and I know I'm going to make people upset, I go anyway. That's cause I like to sway people's ideas." Another positive factor influencing mobility is a person's ability to see himself or herself in novel and unpredictable situations.

Another informant, new to Berkeley, often found herself anxious, afraid of cars, and frightened by the aggressiveness of people in crowded places. In spite of her physical ability to move easily through an environment of curb cuts, delayed traffic lights, and helpful people, she felt "ignored, lost, and small." The first time she crossed a street alone she was "scared to death, afraid people wouldn't see me. I'd get run over; the chair would quit." Others have commented that on the crowded sidewalks of Berkeley, "I feel like I'm in the way. I can't control my wheelchair very well, and I hate always having to say 'Excuse me.' " Peter, however, says, "I enjoy weaving through crowds of people; I like the challenge. Sometimes I enjoy just driving around; being able to travel in my electric chair gives me a feeling of power."

Once the problems of simply maneuvering in public areas have begun to be mastered, there are the added problems of getting lost. Able-bodied people have a variety of approaches in finding new places: they can simply look for landmarks like a steeple or tower and head in the right general direction, they can cruise the general area until they sight their destination, they can consult a map, or they can ask for directions. For a variety of reasons, these methods are generally inadequate for disabled people. Pointing in the right direction does not take into consideration the environmental barriers that could occur between the two locations. For a person in a wheelchair, the most direct route is often inaccessible. Cruising is inefficient, and for a person who depends upon a limited battery or limited physical endurance, it is an unreasonable approach. Maps typically do not indicate curbs, stairs, or steep grades, which makes them untrustworthy as guides,

Going places: business.

and personal directions from able-bodied people rarely designate accessible routes and entries correctly.

One woman mentioned earlier describes getting lost, which happens to her frequently. "I feel like a rat in a maze. I ask people the accessible way, but they don't know what I'm talking about. Sometimes I ask people to go with me; otherwise I have to wait for someone to open doors for me." When she does seek instructions, she finds that people refer to the front or back of buildings. She adds ironically, "I'm never sure which is the front or which is the back. I have never come out of the front of anything." A world made up of back entrances, side doors, detours around stairways and slopes, and streets that can be crossed only at accessible corners is difficult to conceive. Finding routes through such a world can be frustrating and demanding.

One response to the problem of finding usable routes is to determine one route that is effective and then to stick to it rather than explore other paths. Often an attempt is made to find another person in a wheelchair as a guide for excursions into unfamiliar territory. A University of California at Berkeley program that paired incoming students with an experienced and disabled "big brother or sister" formalized this means of getting to know the area for many newcomers. An annotated map of the campus and of the surrounding community, which is now underway, will also address the problem.

Vertical travel often poses a greater problem than horizontal movement. Ramps have been constructed throughout Berkeley in a well-intentioned attempt to increase accessibility, but in many cases they are too steep, too long, or too narrow for safe usage. Some wheelchairs are controlled by muscles with minimal responsiveness; attempting to maintain control on a steep hill or on a narrow ramp can result in overturned chairs. Ramp inclines should be designed with a run of no longer than 30 feet (9 meters) so that the chair does not gain excessive speed or the driver become fatigued; curbs at the sides will prevent a chair from leaving the path and will slow an errant chair.

Steep curb cuts also pose a problem for some: "I have to be very careful when driving. Spasms are a problem for the spinal-cord injured; at any quick motion or involuntary movement a nerve stimulates

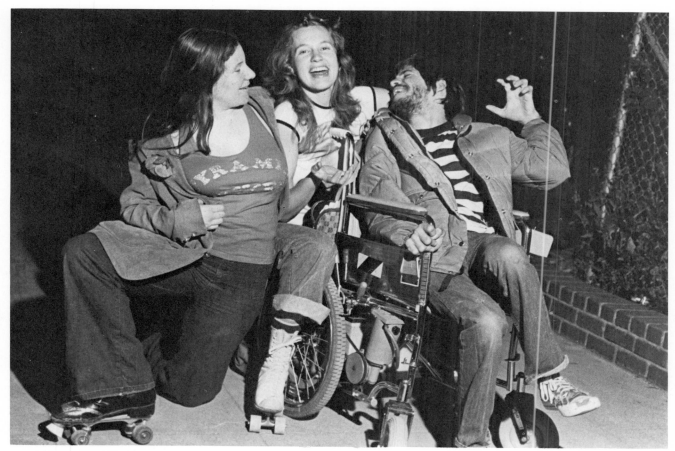

Going places: pleasure.

the muscle. Spasms can be very painful. For example, curb cuts are generally too steep and should be more gradually inclined." Many curb ramps are unusable without assistance for those in hand-operated chairs. They are also unusable for electric chairs when their power is running down. "On many a trip home, I've had to stay in the street the whole way."

Within buildings, elevators are the most convenient form of vertical access; yet they are often hazardous. One former New Yorker reports spending a night stranded in the front lobby of his apartment building because the elevator was out of order. The dangers of fire are increased when the elevator offers the only escape route, a consideration that limits some people to lower floors of otherwise accessible buildings, although fire remains a danger to those on the ground floor. Simply operating the elevator can be very difficult. Call and floor buttons may be out of reach or, worse, temperature sensitive and therefore unresponsive to pressure from a stick. Elevators with doors that pull open and buttons on the entry side are impossible to use. Emergency telephone systems are almost invariably too high. In many elevators there is not adequate space for a chair to turn around in order for its occupant to see the floor level. Doors often close fast and may close too hard. An elevator not flush with the landing may prevent entry or exit.

Public transportation systems are an essential element of traveling. Those who cannot use private cars and do not have access to a van depend entirely upon their chairs and accessible transit systems for entry to the community. In Berkeley, the physical area within which the majority of the most active disabled people live is rather small. Its limits are defined by the hills to the north and east and by a comfortable "wheelchair range" of services on the south and west. Moving out of this area is prohibited by hills too steep to climb, unramped curbs, the limited distance any chair can travel, and uncharted dangers like high crime rates and the lack of familiarity with and acceptance of wheelchairs. Some other means of travel is required to leave the immediate area. Various modes of transportation are available, but only BART and the privately owned vans or those operated by the Physically Disabled Students Program or the Center for Independent

Living are accessible. Buses, taxis, and private cars are generally not usable by those in wheelchairs without special adaptations, which have not been made in Berkeley.

Traveling alone on public transit is a problem for many. One young woman has never ridden on any public transit system alone. Although she is able to walk short distances with braces and could easily take advantage of a nearby bus line, she refuses unless accompanied by someone from her family. "I feel uncomfortable, I don't like to be stared at, and I'm afraid of getting hurt. If I ride with someone, then they are behind me to catch me if I fall. The drivers always take off before you are seated, and I'm not very stable."

Although BART and the vans seem to offer at least a limited form of access to an outside world, they are inadequate. BART is barrier free within the system, but is not linked with any other accessible transit system that brings riders to BART or delivers them to their destinations when they leave BART. Also, the local BART stations are at the outer edge of wheelchair range, which discourages distant destinations, and are not easily used by wheelchair riders, who must summon a station attendant by the telephone call system and wait for the elevator to be sent.

A greater deterrent is fear of the unfamiliar at the other end. While curbs in Berkeley are predictably ramped, streets in San Francisco and other BART communities are often unramped and dangerous. Only a few people in wheelchairs use BART without an attendant. Vans offer direct delivery to a destination, but unless they are privately owned, the necessity of making advance arrangements for the availability of van and drivers limits their usefulness. A lack of familiarity with potential destinations also has a limiting effect, as does the fear of breakdown.

Vans, however, do provide an almost ideal solution to the transportation problem for those who own and drive them. The van can go where any car goes. Special license plates and parking zones enable it to park close to most destinations. But, perhaps what is most important to some drivers, the disabled driver is on a completely equal status with all other drivers.

The van itself, however, can require a complex array of skills to those considering acquiring one. In order to enter the van, either ramps or lifts are needed; if they are to be used without an attendant, they must be electrically operated. Just gaining access to the controls demands the ability to use an adapted key. Lowering and raising the lift is accomplished by using pushbuttons. The extra time necessary (compared with able-bodied travel) is also a consideration, for boarding by wheelchair may require over five minutes. Driving the van requires all the standard skills, but they are often condensed into one or two controls that take advantage of individual strengths; thus, one hand may control the accelerator and the brake on a single continuum, while the other hand steers. Automatic transmissions, power brakes, and power steering are essential. Without these, the van would not be usable for those with limited strength.

Some anxiety about the environmental movement away from large vans and heavy gas consumption is expressed by some disabled people. Peter comments, "It is ironic that, as everyone else should be reducing their gas consumption and mileage, changing to bicycles or walking, disabled people should be increasing theirs. More people should have access to vans, and more destinations should be made available."

Vans have become a political issue, not only because they are gas consumers, but also because of the difficulty in acquiring one under current government programs. Since vans with adaptations usually cost $10,000 or more, very few disabled people can afford to buy a van without financial assistance; therefore, to get one, they are dependent upon support from some agency. As one consultant said, "It's a classic Catch 22! In order to work you need to have a van to prepare for and to find a job, but in order to get a van, you must already have the job."

Although vans do offer considerable freedom and pleasure, they tend to cut off some of the close contact afforded by traveling in a wheelchair. John acknowledges, "Since I got my van I've lost touch with navigating in the chair around town." Daily travels without a van can be important social experiences. A middle-aged man who is confined to a wheelchair by severe rheumatoid arthritis finds that his wheelchair serves two important functions that he would miss if he chose transportation by automobile. First, it puts him in close contact with the people and activity of the street—he often gives the neighborhood children rides on his wheelchair. Second, it gives him high visibility as a traveling assertion that disabled people exist and function in the world. The only uncomfortable aspect of this exposure is the reaction of some older people who give him a "March of Dimes smile" as if he were "the poster child of the month."

This man's comfort with public exposure is reflected in the fact that his chair is equipped with head and tail lights, an important safety consideration for anyone who goes out at night. He is greatly frustrated by the difficulty of convincing friends to take the same precaution; he feels that their "low profile trip" is both absurd and dangerous.

For some, the solution is found by using both forms of transportation. Tom uses his van for recreation, both long trips and local drives, and for assorted distant trips, but his primary mode of transport is his chair. "Riding around in my chair is sort of a consciousness-raising activity. Sometimes I feel like hanging a sign on the chair that says, 'Here I am; can I get into your house?' I deliberately ride on different streets just to increase my exposure."

Meet

The elements of meeting—communication, socialization, education, congregation, and moral concerns—are all interpersonal. The act of meeting may be directly focused on establishing contact with others—seeking intimacy—or it may be coincidental to the performance of a shared task or activity. In either case, meeting is a primary concern of most people, and issues surrounding meeting are some of the first to confront a newly disabled individual. Interaction with others is a major element in the design of spaces. Places to meet, to establish comfortable distances, and to gather in small or large groups are of primary importance both to space planners and to space occupants. Physically disabled people in wheelchairs occupy more area than able-bodied people, but they also have different social needs in the interpersonal environment.

The Developmental Implications

The process of socialization is an essential element of meeting. From birth, each human is trained by others in appropriate forms of behavior and interaction. This early socialization forms the basis for the development of personality and establishes a pattern for the formation of relationships. The warmth of physical contact and the stimulation of communication appear to be elemental in the developmental process.

Youngsters who are disabled from birth generally experience a normal pattern of socialization in infancy. Their needs are probably no greater than those of other infants, and frequently, their limitations are not apparent. Socialization will proceed normally until the baby or child is unable to accomplish a desired skill. At this point, some differences become apparent; parents may choose to accept the limitations and encourage normal socialization within the limits of the disability, or they may focus on some aspect of the disability and attempt to overcome it to make the child as "normal" as possible. The ability to walk is a typical focal point in such cases; the fear that the child will be totally dependent or socially rejected leads some parents to channel considerable energy into the acquisition of this single skill.

Mary Ann experienced this and feels that it created an unreal situation in which too much pressure was applied to accomplishing this skill, instilling the "magical thinking" that if she walked, everything else would be all right. Peter, also disabled from early childhood, had a very different experience. His parents recognized his limitations and established academic and social goals that were well within his capabilities. He was taught to value activities of the mind and was given the opportunities to develop relationships around these activities.

Those who are disabled later in life may face other problems. Their relationships in the past were often based on a set of social patterns that are not applicable to their new life. Carmen had always been beautiful and wealthy; from early childhood she had been admired. As an adult, she modeled and owned a chain of successful import shops; her home was the center of social gatherings. After her accident, Carmen had an experience that changed her outlook. "I went to my first party in a wheelchair. I had spent the afternoon having my hair done, and I had a new gown. I was perfectly made up and I knew I looked good. I went wheeling into the room, making a grand entrance, and no one even turned around. All of my life, when I walked into a room, conversation stopped. Now nothing. That was when I finally saw how different it was going to be."

Tom, disabled at nineteen, experienced a similar need to re-evaluate his patterns of interaction. An athlete, his friendships with men had been based on physical roughhousing and a shared interest in sports. He had related to women as a high-school hero and had waited for them to come to him. After his accident, he could no longer participate in sports and discovered that he had to develop the ability to take the initiative in his relationship with women. In the cases of Tom and Carmen, their accidents necessitated a period of resocialization in which they learned new ways of relating.

Parents are only one of many socializing agents.

Meeting.

Peer groups, teachers, religious leaders, and relatives all have an impact and communicate values. Subtle prejudices and class structures may be maintained by this socialization process and become one basis for friendship choices in later life. Several of our informants described a conflict arising from the experience of either covert or open prejudices against disabled people. Mary Ann remembers, "I hated crips—I think I saw myself in them. Maybe it was because of their attitude, but I was immature, too." Tom feels that he wasn't actively prejudiced; he simply didn't pay any attention to disabled people. Such slights from others are those that disturb him today.

The Intimate Environment

Meeting, in its most personal form, is the desire to share one's self with another, to achieve intimacy. The personal environment may serve as a vehicle for this sharing of self to the extent that a person creates his surroundings in his own image: inviting a friend to share them is a sharing of the self. Among disabled people problems of accessibility in private dwellings often limit social contacts to the dwelling of the disabled individual. A space within the dwelling for privacy and closeness is important.

When much of an individual's time is spent in a wheelchair or in a bed, the impact of the physical distance created by these impediments should be considered. For example, the area occupied by the bed or the wheelchair may act as a real, if subconscious, impediment to intimate conversations. Physical intimacy may be more difficult for disabled people to achieve because it necessitates altering the normal form of interaction since the presence of the wheelchair tends to produce a certain polite distance. For individuals to feel uninhibited in overcoming this distance, a setting for intimate meeting should assure privacy, both audio and vis-

If the meeting space also serves, as it often does, as a bedroom, it may be essential to deliberately create an atmosphere that is not overwhelmingly "bedside" or to actively convey that it is insignificant that the conversation is bedside. Too often patterns of interaction that are established in institutions in which people are confined to beds are continued in their homes. Although hospital beds or lifts may be necessary for comfort, they can be easily disguised under bright bedspreads and colorful pillows, a technique used by many. The desire to eliminate the hospital atmosphere is reflected in Peter's belief that "appropriate ways of dealing with the sick or injured in a hospital setting just don't

work with physically disabled people. People who persist in using this approach gradually fall out of the circle of those you take seriously."

As for interaction with able-bodied people, Gary says:

> I think there's a lot of education that has to happen on both sides. I think a disabled person, if he or she really wants to make contact with a nondisabled person, has to be aggressive to a certain extent. Go out there and say "Hi." But there's another side to that: the people who really feel comfortable about themselves will usually make contact with me whether I'm disabled or not. Like my neighbors over there—to them I'm just Gary, their neighbor, and to some of the others, although they're feeling more comfortable now, since I've lived here eight months, I can always tell that there are a lot of questions that go on as they talk to me. Sometimes they're really careful in what they say and how they say it to me, because I'm supposed to be frail or something. I feel that there still are two groups [disabled and nondisabled people], but see, it depends. It's a very individual question; it depends on the circles you travel in; there are people in Berkeley who still, if I'm going down the street, sort of look at me [Gary is blind] and say, "Oh, you're one of them."

The Dwelling Environment

The dwelling is a common gathering place in which well-established roles are played by both the host and the guest. "Hospitality begins at home" is a maxim particularly applicable to disabled people. Tom is very sensitive to the limited accessibility of private residences in Berkeley.

> I don't consider a town where you can't go into anyone's house but another disabled person's very accessible. There's hardly a living room in Berkeley that you can get into. Every house has steps. People in Berkeley don't seem to gather in public places. What they do is meet in private homes. Well, that usually excludes me. It's pretty hard to be part of a social group when there's no place to get together or it's always your place. There's no dropping in for me, no casual contacts. I think it's very hard to meet people.

The concept of social reciprocity is elemental to most interaction. By maintaining a balance of give and take, an equal distribution of power is assured, and stability is increased. The formal expressions of this social code are seen in the rules of etiquette, which require that all invitations be returned, all calls answered, all gifts reciprocated. On a less formal basis, most relationships develop a pattern of balancing favors, services, and attentions. If a situation develops in which one person is constantly giving, the other constantly receiving, the imbalance places great stress on the relationship.

For disabled people interacting with able-bodied people, difficult issues of reciprocity arise. If the home of the able-bodied person is not accessible, the accepted method of returning an invitation is not available. Although it may logically be more convenient and comfortable to always meet in the home of the disabled person, the situation will remain one-sided. The problem lies not only in the difficulty of visiting other homes, but also in the problems related to offering conventional hospitality. It is easy enough to ask close friends to help themselves to coffee or drinks and to assist with food; but for many disabled people, asking for assistance, especially with new acquaintances, is painful or unacceptable. A setting that may make it possible for a person to meet his own needs will not necessarily work for entertaining others. When this is an important consideration, special adaptation may be helpful. Snacks prepared in advance by an attendant or a conveniently located bar for drinks can make entertaining more comfortable.

Arrangements of spaces and furnishings within the dwelling may have a direct impact on the type of communication that occurs. Numerous studies have documented the effects of varying head elevations and the placement of seating in determining power structures within groups. The occupant of a wheelchair typically sits higher than conventional seating, and in a conversational group this difference in height reduces eye contact and tends to exclude a person at a different eye level. The consultants have dealt with this issue in various ways. Mary Ann has raised the legs of her couch to a level that is equal to the level of her wheelchair, which also makes it possible for her to transfer onto the couch. Peter has furnished his apartment exclusively with assorted wheelchairs, which gives both able-bodied and disabled members of a group equal status. Ron, a large man, has had an out-sized couch constructed which on first glance appears no different from a normal-sized one. By raising the scale of the furniture in his living room to that of himself sitting in his wheelchair, the whole interior is visually normalized around him. Carmen has separated the spaces for wheelchair gathering and for sitting on traditional furniture. One room is furnished only with a piano and a studio couch. It is used regularly for gatherings of people in wheelchairs; able-bodied individuals sit on the floor. A second room is conventionally furnished with a carpet on the floor; people in wheelchairs enter only one side of this room and generally choose to use other spaces in the house.

Carmen spends a great deal of time in her bedroom, which is the social center of her household, and during most of her waking hours people are gathered there. The room is arranged with a low coffee table at its center. Several small, low, comfortable chairs are placed in a semicircle along one side of the table, and her bed, pushed up against it, forms the other side. Carmen lies on her stomach with her head toward the table. From this position, raised on her elbows, she confronts those seated in chairs at eye level and in this way is firmly part of the gathering. The coffee table is usually laden with bowls of fruit and cigarettes. The table, so placed against the end of the bed, is closest to Carmen, and its contents are within her reach. The coffee table is an unobtrusive device to draw the group's attention toward her. Raised up on her elbows she can, even with the limited use she has of her arms, serve herself from the table and also demonstrate with vigorous gestures her great vitality. From this position as well the shape of her attractive bosom may be revealed. Thus, Carmen remains in character, a great beauty, surrounded and admired.

Often, the dwellings of disabled people in Berkeley are very busy places; meeting people is not only possible but unavoidable. Peter and Mary Ann each live with a disabled roommate, a common arrangement that is financially beneficial and permits the sharing of some services. Each of them has three attendants a day, some household help, and an assortment of friends and neighbors who frequently stop by. When you visit either apartment, you meet people coming and going. Loneliness is not a problem; finding the time and space to meet without interruption is. The dwelling, in itself, is not always an ideal place to meet. When casual contact within the home is part of a pattern, it may be necessary to break out of the pattern, to move to another space in order to interact on a more direct level.

The Community Environment
Making social contacts at the community scale is a problem for many. The environment tends to discourage casual gathering by those in wheelchairs. Sidewalks are wide enough to permit standing groups to stop and talk but are so narrow that a wheelchair will tend to block passage. Benches arranged along the edges of paths may place their seated occupants out of the way, looking toward the action, but wheelchair-bound people talking with bench sitters have to sit in the flow of traffic, looking away from passersby.

Groups of wheelchairs occupy a great deal of

A party.

space, and access from every direction must be allowed for as well. Space planners typically allot meeting area sizes based on the maneuverability of the walking person; wheelchairs are not only larger than a person, but require additional space to turn. Besides, many disabilities limit neck or upper-body motion or vision on one side; people with these problems rely upon the realignment of their wheelchair to direct them toward another speaker, a process that requires the constant adjustment of position. The wheelchair does have an inherent advantage in planning spaces for meeting. It functions basically as a flexible piece of furniture that can adjust to the locations of fixed pieces, and this mobility can be used to good advantage if considered in relation to the planning of fixed seating, such as in a lecture hall or theater.

Gathering in public places like coffeeshops or cafes plays an important role in the lives of some of the informants. Two accessible cafes have become hangouts for groups in wheelchairs as well as for a wide variety of others who relate to the disabled community. Both of them are furnished with an assortment of table sizes that allow customers to select a table for themselves or permit them to join others

at another table. Especially when the cafe is crowded, it is an expected and accepted practice to informally join others, who may be strangers. Thus the environment of the cafe has high potential for social interaction. The two cafes most popular with disabled people are known as hangouts for those associated with counterculture lifestyles. Since the informants have, in various ways, reported that they identify with those who pursue an unconventional life, this mixed company may well explain why these particular cafes are desirable environments. Those encountered are no more "freaky" than many others in Berkeley, but more important perhaps, they meet others and form conversational and other types of friendships. A disabled informant who has been living alone or in a care facility in which most residents are heavily sedated has found the lack of readily available companionship one of his greatest problems. "Life is not meant to be lived alone," he said. "I need to talk or I forget how to use words. When I come back from a football game I want to talk about it, to discuss the day, but I have that letdown that comes from living with people who can't talk."

Within the disabled community, a set of dynamics based on the type and degree of functional impairment is superimposed on the more conventional bases for relationships. Disabled people have a common bond in their disability; they share an interest in the means of dealing with the unadapted outside world and face many of the same problems. These common ties may overwhelm the ethnic or social distinctions that are normally operative, but they do not prevent the formation of subcultures within the disabled community, nor do they rule out relationships with able-bodied individuals. Many of Berkeley's disabled population have little or no involvement in the disabled community. John sees these subcultures as possessing a distinct set of values: "There is a disabled community in Berkeley but everyone who is disabled doesn't belong. There are several communities actually; some distinguished by a certain disability. CPs are real tight, spinal-cord injuries are real tight, deaf are real tight. Some by other concerns—gay men and gay women—are real tight." Others comment that although distinct groups and schisms do exist, they are balanced by cross-group relationships.

Mary Ann encourages the development of relationships in the community. "A disabled person will create his or her own social setting. I don't see any way that could be changed. I try to ask new disabled people in Berkeley to parties in order to introduce them to other disabled people in the community. If they want to be part, they will come back. If not, they won't. Disabled people, like everyone else, will seek out a social situation if they want to. They will be alone if they want to be."

John attempts to achieve a balance in his friendships. "I try and balance my relationships with others between those who are disabled and those who are not. I don't want to swing either way, but to socialize with people of both groups. I try to combine these various friends socially. If I'm going swimming I will call up a client [John is a peer counselor at CIL] and an able-bodied friend."

Social interactions are somewhat determined by the support and comfort possible from associates with similar histories or problems, but for many these interactions form only a small portion of the total range of interactions. Support from people with dissimilar histories is also important for an enriched viewpoint and development as a person.

Compete

Competition plays an important role in the development of a self-image. Dominance testing and agonistic rituals establish a place in the social hierarchy; defense and aggression characterize the struggle to maintain the position that has been achieved and to move higher. Chauvinistic conflict and competition in the relationships between the sexes extend competition into most arenas of life.

The Developmental Issues
In infancy, competition among siblings and peers for toys and attention is common and helps children learn to master frustration when the desired goal cannot be attained. The disabled infant may be withheld from this early exposure to competition, or he may be so limited that competition is one-sided. The experience of frustration and the stimulation of competing are developmentally important. The parents of some disabled children tend to overprotect by spoiling them; rewards are not associated with achievement but given indiscriminately. The effect is little sense of accomplishment and no preparation for competition.

Many childhood games are competitive; they symbolize the battles for power or prestige carried on in the adult world. During this period an effort is often made to separate disabled from able-bodied children to equalize competition. Schools are frequently segregated, and play groups or social organizations have been established to provide a sheltered social environment. A young woman with cerebral palsy spent her early school years in special classes with a limited number of children, all performing at their own rate. "The teacher gave us assignments and we did everything ourselves; sometimes the teacher helped with reading but mostly you taught yourself. With the individualized emphasis the kids get behind; they never learn how to compete. You graduate from high school and you've never been out in the real world. Now the kids go to a regular grammar school. I think it's good. I didn't know better at the time."

Many of those interviewed felt unprepared for competition. The special schools were heavily criticized for "catering to the lowest level" and for over-emphasizing art and therapy as if standard academic skills were unimportant. When students did shift into regular schools, many of them had to repeat one or more years to catch up with faster-moving classes. The reasons students were given for being unable to attend conventional schools were both environmental—that is, the school was inacces-

The computer science course: preparing oneself for the job market.

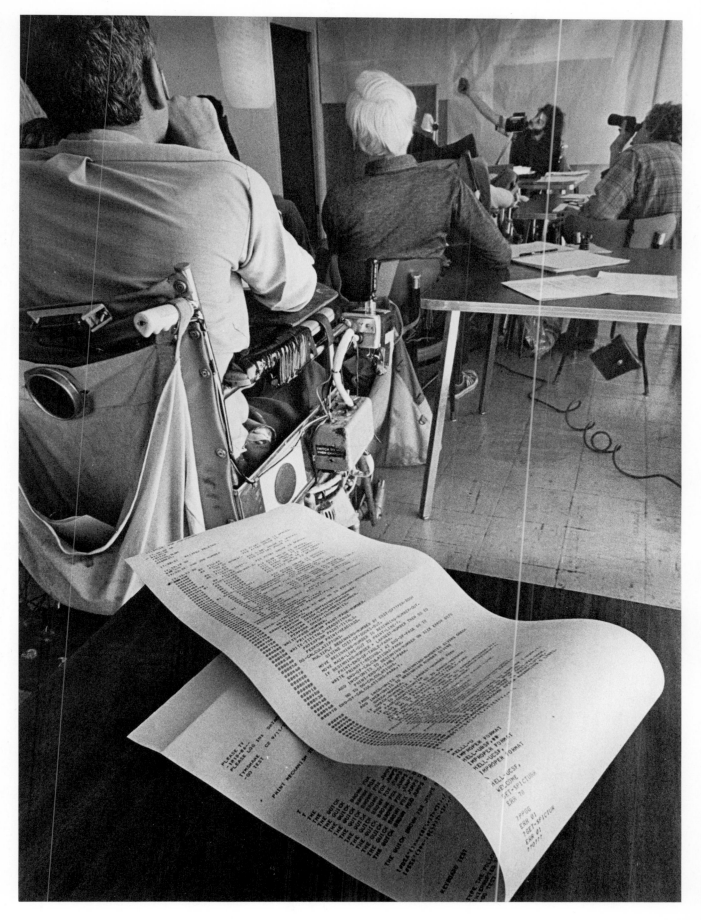

sible, space was inadequate, or the equipment was not adapted—and attitudinal—there was not adequate staff, disabled people need extra attention, disabled people will not be able to keep up with the work.

When parents are able to see their children as individuals and stress their areas of competence as appropriate areas for competition, a normal social pattern is possible. The most difficult situations are probably experienced by less severely disabled people who are urged to overcompensate to compete in all areas. Gary says, "There's something that I've been trying to get rid of over the years. There's a certain image that goes along with being disabled, and that is that someone has to be unusually strong and unusually good; it's the whole idea that because you're disabled the image is super crip."

In another area, competition is often avoided all together. Among adolescents, competition tends to focus around sexual display. The symbols of adulthood and sexuality assume great importance. Rituals based around cars, clothes, or sports are a major focus and consume considerable time and energy. Disabled teenagers may be totally excluded from this experience; they frequently cannot compete in terms of symbols. Often they do not drive, are not athletic, and do not display clothes well. They are not regarded as sexual beings by the able-bodied world. Sexual competition is not expected to occur or is thought to be so problematic that it is avoided, resulting in another reason for resocialization later in life if independence is to be achieved.

During both childhood and adolescence, an effort is often made to channel competitive energy into intellectual or academic pursuits. Education is stressed as a route to competitive success. "You are going to have to use your head rather than your hands" is a common adage, often applied indiscriminately. Susan O'Hara, head of the university dorm program, says, "My impression is that most of the people who come here are men. Men are often nonacademic as teenagers and most of the traumatic quads are men. The kid who reads books and bird-watches is not the kid who is diving. Men who are not academically oriented before the accident and then choose to pursue a life of academics are not always able to make the switch successfully."

Among disabled people high value is placed upon competition as a way to validate a social role, and for those who are personally and intellectually suited for academic competition, opportunities to

Taking part.

compete and to succeed are readily available. "Unfortunately," continues Susan, "the person who lacks the emotional strength or the intellectual skill to be a superquad falls into an ambiguous position. They depend to some extent upon the leaders [in the disabled community] who have strong feelings that everybody is entitled to supports and assistance despite varying ability to contribute." Often the competitive drive seems to be channeled into a search for group rights rather than into competition on an individual level.

Peter, who expresses this philosophy, admits to being competitive on both levels. "As a child, I was fiercely competitive and show-offish. When I went to regular schools I was sometimes asked very hard questions I knew the answer to. I was very concerned about getting the best grades, all As, being smart, being Phi Beta Kappa. I cared about performing well and having people admire me." Peter's goals now are both to work for continued recognition of disabled rights and to seek employment teaching at the university level in the able-bodied world. Still competitive, he wants success at both levels.

The Intimate Environment
Although competition is usually interpersonal, the traumatically injured disabled person often carries his competition within himself. The person before the injury is frequently viewed as a separate identity. The "new me" must compete with his own and others' image of the "old me" to reestablish relationships. While acquiring independence is a gradual and largely unconscious process during normal development, it is a very conscious and compressed process after an accident. A young quad constantly compares his current skill level: "I'm seeing if I can do it on my own, and I've found that I can, coming out of the hospital doing zero, and finding that I can."

What seems to be required for the disabled person seeking independence is a certain degree of challenge in his personal physical environments. If everything is made accessible and usable without the intervention of the user or inhabitant, there is little sense of competitive achievement. Under such circumstances, what has been physically done to the environment has been done *for* the disabled person, not *with* him.

The Dwelling and the Community Environments
Suitable arenas for competition in the public environment are rare. The presence of able-bodied indi-

119

viduals unbalances competition in many areas, and this aspect of competition—of competing with able-bodied people—is continually present. Speaking about his expectations of himself, Peter says, "You define normal either around what is normal for an independent person with your disability or around yourself at your best, not around what is normal for the able-bodied person."

Competition tends to be regulated by what is possible. Attempting to achieve the same goals as someone who is better able physically to succeed is simply frustrating. Peter continues:

> What the disabled person is usually concerned with in regard to the able-bodied person is overcoming certain prejudices, not direct competition. Among disabled people a significant number have quite a high competitive drive. Consider the model of superquad who is as physically independent as possible, active in many organizations and programs, maybe going to school or working as well. There are some who work on crip service things, are involved in community programs seven days a week, late into the night. Among some there's an admitted ruthlessness, a cold-bloodedness in their attitude toward able-bodied people. There's a lot that has to be done; a revolution has to be won. It takes a fatal commitment to the cause and a willingness to use whatever means you have access to, to carry it out.

The school environment, if not segregated, is often developed in a way that encourages fairly equal competition. In intellectual pursuits, the ability of a disabled person to interact as an equal may simplify contact in the social arena. For example, a young woman who attended boarding schools had a unique advantage in the competition for attention from the boys. Although she is normally confined to a chair, the school was inaccessible, and so she attempted to manage on Canadian crutches. She moved slowly and was unable to make it to classes on time, a problem solved by the boys who gave her piggyback rides. She commented, "I got along better with the boys than the girls" and feels, in retrospect, that the attention she received from the boys, combined with her status as an honor-roll student, made her a threat.

Competition that is designed specifically for disabled people, such as the Wheelchair Olympics, offers an opportunity to be involved in the American mania for athletic contests at a level appropriate for the individual.

Environmentally, competition encompasses so many social and psychological implications that the physical environment, to assist the disabled individual, must respond to the specific disabled population. Otherwise, important subtleties and implications will be lost, and the physical environment will place unnecessary strain on the lives of those who use it.

Work

Work entails hunting, earning, gathering, building, and making. In contemporary American culture, earning is the primary activity associated with work. To earn, however, one must have a skill, profession, or talent that is marketable. Many social activities center about exercising this skill or profession; many pleasures are financially possible only because one works. The sense of personal achievement and view of one's own social status are also strongly related to work. Contentment in work is likewise necessary for a sense of individual well-being.

The Developmental Implications

For children in contemporary American culture, work is a part of life that is typically regarded as separate from the rest. Fathers go off to work in the morning, carrying out this activity in a setting that may be completely alien to the child and performing tasks that are equally remote. Mothers who work also usually leave the home; the routine care of the household, maintenance, and other chores familiar to the child are less likely to be described as work, a term reserved exclusively for employment. In recent years, there has been some change in this scene. As more mothers return to work (almost 50 percent by recent statistics) and fathers are drawn into the child-care role, working at home is becoming more common. Children growing up today will have some exposure to the actual business of work and a broader concept of the variety of activities covered by this term.

Most of the disabled people interviewed were brought up in a conventional setting. Unable to move about easily, they were more removed from the working world than able-bodied children. Although their parents and teachers may have held limited expectations for their future, all of them were exposed to the cultural expectation that children spend their early years preparing for the time when they will grow up and go to work. Children who are disabled from birth are rarely asked, "What are you going to be when you grow up?" but they have the same fantasies as able-bodied children; they plan to follow in their parents' footsteps

Carmen Anderson: the business woman.

or become "heroes." Attempting to fulfill childhood expectations is a particular problem for disabled adults who grow up in families in which there is little intellectual orientation; they may lack role models in work that is not physical in nature.

The work orientation is subtly stressed in both homes and schools during the developmental years: chores are given to develop responsibility, schoolwork is task- and success-oriented, skills are stressed that will contribute to later success in work. Disabled children may have only a limited exposure to such influences. Schools for the handicapped are described by the consultants as almost uniformly poor in developing academic skills or preparing students for an independent future. The role of many such schools is that of caretaker. Gary describes the special education schools that he attended: "Teachers and administrators felt that the basic way you raise a disabled kid, or teach a disabled kid, is to make him as normal as possible. In other words, the idea was, 'Don't show your disability,' so that was pushed on me a lot. Learning to dress oneself was sort of a standard for all disabled people."

The impact of this education was to leave him without salable skills and filled with resentment at learning tasks that he was not doing for himself. The focus of many activities seemed to be to make things easier for the caretaker, rather than to educate or stimulate the student. Peter relates:

> Sometimes, there is a real conflict, especially in growing up, between adjusting to being a crip and adjusting to the greater world. One example is the choice between trying to learn lip reading so you can communicate with the hearing or learning sign so you can communicate with the deaf. The same problem arises in trying to choose between making it in the larger society, [having a] conventional job and friends, versus having crip friends and role models and making it in the crip world.

Too often this conflict is resolved only because environmental barriers limit the real choices available. Either choice is valid and may suit a given person. What is essential is that the choice not be predetermined by attitudinal or physical barriers. Peter also spent many years in special schools or special classes and felt most hampered by the assumption that all handicapped people have similar educational needs. He was often grouped with others of a similar age who were mentally retarded or slow learners or had problems requiring special atten-

Lennis Jones: the academic dictates a book.

tion. The teachers were so busy that any real education was almost impossible. Peter, a bright student, was unable to learn in this setting and finally completed his education in standard schools. The stereotypes that group disabled people under a single banner are a disservice to all. They deny individuality and the opportunity to develop as a unique person.

The problem of limited opportunities and training for stereotypical job assignments is typified by the sheltered workshops in which many disabled people are placed. Gary says that "people get put into them because they don't know where else to go. There are a lot of disabled and blind people there on the lower end of the scale, not really retarded but slow because of their background and where they came from. They were there to work outside their usual environment." The work that is available is often limited, geared to the minimal abilities of the workers, and is not preparation for future occupations. The mother of a disabled man said, "Oh, we know it's mainly social; it's just a chance to be out of the house and have some other life." The importance of this "other life" cannot be denied, but the large number of disabled individuals who are capable of greater independence should not arbitrarily be grouped with the much smaller number who need the protection of a sheltered environment.

Job training programs established for disabled people may suffer from the same narrow categorization of employment supposedly suitable for disabled people. Traditionally, watchmaking, telephone services, piecework, or assembly-line jobs have been viewed as suitable. More recently computer programming has been the focus of training programs. (The Center for Independent Living sponsors one.) The advantage of training for these few fields is that a pool of potential employers, familiar with the abilities of the disabled employee, develops, and job placement becomes progressively easier. The disadvantage is that such employment appeals to the interests of only a limited group; the majority must find their training in the mainstream or accept jobs that do not fit their interests.

Both training and employment pose special problems for disabled individuals with special needs. Often, working an eight-hour day is physically impossible; it may be impossible to sit this long, or the worker may fatigue and need rest periods more frequently than others. Aid may be required to use the bathroom or to eat, which may be awkward or impossible to arrange in a work setting.

Frequently, one of the major barriers to employment is the idea, carried by both the employer and the potential disabled employee, that a job must fit into a standard form: eight hours at a desk, typical sign-in routines, and so forth. As other employment groups also begin to recognize the value of flexible schedules, shared jobs, and innovative approaches, this aspect of the employment problem may begin to ease.

The financial aspects of working continue to pose major problems for disabled people. The realities of disability often include expensive medical and attendant care unknown to able-bodied people. Financial aid from the government in the form of special allotments for attendants and medical coverage solve this problem for Berkeley residents as long as they do not have a minimum income. Unfortunately, there is no current program to cover these excess expenses until income or benefits are sufficient to meet them adequately. In many cases, income will never meet expenses, yet the experience of working is valued. Most entry-level salaries do not approach the amount of income needed to survive; as a result, employment is impossible. For many, uninsurability is an added problem; they are only assured of medical coverage if they are eligible for a Medicare program, which is terminated when the income reaches a given level. Peter informs us that "there is a decided devaluation of boring 'crip jobs' and a valuation of working in relevant fields, even if the pay is poor. If you are performing a worthwhile function, then it's okay if the government supports you through SSI [Social Security Insurance]."

Work for the disabled person may never fit the typical image; the most well-suited involvement may be part-time, voluntary, temporary, or sporadic. An important part of the development process is learning to value the contributions that one is able to make, the abilities rather than the disabilities. It is important for the self-image that a person feels productive. Thus, exploration of personal potentials is a major task, for the disabled as well as the able-bodied person. One young man says, "I choose not to work at a job." He receives Social Security Insurance benefits and feels that he probably uses his time more productively by being able to work with the projects and in the areas he feels comfortable. At the moment, he is doing counseling at Vacaville Correctional Facility with disabled prisoners. He said that many of them were not disabled before going to prison but that they were wounded while being brought in or during prison fights. He feels that people do not have much respect for volunteer work and suggested an advertising campaign founded on the idea, "Look, are you unemployed and bored—or even employed and bored?" Volunteering can be helpful to both the self and to society.

A major element in the work environment of disabled people is the Department of Vocational Rehabilitation. While able-bodied people usually face the employment struggle alone or with the aid of a selected employment agency, disabled people typically seek training and employment through a government agency. The Department of Vocational Rehabilitation has a broad range of services and powers. Its offerings range from training programs, through securing such job-related necessities as electric wheelchairs or adapted vans, to job recommendations. The effectiveness of the programs offered, however, seems to depend on the ability and empathy of the counselor. Because the department has the power to support a plan for education or employment with both finances and equipment, it is extremely important to work with counselors who are interested in a pattern of independence and will support progress in that area. Peter says, concerning qualifications for those who work with disabled people in capacities such as rehabilitation counseling, physical therapy, and so on, "The emphasis is on communications abilities, on being empathic, more than upon having a certain set of skills such as extensive knowledge of prostheses or Braille. It's more important to have been part of a community of disabled persons as a prerequisite for such work."

One veteran of programs sponsored by the Department of Vocational Rehabilitation has found that it is essential to understand how to use the grass-roots organizations as a source of information on techniques for handling the formal systems in getting job or work assistance. According to this informant, "Getting services and support from rehabilitation means knowing how to manipulate the system. They will pay thousands of dollars for college but will not make loans to start businesses. If a business were to fail, it would look like their failure." His wife adds, "If rehabilitation places you in a job and it doesn't work out, they may or may not reopen your case." Some do not always feel they can turn to the Department of Vocational Rehabilitation for instant support. "I have had to struggle for whatever I wanted; there was always a fight. If you don't know what you want, you are at a tre-

Greg Sanders: the carpenter-craftsman.

mendous disadvantage. A lot of disabled people don't think they deserve things, don't think they should be hired. In practical terms, they lose out."

The Intimate Environment
The most intimate setting for work includes the immediate space surrounding the worker and any adaptations this space requires. The adaptations may be either physical or organizational; often the most significant changes made are those involving the scheduling of tasks to permit the disabled worker to use his available time and skills most effectively. In seeking employment, the disabled job seeker must expect to be faced with questions regarding the type of adaptive devices or conditions he will require to work effectively. A thorough knowledge of personal requirements and the willingness to describe them will often set an employer's mind at ease, for the barriers to hiring are composed primarily of a lack of understanding of just what special accommodations may be required.

For the disabled in wheelchairs, changes may range from rearrangement of office furnishings to permit the passage of a wheelchair, through adjustment of working-surface heights, to the purchase of special equipment like voice-activated telephones, electric typewriters, or calculators with touch-responsive systems, and hand rails or grab bars. The work space itself can often be made more efficient by careful organization: open storage for frequently used items, touch-responsive catches on drawers or cabinets, a well-stocked supply of materials, and the strategic locations of telephones. Jobs requiring special machinery may demand some adaptation; extensions on controls to place them within reach, modifications to permit leg room or space for a wheelchair, and a hand rather than foot control may be needed.

Changes in strategy may reduce the need for physical adaptations. In some cases job descriptions may need to be modified to permit a disabled employee to handle parts of a task that do not require physical dexterity while another employee covers those parts that do. In other cases, part-time work or flexible schedules that allow for split shifts or versatile hours may permit the employee to work out arrangements for attendant requirements around the work schedule. Working at home, either full- or part-time, is another option that may result in increased comfort and flexibility.

Gary works as a part-time disc jockey for a radio station. Blind and confined to a wheelchair, he has solved accessibility and physical limitation problems in a number of ways. He does some of the preparation for the show in his apartment; there his personal record and tape collection is labeled in Braille and indexed on tape. At the station, which was physically accessible when he got the job, he uses an attendant-reader to help with tape selection and organization. The program itself is carefully planned ahead of time so that there is no need to leave the microphone during the show. By working part-time at a job that is both challenging and satisfying, Gary has gained entry into a field that has always appealed to him; as a result he has found new opportunities, such as serving as an on-the-scene reporter during a recent sit-in.

Tom has taken another approach. A journalist and aspiring novelist, Tom works from his own home, making contacts by telephone or mail. His workspace is perfectly adapted to his needs and entirely within his own control. The typewriter, telephone, reference materials, and record collection are all close at hand, and he can schedule his working hours to suit his own needs.

Mary Ann is typical of another pattern followed by a number of Berkeley's disabled population. Supported by Disability Insurance, Mary Ann has an earnings ceiling above which her benefits will be cut. She works for the Center for Independent Living on a part-time basis and is paid little enough so that her benefits are unaffected. Her work, however, contributes to the existence of a program she believes in and forms the basis for future employment. Her work environment, located in a place designed for disabled people, is already fully adapted. Most of the employees at the Center for Independent Living are disabled themselves, so they function as role models as well as service renderers for CIL's clients.

The Dwelling Environment
Work, whether it takes place at home or in another setting, demands adjustments in the home. Schedules must be adapted to the demands of the job, and time must be structured to permit all the necessary tasks to be accomplished there. This often requires the establishment of a system of trade-offs. Many of the tasks of daily living are very time consuming for disabled people; it may be possible to dress oneself, to prepare and eat meals with aid, to clean and maintain one's surroundings, but hours are required for these tasks. In order to gain time to work

at a satisfying job, it may be necessary to turn over some of these support activities to attendants.

The Community Environment

Many of the significant barriers to working occur at the community scale. The problems are numerous: public attitudes and beliefs; physical barriers, such as curbs, staircases, narrow doorways, or inaccessible bathrooms; transportation problems posed by inadequate or inaccessible transit systems; rigid concepts of job requirements; poor or distant support facilities, such as restaurants or libraries.

These barriers begin to have an effect as soon as employment is contemplated. The geographic area that is realistically accessible may be a primary consideration in the job search; buildings with staircases, multiple levels, inadequate or inaccessible parking may have to be ruled out. Buildings that are accessible but have no support facilities may be too inconvenient. Once physical access to potential employment is assured, greater attitudinal hurdles must be faced. Images of successful employees as vigorous go-getters may subtly influence employers, as do considerations of extracurricular business activities or after-hours meetings, which may not fit the schedule of a disabled individual.

Countering the biases against hiring disabled employees are statistics indicating that the disabled employee has a better-than-average absenteeism record and is often more able to sustain interest in limited tasks over a long period of time. Recent publicity has shown disabled individuals holding important positions in government and law, and academic roles have been held for some time. The super-crip image, however, poses a problem for many more-average individuals who feel, "That's fine for her, but I'm no Helen Keller."

Often a psychological pressure to achieve beyond a comfortable level is counterproductive. Several of the consultants referred to the difficulty of self-acceptance in an environment that stresses excelling in every aspect of life. The struggle for a personal sense of independence based on achievements rather than on the continued need for support and assistance is one faced by many disabled individuals. For many, a satisfying resolution can be found in volunteer or part-time work; for others, a job within the disabled community may offer the flexibility of work schedule that is required.

Because of the informal networks, there are job opportunities for disabled people that do not require specific training. On occasion, the Physically

Disabled Students Program or the Center for Independent Living, with their various programs, will hire someone on a provisional basis. It is not unusual that disabled people come to Berkeley to attend the university and then, after finding some work opportunity, do not attend the university after all; they go to work. In these cases, the academic pursuit tends to fade behind other interests generated by the taste of an independent life in a supportive community. However, without the developed facilities of the Berkeley community, these opportunities would not be possible.

Occasionally, the experience of such jobs will lead to a desire to work in a broader context, though it is at this juncture that disabled people begin to confront a certain reality: Berkeley cannot provide for them. John finds work within the disabled community as a peer counselor at the Center for Independent Living to be satisfying, but he feels this is only temporary, because he wants to have a larger social experience as a peer counselor and this means working with able-bodied people as well.

> Eventually I will have to branch out, to have a more balanced view. If the job is unbalanced, the life is unbalanced. Working with only disabled people, I cut myself off from regular society. But working with disabled people is also very important, because they offer a model for restructuring society. [Many disabled people express a similar attitude: because of their experience, they have a clear understanding of the real values in life.] Working and living exclusively within the disabled community I run the risk of getting burned out. I get sick of hanging around all these disabled people with their problems. A lot of people get burned out. Social life, disabled life, all disabled people. I feel I must begin to integrate my work with being in the non-disabled world as well so I don't get bogged down in a routine and forget how to relate to others.

However, the image of disabled people working within the community is still foreign to many, including disabled people themselves. Carmen says, "Most crips don't know how to manage without rattling the proverbial tin cup." While this exaggerates the degree of lack of awareness, it is woefully true that there are few role models for those who wish to work in their own community, yet do not want to work directly with disabled people in some helping capacity. Carmen is attempting to break new ground by opening and managing an import shop, a job she held before her disability. Her goal is to become a "capitalist model" for others who want to tailor a work situation to their own needs and abilities.

The private world of Carmen Anderson.

Part 5
How to Research

This part will be a discussion of some techniques that we evolved to enable us to enter the lives of physically disabled people and design environments for them. It will deal primarily with those techniques, but first we want to explain the philosophical framework and conceptual basis behind them.

Empathy and Intentionality

Our underlying premise is that the environmental needs of physically disabled people are complex and not readily understood by able-bodied people who do not have direct interaction with them. This thesis is supported in certain previous and ongoing research concerned with disabled people, other vulnerable populations, and user participation in environmental design. These studies have shown the importance of creating new and imaginative ways to bring the disabled user into the design process and thus open the way toward making environments that are truly accessible.

As discussed in Part 1, we chose interactionism as the vehicle by which to enter the world of physically disabled people, for it is the stance by which to assure others that one values their world and is not merely observing or judging it. *The fuel for interactionism is empathy.*

Empathy has been carefully studied and proved effective in counseling, education and the field of social relations in general.[1] Carl Rogers defines empathy as a process:

> The way of being with another person which is termed empathic has several facets. It means entering the private perceptual world of the other and becoming thoroughly at home in it. It involves being sensitive, moment to moment, to the changing felt meanings which flow in this other person, to the fear or rage or tenderness or confusion or whatever, that he/she is experiencing. It means temporarily living in his/her life, moving about in it delicately without making judgments, sensing meanings of which he/she is scarcely aware, but not trying to uncover feelings of which the person is totally unaware, since this would be too threatening. It includes communicating your sensings of his/her world as you look with fresh and unfrightened eyes at elements of which the individual is fearful. It

means frequently checking with him/her as to the accuracy of your sensings, and being guided by the responses you receive. You are a confident companion to the person in his/her inner world. By pointing to the possible meanings in the flow of his/her experiencing you help the person to focus on this useful type of referent, to experience the meanings more fully, and to move forward in the experiencing.

> To be with another in this way means that for the time being you lay aside the views and values you hold for yourself in order to enter another's world without prejudice. In some sense it means that you lay aside your self and this can only be done by a person who is secure enough in himself that he knows he will not get lost in what may turn out to be the strange or bizarre world of the other, and can comfortably return to his own world when he wishes.[2]

Rogers goes on to show that this "deceptively simple empathic interaction" has a number of profound effects:

> 1. In the first place, it dissolves alienation. For the moment, at least, the recipient finds himself/herself a connected part of the human race.

> 2. Another meaning of empathic understanding to the recipient is that someone values him, cares, accepts the person that he is. The message comes through to the recipient that "this other individual trusts me, thinks I'm worthwhile. Perhaps I *am* worth something. Perhaps *I* could value *myself.* Perhaps *I could care for myself.*"

> 3. Still another impact of a sensitive understanding comes from its nonjudgmental quality. The highest expression of empathy is accepting and nonjudgmental. This is true because it is impossible to be accurately perceptive of another's inner world, if you have formed an evaluative opinion of him.

> 4. When a person is perceptively understood, he finds himself coming in closer touch with a wider range of his experiencing. This gives him an expanded referent to which he can turn for guidance in understanding himself and in directing his behavior. If the empathy has been accurate and deep, he may also be able to unblock a flow of experiencing and permit it to run its uninhibited course.[3]

With interactionism, one steps into another's world. With empathy, one tells the other one he *values* his world. Now there is the possibility of understanding how he gives meaning to his world, because now he is open to revealing it.

As a tool for dismantling the complexities of another's experience, we used the concept of *intentionality*. Intentionality encompasses two aspects of human experience: first, the way in which one brackets aspects of experience so as to see the parts in relation to the whole and not be flooded by the complexity of an experience; and second, the way or ways in which one relates subject and object. One steps into a person's world and one sees him act. But what lies behind the act? Rollo May says that "you cannot understand overt behavior except as you see it in relation to, and as an expression of, its intention. Meaning has no meaning apart from intention. Each act of consciousness *tends toward* something, and has within it, no matter how latent, some push toward a direction for actions."[4] Thus, as many have pointed out, intentionality is what moves a person, what gets him out of bed in the morning. It is one's "imaginative participation in the day, and the events of the day, which is reaching out to him, grasping him, that accomplishes the getting up."[5]

In relation to design, recognition of intentionality is a major matter, for it can result in the transformation of all aspects of the built environment—social, political, and cultural as well as built—that affect the client. However, the goal of design is not to arrive at environments that perfectly capture user intentionality. The accommodation of intentionality is not a matter of creating an environment so specialized and exactly fitted to momentary needs that, like Cinderella's slipper, it neither fits anyone else nor offers the possibility of doing so. Rather, it is a question of providing a suitable context for human activity, a *mise en scène*.

An analysis of Le Corbusier's drawings provides an example of intentionality. Peter Prangnell has pointed out that Le Corbusier's drawings of buildings and interiors convey, first and foremost, a sense of a particular scenario of human interaction, which we recognize and identify with and which allows us to place ourselves in the environments he portrays and sense their attributes. He shows us the kitchen of a small house, but we come away with an impression of its occupants: we sense the aroma of their coffee and anticipate the man's remark, as he reads his morning paper, that his stocks have gone up or that a certain movie might be fun to see. The building itself provides only a setting, which others inhabit and mark with their particular imprint. Le Corbusier's drawings convey his empathy with a particular segment of humanity and reveal, in his choice of objects, clothing, positions of body, gestures, and so on, a sense of these people that enables us, too, to empathize with them and put ourselves within the scene he has depicted.[6]

Any discussion of architecture that proceeds from an understanding and recognition of intentionality must include Aldo van Eyck who, through both his architecture and his writing, is a most eloquent spokesperson for this orientation in design. One can construe Van Eyck's use of the terms *form* and *counterform* as being similar to intentionality and the built world, respectively. Van Eyck argues, "Cities should again become the counterform of society's reciprocally individual and collective urban reality. It is because we have lost touch with this reality—the form—that we cannot come to grips with its counterform."[7] His image of the house as a tiny city is most memorable:

> Space has no room, time not a moment for man. He is excluded.
>
> In order to "include" him—help his homecoming—he must be gathered into their meaning. (Man is the subject as well as the object of architecture.)
>
> Whatever space and time mean, place and occasion mean more.
>
> For space in the image of man is place, and time in the image of man is occasion.
>
> Today space and what it should coincide with in order to become "space"—man at home with himself—are lost. Both search for the same place, but cannot find it.
>
> Provide that space, articulate the inbetween.
>
> Is man able to penetrate the material he organizes into hard shape between one man and another, between what is here and what is there, between this and a following moment? Is he able to find the right place for the right occasion?
>
> No—So start with this: make a welcome of each door and a countenance of each window.
>
> Make of each place, a bunch of places of each house and each city, for a house is a tiny city, a city a huge house. Get closer to the shifting centre of human reality and build its counterform—for each man and all men, since they no longer do it themselves.
>
> Whoever attempts to solve the riddle of space in the abstract, will construct the outline of emptiness and call it space.
>
> Whoever attempts to meet man in the abstract will speak with his echo and call this a dialogue.
>
> Man still breathes both in and out. When is architecture going to do the same?[8]

Designing with Empathy

For the designer, then, the use of empathy comes down to this: It makes it possible to picture another's situation accurately and to create in one's design the sorts of setting that allow others' lives to unfold freely. As Peter Prangnell also points out, people learn to treat others as human beings who shape the environment with the force of their existence.

To show how the concepts of empathy and intentionality, drawn from psychology, can be put to use by the designer, let us compare two radically different approaches to designing for disabled people. One example is that of a time-lapse film we once made of the use of the outdoor campus environment by disabled people. Our interest was in understanding the nature of what was going on. What occurs when a half-dozen disabled people in motorized wheelchairs group together informally in a public space? Can the design of a public space be considered with this potential occurrence in mind? What knowledge can we extrapolate from this occurrence that would be useful in the design of other kinds of places?[9]

One thing this movie showed was that people who use wheelchairs space themselves in a conversational grouping much farther apart than one might imagine—far enough apart, in fact, that one might not guess they were interacting with one another. The purpose of this arrangement is to allow for any participant in the conversation to come or go without creating a disturbance.

We learned about this scenario from viewing the film with the disabled consultants, who explained what was taking place and, more importantly, how they felt about it. Other scenarios revealed that the environment worked well for disabled people, accommodating their activities and meeting their needs, or, alternatively, revealed the extent to which the environment prevented or inhibited interaction, the accomplishment of a desired action, or access to a desired setting. Thus by modeling the environment and modifying it in interaction with the consultants we were able to arrive at a picture of settings that might better recognize their needs.

We came to an understanding of a particular scenario, first by observing and documenting it, then by understanding how it was perceived by those who experience it. Through this analysis, we came to understand the nature of their present situation. Then, by simulating the present situation, we could discuss its alteration and test new settings to see how they corresponded to the desires of those who experience them.

As another approach, consider a community that after surveying its disabled population, determines that "accessible housing" is their highest priority. It therefore hires an architect, asking him to make proposals for the modification of existing dwellings and the design of new ones that will ensure their accessibility. How does the architect interpret this? How does he understand the term "accessible housing," and what assurance does he have that what he is being asked to do is the proper means of meeting this demand?

With no particular knowledge of disabled people, the designer might conclude that accessible housing is housing that they can get in and out of. If he turns to the design manuals that discuss the accommodation of disabled people, he may also decide that it involves the dimensioning and arrangement of the house. This definition allows the disabled person to move in and around his dwelling, but it fails to convey any sense of what he does there. It lacks any feeling for the everyday life of disabled people, seeing them instead as abstractions or as extensions of the designer or people like him.

Some existing design manuals add to this distortion by picturing disabled people in a way that seemingly compensates for their disabilities. A person who has spent any time with wheelchair-using paraplegics or quadriplegics comes to realize that their physical problems are often more substantial than mere problems of mobility. Even with paraplegics, the same problems that have paralyzed or rendered their lower bodies uncontrollable may have had an enervating effect on their upper bodies as well. When a person familiar with disabled people looks at design manuals and sees drawings of a wheelchair-bound *übermensch*, his muscular arm stretched out from his body like a basketball player's, he can only shake his head. Although this image is sometimes appropriate, it is equally often a distortion, for it implies a robustness or a level of health that is frequently lacking, the absence of which has some particular design implications.

A comparative analysis of the two approaches is unnecessary, because the conclusion is obvious: rather than only using the conventional guides, the designer must learn a new dialect—the particular set of meanings about the environment held by the disabled people in his community. This can only come from direct interaction with people who, as the representatives of a larger body within the community, can serve as "native guides" in a landscape the designer sees only vaguely.

By coming to see the community through the eyes, ears, and hearts of his consultants,[10] the designer gains an awareness that approximates the community as it is seen by its disabled population. Soon he will have learned that accessible housing is something quite different than he imagined—that it expresses a deeper desire for access to the community as a whole.

Techniques

How might one develop a program that would convey to others, or raise one's own awareness of, the environmental needs of disabled people? Such a program could be constructed using the techniques outlined in this part. The program would have several stages, aimed at bringing the person from an awareness of himself to an awareness of others, and it would provide several means of evaluating the extent to which one had gained in the ability to empathize with the situation of others and perceive their particular values and needs, both in a general and in a design-specific sense.

The following four sections constitute such a program. The first section, Using Existing Information, outlines some current literature and visual material. It suggests sources that can lead the reader to others, while providing in themselves a reasonably representative picture of what has been done in the area of design for disabled people and giving the reader some familiarity with the situation of disabled people as they have described it themselves.

The second section, Interviewing Disabled People, begins the process of working directly with disabled people to learn more about their situation and, ultimately, their intentionality in terms of new settings. At this stage, the designer should not attempt to affirm what he has learned through reading or viewing existing material, but rather, he should seek to expand his knowledge and test his assumptions against others' perspectives.

The techniques of interviewing suggested in this section are ethnographic; that is, they are aimed at uncovering as much as possible about the nature of the lifestyles of people whose situations and settings are representative of the range of disabilities to be found within the community. Such informants must be selected in part for their own commitment to changing the community, or the information gained will be an affirmation, rather than a critique, of the existing environment and will fail to point toward any other possibilities.

In both this section and the following one, Visual Documentation, the idea is to make use of settings or representations of settings as projective tools in eliciting a greater-than-usual amount of information about what the person really thinks of the setting, how it functions for him, and so forth. By filming or photographing human action or interaction in the environment, it becomes possible to analyze what is happening in terms of movement or grouping patterns, proximities, and other dynamics. However, only through discussion with one's informants of what is being depicted or experienced is it possible to understand how what has happened affects them and to get at their feelings about how the settings in which these actions and interactions occurred could be modified to work better.

At each step in the process of learning about disabled people, the designer can turn to his informants to check his understanding against theirs. The fourth section, Scenarios and Modeling, suggests a series of techniques by which the designer can approximate, in increasingly accurate detail, the environmental needs his informants have expressed. These representations of physical settings can then function as projective tools in learning the environmental values held by informants in more concrete terms. If the techniques are used collaboratively by the designer and his informants within a participatory process, they provide the means for testing values and assumptions against the larger public.

Movement throughout the four states of this program is really a process in which the designer and his informants reveal themselves to each other, becoming increasingly conscious of how they use and view the current settings in which their lives unfold; of how these settings, if they were to change, might better accommodate their real needs; and of how such changes might actually be expressed—how these new settings might look and function.

In the course of this process, the designer gradually sheds his assumptions about his informants and their needs, as his informants clarify who they are and what they want from the environment. In developing an empathy for disabled people, the designer's major responsibility is to maintain a receptivity. The major assumption behind the use of these techniques is that they can help establish a trust between the designer and his informants that will lead to their revealing what is genuinely significant to them about their lives and their interactions with the environment.

132

1. Using Existing Information
A first step in learning about a group of people with whom one is unfamiliar is to refer to existing information about them. In the case of disabled people, there is a substantial amount of material available.

One place to begin is with general sources like the journal, *Rehabilitation Literature,* which reports on forthcoming publications and ongoing research, providing frequent excerpts and summaries of important new documents and developments in the field.[11] Also a book like Laurie's *Housing and Home Services for the Disabled,* although addressing a specific problem area encountered by disabled people, provides an overview of everything pertaining to the use of housing by disabled persons. It contains some specific design information, but it is most useful as a directory to other sources of information.[12]

More design information can be found in such publications as the American Society of Landscape Architects Foundation and the Department of Housing and Urban Development's *Barrier Free Site Design*[13]; Tarrant and Subiotte's *Planning for Disabled People in the Urban Environment,*[14] an English publication; and Harkness and Groom's *Building without Barriers for the Disabled.*[15]

Some publications address the problems of disability in terms of ameliorating them through physical design and human understanding or both. Robinault's *Functional Aids for the Multiply Handicapped,*[16] which deals with cerebral palsy, and Lowman and Klinger's *Aids to Independent Living: Self-Help for the Handicapped*[17] are examples of books that suggest "hardware" solutions to the problems of disability. Planned Parenthood of Snohomish County, Washington, Task Force on Concerns of Physically Disabled Women has published one booklet, *Within Reach: Providing Family Planning Services to Physically Disabled Women,*[18] which considers physical and social modifications to existing service organizations. Another of their publications, *Toward Intimacy: Family Planning and Sexuality Concerns of Physically Disabled Women,*[19] is aimed at helping disabled women themselves discover, rediscover, or cultivate their sexuality.

Special note should be made of *Barrier-Free Environments,*[20] edited by Michael J. Bednar, which contains several articles that address the psychosocial dimensions of barrier-free design, especially Edward Steinfeld, James Duncan, and Paul Cardell, "Toward a Responsive Environment: The Psychosocial Effects of Inaccessibility"; Wolf Wolfensberger's "The Normalization Principle, and some Major Implications to Architectural-Environmental Design"; and R. Christopher Knight, Craig M. Zimring, and Margaret J. Kent, "Normalization as a Social Physical System."

There are other categories of information as well—more art forms than social science—which are increasingly recognized as being important to understanding. These include film, autobiography, the novel, and journalistic reporting. A list of these is included in the Selected Bibliography.

Certain films describe disabled people and, more importantly, give the viewer a sense of their everyday lives. Perennial Film's, *Like Other People*[21] and the Easter Seal Society's *The Surest Test*[22] are examples of such films available from national distributors. Some interesting films by independent film companies are also available, such as Barry Spinello's *A Day in the Life of Bonnie Consolo*[23] or his *Daily Routine in the Life of Dave Harvey.*[24] These films depict real people in real situations and help to dispel two preconceptions about disabled people: that they are less than human and that they are unaffected by their disabilities.

Understanding the lives of several disabled people, as they themselves have chosen to present them, gives the designer an initial impression of experiences that may be markedly different from his own. In sifting through the most personal data, the designer can also reflect on how one extracts from a subjective view of the world a picture of intentionality and, moreover, how one relates this intentionality to the environment. He can begin to get a sense of the boundaries and the rhythm of these lives and of their aspirations.

These are the lives of people who came to grips with their situations and clarified them for themselves and for others. In doing so, they sought their place in society, their place within humanity. One of the reasons their lives are important is that they serve as potential role models for others—they are there for all to see, in the richness of their frustrations and desires. Such people make good respondents and collaborators, because they have the requisite energy and determination to explore their own possibilities. More importantly, they believe that they have possiblities, and they are capable of envisioning new situations in which these possibilities are realizable.

Autobiographical works like Richard Brickner's *The Broken Year*[25] and *My Second Twenty Years*[26] or Ron Kovics's *Born on the Fourth of July*[27] chronicle, in greater and more-personal detail, the experiences of disability. These particular books concern the lives of people who became disabled in their twenties. There are other books that describe the lives of people who have been disabled since childhood. In either case, the reader begins to get a more subjective view, which provides a basis for empathic understanding.

These various sources of information, which are meant to be indicative rather than inclusive, provide the reader with a place to begin—they offer a sense of the types of problems that disabled people encounter in our society and of some of the solutions put forward to counter them. They also provide an idea of the resources to which one might turn for further information: organizations, people, and communities.

In general, the designer might pick his sources with the aim of getting an overall picture of "disability" and "design for disabled people" as topics. From bibliographies and from publications like *Rehabilitation Literature,* the designer can select representative, recent publications that provide an overview of current programs, services, and research, as well as specific design information relevant to the immediate design problem. To this, he can add films and books that deal with disability more subjectively or personally, considering the lives of individual disabled people within the context of the everyday environment or within a particular social situation. These provide an important counterpoint to the generalities and abstractions of the other publications, giving the designer a preliminary feeling for the human dimension of disability, which, in fact, is the real link between himself and disabled people.

2. Interviewing Disabled People
If autobiographical and documentary material can bring one to the threshold of empathy for disabled people, then the process of interviewing is the means to cross over and enter into the realm of their experience. Interviewing is a fundamental technique in the social sciences and has been developed in different ways to retrieve specific kinds of information and understanding.

In writing this book, we needed a certain kind of understanding of informants' lives, and this was gained by scheduling a series of interviews with each informant, in which each interview took place in a different environment of the informant's choice. The interview was basically unstructured or free in format; this allowed for the environment in which the interview took place to be a primary subject insofar as the informant desired. This technique was extremely useful in gaining a breadth of awareness of the environmental situation of the informant: What aspects of physical access were worth noting? What social and physical factors made this particular environment a place worth noting as part of the informant's daily life experience? How did the informant *feel* about going there and being there? Also, this interview-in-place gave the participants a shared experience that was invaluable in reaching the deeper meanings the environment held for the informant.

SELECTING INFORMANTS
Norman Denzin defines the role of the informant in the following way:

> By informant I refer to those persons who ideally trust the investigator; freely give information about their problems and fears and frankly attempt to explain their own motivations; demonstrate that they will not jeopardize the study.... The primary functions of the informant are to act as *de facto* observer for the investigator; provide a unique inside perspective on events that the investigator is still "outside" of; serve as a "sounding board" for insights, propositions, and hypotheses developed by the investigator; open otherwise closed doors and avenues to situations and persons; and act as a respondent. Informants serve multiple purposes for the investigator, acting simultaneously as expert witnesses and as transmitters of information, and finally as informal sociologists in the field.... Furthermore, they will be knowledgeable in that they are exposed to the situations and topics central to the study.[28]

The selection of key informants is actually the last step in a process of making contact with and gaining the interest of the people in whom one is interested. As the ratio of contacts to key informants is roughly 10 to 1, it is important that one be in a position to make contacts easily, whether directly or by referral.

One cannot expect to interact with others on any significant level unless the others discern some purpose to the interaction for themselves and for the other. For this reason, it is important that the desire to develop an empathic awareness of the environmental needs of disabled people be part of a larger and legitimate interest in improving the situation of disabled people within one's community—an interest that shows itself in active participation in community affairs, whether through service on committees, collaborating with organizations representing or serving disabled people, or other means.

Not only is such active participation a prerequisite for any significant interaction with disabled people, but it makes the process of interviewing far more interesting for oneself and one's informants. It makes it possible for them to understand their role as an informant as being a contribution toward an objective of mutual interest. They are party to an interaction in which both participants are giving and receiving. The designer contributes his expertise; in return, he learns more about disabled people. The informant contributes his expertise; in return he has a greater influence on the design or planning of his community. Through this means, they become collaborators. On this basis, each selects the other.

It is extremely useful to develop a working relationship with organizations in the community that represent or serve disabled people. And the more these organizations are dedicated to improving the situation of their membership, rather than being preoccupied with maintaining them in the present situation, the more useful they will be as a source of the kind of informants who, as noted earlier, have wants they are in the process of meeting. Ideally, this would be a group with disabled people in charge. Such organizations can help provide initial contacts and referrals and can also help provide a picture of the range of disabilities and the number of disabled people in the community.

Where no such organizations exist, one can look for informants within situations likely to attract independent disabled people—in offices and schools, for example. Even in communities where very little has been done to accommodate disabled people, it is now more probable that government-related buildings will permit access to and employ disabled people.

The Interview-in-Place

If it is one's intention to understand the present situation of disabled people in the community, particularly in relation to the physical environment, then one must develop an approach to interviewing that allows both discussion of specific environments and observation of the informant within them. Furthermore, one must come to understand the range of environments that the informant experiences. This requires seeing the informant many times within different settings and different situations.

Our approach was to begin the interview series by making initial contact with a potential informant, explaining the nature and purpose of our study, and asking him if he would meet with us in a setting in which he felt comfortable and discuss matters pertinent to the study—in particular, his reactions to the setting in which the interview would take place.

The initial reason for asking the informant to select the meeting place was to set him at ease, but in fact these settings became the focal point of our discussions. As the interviews progressed, we selected settings that clearly offered or denied something to the informants, so that we could begin to understand what these places were about.

Rather than developing a set of specific questions, we used an unstructured interview style and at the end of our study relied on several conceptual frameworks to organize the material we were collecting from the informants. Such frameworks or typologies can be helpful in sifting through data that have come to one piecemeal and without much order. One must be careful, however, that such a schema does not begin to override the data, so that one does not push information into arbitrary categories. One way to avoid this is to select several such frameworks, which then work complementarily and permit the data to be organized in several ways.

The first series of interviews we conducted were carried out by some ten or twelve interviewers and involved two to three meetings with each informant. The series of interviews was one of the tasks of the seminar we had formed to study the use of housing by disabled people in Berkeley. It could just as easily have been a committee, a workshop, or an informal working group within a design office.

The seminar gave the interviews a context (it provided another forum, in addition to the interviews themselves) in which the informants could participate—interacting with each other, the people conducting the study, and invited guests. It was the means by which we were able both to attract people who could give us information of remarkable richness and to develop a coherent respondent group to whom we could turn as we began to develop the material and draw conclusions about how disabled people use the environment.

On the basis of the initial interviews, we selected several key informants. Next, through interviewing in depth, we obtained detailed profiles of a number of disabled people. From these we selected seven whom we felt could convey the story to others. Although it is not possible to draw conclusions about the disabled population as a whole from the profiles of a few individuals, it is nonetheless easier to understand the cumulative effects of varied situations, the development of attitudes and beliefs over time, the intensity of feeling for the social and physical environment if selected individuals are profiled and their responses to those environments are seen in the context of each life history. Such profiles serve

Lawrence Berkeley Laboratory Transition Plan Study *Of Transportation* *and Emergency Procedures*

IV: TRANSPORTATION PLAN: ~~Personal Vehicles~~

A1. Physical Obstacles that limit Accessibility ~~(Off-site to On-site)~~
    1. Off-Site - On-Site
    (b) Personal Vehicles

    a) No handicapped parking at Buildings 390 and 391 (Center STreet and Hearst Street)

    b) No curb cut at Building 390 (Center Street). Access from street for wheelchair bound handicapped through service cut at east end. Dangerous and hazardous with loading/unloading traffic dock.

(4.33)

B1. Recommendations to make Facilities Accessible
    1. Off-Site - On-Site
    (b) Personal Vehicles

    i a) Provide handicapped parking under shelter in yard of Building 390 (building clearance adequate at rear, not adequate in covered parking along front of building)

    ii b) Provide curb side standing zone (by city) at front of both Building 390 and 391. Provide adequate clearance at rear of parking for loading and unloading (estimated 15 feet).

    iii c) Provide curb cuts appropriately placed in relation to parking and front entrance of the buildings.

    iv d) All handicapped parking should be clearly marked with signage.

Curbside Bldg. 391 Hearst Street

(8.23)

Curbside Bldg 390 Center St.

yard. Bldg 391 (6.0)

No access from street Bldg 390 center st. (8.22)

(6.3)

Worksheet: the Lawrence Berkeley Laboratory site evaluation.

two other important purposes: they provide a sense of human reality and continuity, and they eliminate many of the mysteries that surround disabled people.

Statistical data, case studies as anonymous examples that fulfill theoretical assumptions, or laboratory tests all set a distance between us and disabled people. The profiles, however brief, let us see whole human beings in the world, acting in and determining that world. We see more than the disability or the wheelchair; we see the person behind the disability, who can become blurred if we focus on the attributes that make him seem separate from us.

With the key informants, we continued the interviews in a similar manner to the first series, meeting always in settings relevant to the disabled person as the embodiment of a particular environmental value. Because our emphasis was on housing, we tended to focus on environments that were residential or supportive of the residential environment. We also began to go into the backgrounds of our informants in an effort to understand how they had arrived at their present situation and how they had developed their present values and assumptions about the environment.

Through these discussions and from participant observation, we began to understand how particular environments are perceived and used. We also came to understand how disabled people make use of the community as a network of supports and services—that is, how well the community as a whole functions for them. Through this means, we were able to form a picture of their existing situation in terms of both its assets and its inadequacies.

THE PERFORMANCE INTERVIEW

A variation on the interview-in-place is the performance interview. This is a useful technique by which to obtain firsthand knowledge of how a disabled person manipulates a given environmental situation in order to evaluate either how accessible a particular environment is or how accessible a proposed environment might be once built. When confronted with a certain terrain, how does a person in a push chair or a power chair negotiate? When a person with impaired vision traverses a certain kind of public environment, what obstacles is the person likely to encounter? What are that person's feelings in such a place? At noonday? At night? In bad weather?

The technique has two aspects: the first is based upon observing the informant carrying out a given environmental movement (usually within a given time frame); the second is based upon a later discussion of that task experience with the informant.

We used this technique extensively in 1977 when we were commissioned to carry out a site evaluation of the Lawrence Berkeley Laboratory, a multi-acred, steep terrain across which numerous large buildings are scattered. What problems did this environment present to physically disabled persons as visitors or employees? In accord with Section 504 of the Rehabilitation Act of 1973, we were charged with bringing disabled persons into the evaluation procedure.[29]

Because there were few disabled individuals presently employed at the laboratory and none who were confined to wheelchairs (nor any who drove their own modified vans), we set up a series of performance interviews with disabled consultants brought to the site for that purpose. The consultants were first observed and then interviewed as they engaged in occupying a given environment for a particular purpose, in moving between destinations within buildings or across the site, in planning an itinerary using the laboratory's public information maps or in responding to a simulated crisis situation.

Their involvement in the evaluation process was crucial. On the one hand, we had come prepared with a checklist of hazards and obstacles drawn from government and institutional sources by which to examine the environment. This brought our attention to the obvious problems. On the other hand, through the consultants, we were able to observe the implications of hazards and obstacles when encountered by people of differing disabilities. More importantly, we observed additional situations that could not have been noted without their participation.

In the discussion portion of the interview we were able to involve would-be users in determining the best ways to solve the problems encountered. More significantly, through their presence we derived a point of view about the environment as social and physical milieu that could not have been determined otherwise. Thus, the performance interview may be used either to evaluate an existing environment or to gain insights into the design implications of a proposed environment. It is a low-risk, economical way of determining beforehand whether or not a proposed design will work.

Ethnography

Ethnography—a technique used in anthropology—aims at understanding the situation and structure of a particular organization or what happens within a particular setting. The use of ethnography as a tool in the design process has been suggested by Galen Cranz,[30] who has adapted the ethnographic approach outlined by James P. Spradley and David W. McCurdy.[31] Cranz's approach is to find a key informant within the setting in which one is interested and to supplement the information gained from this informant by direct observation of the setting.

Irving Zola has suggested another anthropological technique that would lend itself to gaining an empathic understanding of disabled people. He proposes that the designer in effect immerse himself in the everyday lives of his informants by spending a 24-hour period with them or perhaps by spending three 8-hour periods or four 6-hour periods, which would, in their totality, approximate a 24-hour day. His point is that only through such an intense observation will it be possible for an able-bodied person to get an accurate sense of such dimensions of disability as, for example, the time it takes to perform daily activities or the distances that a disabled person can cover within a given time period. Such immersion gives the observer an intuitive sense of the disabled person's situation—a feel for the tempo of his existence and for its particular priorities.[32]

In addition, this technique gives the designer a feeling for how the disabled person copes with his situation through organization—both of the environment and of his time. Such organization is extremely important; in our experience, it is one of the foundations of an independent existence.

To Zola's proposal, we add one of our own. Rather than attempting to make these observations within a very short period, it might be preferable for the designer to take an active role in the everyday environment of a disabled person—for example, to act as an attendant—and thus come to understand the situation of this person over a longer period. Although this approach may not be practical for every observer, it offers the best possible opportunity for a more leisurely and varied view of the situation. Such a view, particularly in conjunction with other kinds of interaction (such as the interviews described previously), can make it possible to reach a very detailed understanding of the other—an understanding that can provide the firmest possible basis for empathy.

THE ENVIRONMENTAL HISTORY
Clare Cooper Marcus has developed a technique—the environmental or residential history—that is a valuable means for understanding more clearly

those aspects of a person's background that have a direct bearing on their present environmental preferences. The technique consists of tracing one's environmental history back to childhood, beginning with the earliest residence one can remember, and then moving forward to include others that were significant. In general, these environments are first organized chronologically; it is also possible to categorize them as "supportive" and "unsupportive," "comfortable" and "uncomfortable," or according to other perspectives.[33]

The aim of the technique is to make a person's environmental values and assumptions explicit and to uncover the patterns that underlie one's choice of settings, residences, and other environments. Understanding these things makes it also possible to move beyond them. As Florence Ladd has written, "After considering where he or she has lived in the context of other possibilities, the student of residential environments often sheds some fixed ideas about the configuration of home."[34]

A final note on interview techniques should be made. Empathic simulations have proved to be an effective means of giving able-bodied people an understanding of the environmental experiences of disabled people: the use of wheelchairs, crutches, blinders, and so on provides first-hand experience of various disabilities in an important even though extremely limited sense. A few of the problems should be mentioned. The able-bodied researcher is experiencing only one aspect of another's condition, which can give only a limited insight. In addition, the researcher may well experience stress—due to the sudden immobility or impairment—that the disabled person has found ways of overcoming. Thus, there is the danger of projecting onto the disabled person a certain affect that is not there. However, if an empathic simulation is used in conjunction with an interview procedure in which the disabled person *guides the researcher* through the simulation, much of the risk can be reduced and the benefits magnified.

3. Visual Documentation
The use of different techniques of visual documentation of the environment can be helpful in understanding how the environment is used by disabled people. Earlier in this part we discussed the use of films made by others. In this section we will describe film techniques the designer may use.

THE VALUE OF VISUAL DOCUMENTATION
Techniques of visual documentation like photo-

graphs and films have two major values when used in a process of developing an awareness of the environmental needs of disabled people: (1) they help make explicit the use of the environment by disabled people, and (2) they function as projective tools in discussion and interviewing.

The visual documentation of specific interactions between disabled people and the environment can provide a record of such interactions that can be analyzed fully in terms of the problems the environment presents to the disabled person or in terms of the adaptations the person makes to it. As Paul Byers has written:

> Human behavior is patterns of patterns of patterns, decreasing in scope beyond normal social seeing. Seeing is learned and culturally influenced; we learn what to see and what not to see. In the still photograph, we can find relations frozen that are, in life, too fleeting for our eyes. . . . The still camera provides a new order of seeing based on a change in time.[35]

This is true also for time-lapse photography. We have found that the repetitive viewing of conventional motion pictures also makes it possible for observers to gain increasingly detailed understanding of what is occurring within the setting depicted. This is particularly true when observation occurs within groups and discussion is possible.

John Collier, Jr., has pointed out the power of the photograph as a projective tool:

> Photographs are charged with unexpected emotional material that triggers intense feelings. It is probably more difficult to lie about a photograph than to lie in answer to a verbal question. . . . The thematic qualities which can be found in photographic content, in intimate studies of the informant's life, evoke emotional statements of value—a positive "yes" and a positive "no."[36]

For this reason, photographs and other visual material can be especially helpful in generating discussion with informants. They provide clear images of the environment which disabled people can respond to and elaborate on. Through this type of process, it becomes possible to understand a great deal about the informants' perspective on the environment.

Consider, for example, a film of a disabled, wheelchair-using person moving along a crowded sidewalk, taken at the eye-level of the person in the chair. When the able-bodied person first looks at this film, he typically fails to see anything unusual. The disabled person, however, can place himself within the picture. He knows what the disabled person sees within this situation—an ocean of bodies, viewed at midsection. Except for those in the distance, able-bodied people pass by without making eye contact with the disabled person. He remains an object for them.

The able-bodied person might imagine that it is a simple matter for the disabled person to look up and establish eye contact. But the disabled person knows that his attention is directed to maneuvering his wheelchair through heavy pedestrian traffic. The device he uses to move himself through space is cumbersome and somewhat too fast for the sidewalk. At the same time, it is much too slow and too vulnerable to contend with other vehicles.

Thus, from a single photograph, the able-bodied person, working together with the disabled person, can begin to understand much more about the world of his informants than he might learn through discussion or interviews which lacked such a catalyst.

THE FILM JOURNAL
In our work with disabled people, we made valuable use of time-lapse movies as research tools in learning how disabled people negotiate the physical environment and contend with social interactions. Time-lapse movies allow a great deal of information to be recorded without losing a sense of the movement of the informant across the terrain or within the setting. The process allows informants to control the filming themselves and thus have autonomy over selection of exactly what to record.

Our approach was to mount Super-8 cameras, modified for time-lapse, on the back of electrically powered wheelchairs. These were fitted with remote switches adjacent to the chairs' control boxes. The time-lapse feature made it possible to film for a considerable amount of time without having to reload, which provided economies in terms of the amount of film used and made it easier to let the disabled informants operating the cameras work independently.

Initially, the filming was made at a rate of one frame every two seconds, but this omitted too much activity. The rate was then adjusted to one frame every half second. The camera was mounted so that it approximated the field of vision of the informants, who were able to aim it by pointing their chair in the direction of what they wanted to record, using their outstretched feet as a pointer. Each camera was fitted with a wide-angle lens, which put part of the chair into the film as a point of reference.

The informants made their films both independ-

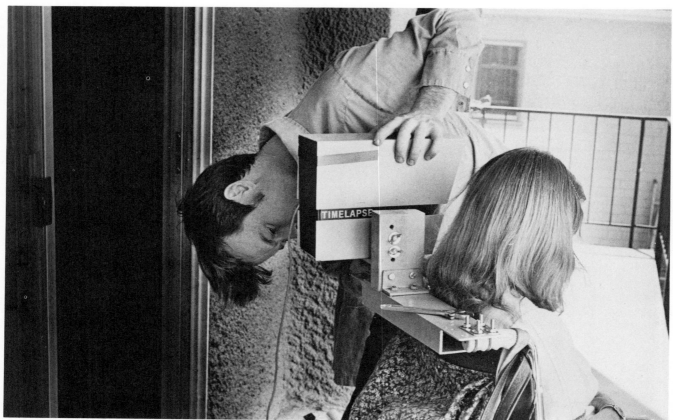

Making a film journal: mounting the Super-8 camera.

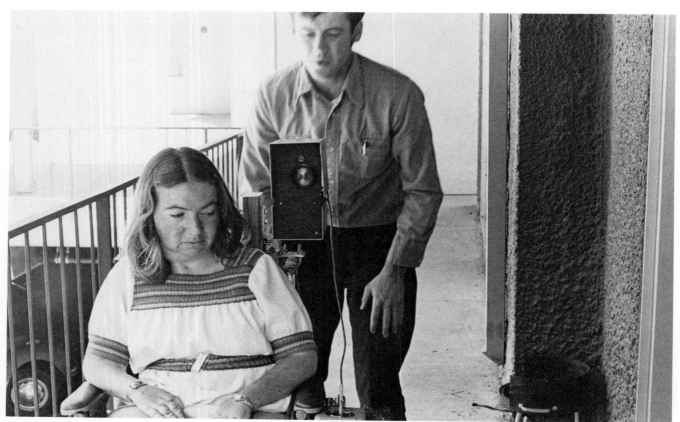

Making a film journal: the camera lens—tilted forward—approximates eye level of the cameraman.

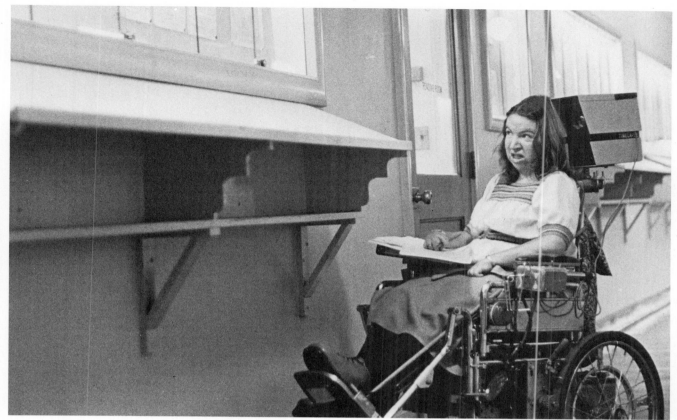

Documentation process: confronting a barrier.

ently and with one another. One part of their footage was predetermined by the researchers, while the remainder was left to their discretion. Most of the particularly valuable footage was taken by the informants in the course of their daily activities. They developed a technique for filming that proved quite effective. One informant would film the other in a particular situation, while the other filmed the situation from his viewpoint. Thus, we got two views of the same situation—one showing the personal and the other showing the contextual perspective of the event.

To get an overview of the use of the environment by disabled people, we also filmed more general situations from a tripod, placed sometimes at ground and sometimes at second-story level. These sequences include disabled people crossing the campus and disabled people and others making use of several large public spaces. These added the perspective of the distant observer to the more immediate perspective of the informants.

In general, the cameras were quiet and unobtrusive enough to be inconspicuous, allowing the filming to occur without disrupting the normal flow of events. Since the cameras could be simply operated, the informants never appeared obviously preoccu-

pied with their use. Consequently, the footage reveals with reasonable accuracy the environment disabled people normally experience.

The analysis of the resulting films was carried out in conjunction with disabled informants and others in weekly sessions held over a two-month period. The time-lapse feature allowed us both to scan the films for sequential events and to study single frames of film in isolation. It was sometimes necessary to view sequences in reverse in order to understand them fully.

The simulated eye-level view of the films gave the viewer a sense of the perspective of the disabled, wheelchair-using person. This allowed able-bodied viewers to quickly develop a feeling for the wheelchair environment and to contrast the experiences of the disabled person with their own.

The time-lapse technique made for a choppy presentation. This was in some ways valuable, because it helped to convey to the viewer a sense of the anxiety of the wheelchair-user in many situations, but the insertion of a lead-in sequence filmed at normal speed would ease the transition to the time-lapse format.

The preset focus and aperture gave the films a bland quality, which perhaps made them less striking as visual documents than if exposure had been better controlled. This blandness did not, however, diminish their usefulness as research tools.

VARIATIONS
The film journal was our technique for allowing informants control over the process of recording what is significant to them in their environment. There are a number of other ways to accomplish this as well.

One approach is to substitute conventional 35mm or Super-8 cameras for time-lapse equipment, providing a remote switch and some mechanism for winding the film (available now for many 35mm cameras). Although this would result in photos or in footage that would be less informative than time-lapse movies in terms of recording both the elements of a given setting and movement within it, it would nonetheless provide a permanent record of a particular event that could be subsequently analyzed by the informant and others.

Where the informant's disability does not preclude his use of cameras in the conventional manner, such filming could be accomplished without special equipment. Likewise, informants could be accompanied by able-bodied assistants who could photograph or film according to the informants' directions. The use of Polaroid cameras would make it possible to check the accuracy of recording on the spot.

The material gathered through these different methods could be used in what we call a "photo essay." This consists of photographs or filmed sequences of aspects of an environment or environments in which the informant believes there is evidence of a good or bad relationship between the built environment and human behavior. It requires, therefore, that the informant develop a set of criteria for making such observations. In presenting the essay or essays to other informants and members of the design team, the informant exposes the personal values that influenced his choice of settings.

This presentation also gives the group a range of images and shared experiences that can be referred to when discussing proposed environments later on. For example, one might say when discussing a particular design problem, "It's the same situation that occurred in George's picture of the entry to the Mexican restaurant." In this way, the photographs often serve as references for clarifying ideas presented in other situations. In using a camera or in observing settings carefully, the informant (and

the able-bodied assistant) gains in visual awareness and learns to discover and become sensitive to those images, details, and qualities in the built environment that are the stock-in-trade of good environmental design. By exposing the recorded settings to a larger group, this awareness is also shared with others.[37]

Visual documentation techniques can also be used to generate dimensional data about one's informants within the context of typical situations and settings in the community. Such data can go far beyond the information found in design manuals, providing material on the interaction of disabled people with each other and with able-bodied people.

The development of such data has two components: an understanding of present patterns of use within the setting, and an understanding of patterns of use that would eliminate the present difficulties a setting imposes on its users.

4. Scenarios and Modeling
The techniques outlined in this section provide a transition from a focus on the environmental needs of disabled people to the expression of those needs in physical form. The techniques can be carried out directly with informants or can be used as projective tools for testing how well the environmental values and patterns of living that have been discovered in the course of interviewing and ongoing discussion are met in the proposed environment.

These techniques of scenario development and modeling are intended to be heuristic; that is, they are intended to lend themselves to ongoing exploration of environmental values, rather than functioning simply as a rendition of a determined environment. The heuristic quality is not achieved so much through the direct modification of the maps or models, although such modification is to some extent possible. Rather, it is reached through the use of these techniques as projective tools, which enable others to respond to them and to project onto them their own perceptions and feelings about the proposed environment.[38]

In our experience, we have learned a great deal from such use. Our decision to write this book stemmed initially from some work we did with the Center for Independent Living. When asked to assist CIL in formulating a program for barrier-free housing, we were confronted with interpreting the term "barrier-free." A strong intuition told us that barrier free means much more than physical access. As for the nondisabled person, an accessible environment is one in which its physical and social qualities do not jeopardize one's potential for feeling oneself to be a whole person.

To examine this thought and to research its implications for the designer, we conducted an eight-week workshop comprised of sixteen designers and twelve severely disabled individuals. A task related to barrier-free housing design was set by CIL. Design teams of able-bodied designers and severely disabled consultants were established, and these investigated the topic through a design process utilizing the modeling technique. The workshop produced an incredible amount of material—enough to make us realize the importance of grounding ourselves more thoroughly in a first-hand understanding of physically disabled people in the built environment. The results of this experiment in modeling as an heuristic process led us to write this book.

DEVELOPING SCENARIOS

The design of a new environment rests upon its visualization in terms of human interaction. In linking together act and environment, the concept of "scenario" is useful. In our terms, a scenario is comprised of three elements: the support system of the environment (typically those parts that are fixed and immutable: floors, roofs, walls, doors, windows—the structure and constructed elements); the equipment people bring into the environment (all those items that enable a person or a group to make themselves "at home" in the environment: clothes, furnishings, nourishment—material and ephemeral elements); and the human situation the proposed environment has to accommodate (individual acts or interactions—from those that may be thought of as random happenings to those that may be considered everyday rituals).[39]

Our approach to the development of scenarios is to use what we call a "story line" as the means to elicit spontaneous responses about the support system, the equipment, and the situation, together with the emotions that accompany them. Such a story might start with the simple phrase, "having lunch with your parents on a Sunday afternoon in July. . . ." The informant draws or verbally sketches what images this phrase engenders. The sketch is then analyzed for its elemental parts, and the environment is considered in terms of what relevant information is contained to assist the designer with his task.[40]

The value of this method, which is related to the technique of free association except that it deals in images rather than in single words, is twofold. It shows that one must place oneself within a given setting and explore it in order to think about it. It also demonstrates that design is only a response to an expressed human need—to an interaction in which different aspects of the environment coalesce into a whole, a scenario.

The technique allows the designer to gain a much more comprehensive view of an informant's intentionality. For example, if an informant tells him, "I like to cook," this information is not enough for the designer to picture a setting in which cooking might occur. If, however, the informant responds to phrases like "making dinner for close friends," "getting a snack in the evening," or "making breakfast in the morning," then the designer gets information from the responses that helps him form a complete image of where and how cooking occurs, its place in the life of his respondent, and so on.

DEVELOPING THE NEW ENVIRONMENT THROUGH MODELING

These scenarios are the raw material from which the new environment is constructed. Our approach in modeling the proposed environment is to begin by mapping the scenarios, then to combine these scenarios into a coherent whole that can be understood by others.

As the scenarios are developed and integrated into a larger setting, it becomes apparent that they have two separate sets of meanings: one when the scenario is thought of in isolation and another when it is thought of in relation to other scenarios. The problem in developing the larger setting becomes that of preserving one's intentions for each scenario.

Scenario Mapping. The first approximation of the proposed environment may be considered scenario mapping. It is two-dimensional like a collage; and construction paper is used to represent, at ½-inch (1.3-centimeter) scale, moveable and fixed objects, scale figures of inhabitants, qualities that have measurable properties (light, heat, sound), and qualities of a more subjective nature (intimacy, warmth, hospitality, private, public, and so on). Furniture and facilities can be given shapes that connote the actual item. Qualities can be given symbolic shape or color and are placed in the area in which they are to be experienced. If an idea related to a scenario cannot be expressed through shape or color, the participants can write these ideas on the construction itself.

Scenarios that depend on vertical relationships—

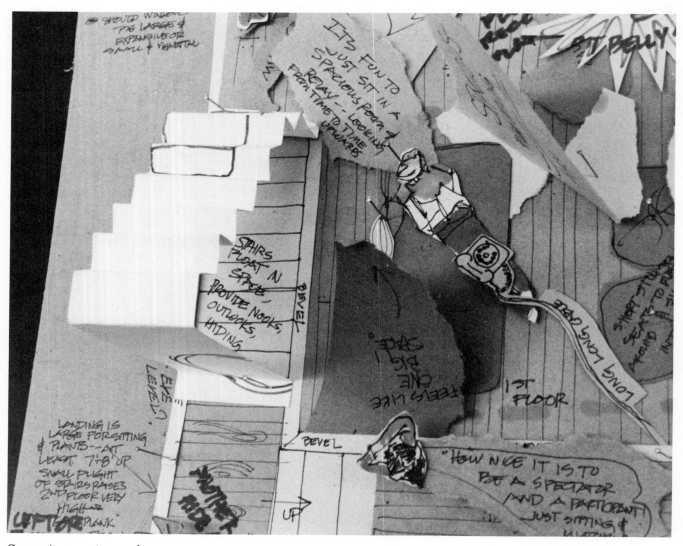

Scenario mapping underway.

playing in the attic, looking down from a loft, going upstairs to bed—are represented by placing settings on top of one another. Each setting, however, is worked out independently according to its own requirements. If two related settings do not correspond in terms of structural dimensions, there will be an opportunity to resolve these conflicts in subsequent models. Floor plans per se are not created in this model; rather, the participants are asked to create spaces around a setting or group of settings, which are then defined by boundaries, such as a strip of paper between accommodations. One of the major objectives of this changeable model is to allow the participants to work as rapidly and spontaneously as possible in developing ideas about the proposed environment.

Through this technique, the requirements of each setting are established in relation to the situation they support. As each scenario is developed, the participants move onto the next until this graphic representation of the proposed environment can be comprehended in visual form by others.

The Three-Dimensional Model. This second approximation of the environment—a three-dimensional model—is not a reproduction in three dimensions of the scenario map produced in the first round. Rather, it is a more advanced version of what has been gained from developing and discussing the types of settings previously explored. The scenario map is intended to serve only as a set of notes for its construction.

This model provides another opportunity to introduce new ideas and discard old ones. Its construction is much like that of the first model; sce-

144

Scenario mapping: a detail of the proposed design.

narios are developed that reflect the needs and values of proposed users and are integrated into an overall setting. However, its instrumental role is in bringing into focus the architectural questions of building construction, such as what materials are appropriate for the new environment? and what type of structure would contribute to the qualities we are looking for here?

In the three-dimensional model, also at ½-inch (1.3-centimeter) scale, the participants use cardboard construction paper, or whatever materials seem to best represent the built forms they want to include. Here, all the details are rendered more precisely. The boundaries established in the two-dimensional model are identified as walls or transition zones. Environmental qualities are articulated in terms of windows, skylights, doors, wall thickness, proximity, area, and so on. Qualities more dif-

ficult to define, such as intimacy, begin to be expressed within the design, in terms of both the attributes and the relations between spaces.

The scenarios are reworked, this time using actual photographs of the participants and others—photographs that represent them at ½-inch (1.3-centimeter) scale, in keeping with the model. The use of such photographs helps make the scenarios "alive" in the minds of the participants. They are also valuable in providing a basis for testing assumptions about dimensions in all proposed settings. On a technical level, these figures give participants a more-precise measuring stick with which to gauge the "right size" and "right relationship" in designing spaces and forms. With this method of "peopling" the proposed environment, the participants can more effectively gauge static dimensions and better determine the needed space for certain

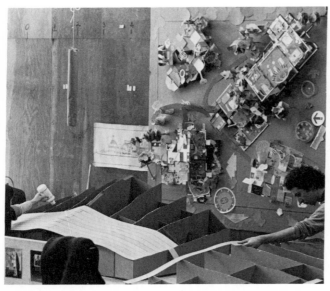

The three-dimensional model: constructing the site (foreground). In the background is the scenario map in plain view as a reference.

Development of the model.

The environment.

Discussions with user-clients.

Examining a design detail.

kinds of social interactions or for individual needs for mobility.

In this model, the emphasis is on questioning all aspects of a setting to ensure that it embodies and offers those qualities or amenities considered desirable. Participants should design even familiar things, such as furniture, fireplaces, doors, and windows, so that these become an integral part of the setting. This makes it possible for them to examine what is typical in the existing environment to see how well it suits the exact requirements of users. If nothing meets these requirements, the participants will have to invent something new.

Detailed Models. The final category of modeling—detailed models—is a construction, at 1-inch (2.5-centimeter) scale, of particular spaces within the three-dimensional model. Again, participants continue to introduce material and indications of construction that help to create an environment with the qualities they consider desirable. By redesigning aspects of the environment at much larger scale, participants once again have an opportunity to reconsider their assumptions about the proposed environment. This reexploration also draws attention to many details of construction that would probably be left undefined at the smaller scale.

Epilogue

An early intention of this book was to write a modest tract that would offer encouragement in the way of role models to physically disabled people who had not moved into the mainstream, but now at the end of our study we have a different slant on what we wish them to know. We have also come to believe that what disabled people have revealed to us is important to relate to able-bodied people, to whom role models are also important in improving their lives.

In the beginning, for all our good intentions and our openness, we were still biased by our preconceptions of what it would mean to be physically disabled. We continually mapped onto the disabled person the persona of the able-bodied person, and where there was a lack of congruence, we felt pain: that in these aspects of life disabled people must experience some difficulty in feeling completely human. However, it was exactly at these points that we began to see that disabled people are not pretending to be able-bodied. They have in fact developed other ways of being in the world.

In Berkeley we have confronted a sizable population of disabled people who know the joy of small, self-sufficient acts; who are very much in touch with their bodies and know what is good for their bodies; who often spend long periods of time alone and have come to know that aloneness is not necessarily loneliness; to whom being alive and well and active in the world is rarely taken for granted. These people are not necessarily sensitive to these things by choice, but through circumstances have come to identify ways of being in the world that are truly life-enhancing and that able-bodied people, with seemingly endless options, casually overlook. We have become acutely aware that each person—able or disabled—has a different capacity for self-sufficiency. We have also become aware that all of us are dependent and that those who are more dependent than others for everyday physical functions do not necessarily view themselves as devalued be-

Moving on: entering the Federal Building in San Francisco on April 5, 1977, to begin the twenty-six-day sit-in that resulted in the implementation of civil rights legislation for physically disabled people.

cause of their dependency. What we have come to see is that all people need to balance their independence and dependence in a realistic way.

Because of this new understanding, we must introduce a minor caveat about how able-bodied people tend to view mainstreaming. Through this study we have learned admiration and respect for those who mainstream; by their willingness to take risks, to do battle, they have changed the environmental possibilities for all disabled people. We admire those with determination, but see that it can have its price. In this society we give status to those who overcome their handicaps, but rarely do we know the price they may have paid to achieve that status. In Berkeley we have become sensitive to how society encourages disabled people to deny their handicap by placing a high value on overcoming it rather than supporting the person as he is. Irving Zola, a disabled person and sociologist with a national reputation and a correspondingly busy schedule, has made this point quite vividly. He reports that for years he would at all times use his leg braces and cane and *walk*, even under very stressful conditions, such as when negotiating a large international airport. Only recently has he allowed himself the comfort of the wheelchairs available at airports—thus heightening his profile as a disabled person in the public environment.[1]

In a certain, perhaps unconscious way, Berkeley too gives status to those who overcome their handicap. This causes some alarm to individuals who may look to Berkeley as a place to come and to some individuals who are already there. To mainstream is often equated with being a "super crip," an image that can be both repelling and destructive. It is important that Berkeley not project a lopsided image as a place of miraculous cures, a manufacturer of super crips, because there is so much more to learn there than that.

What needs to be articulated most is the fact that the disabled people of Berkeley have effected a very special social structure supportive of their goals. The physical environment of Berkeley and the attitudes of the disabled people there are essential components of this process. The ramps, the curb cuts, the pedestrian environment, the varied ap-

149

proaches to accessibility, the informal organizations are all ingredients of an accessible world. The image Berkeley has achieved in the media reflects a reality.

The entire Berkeley phenomenon, however, is best viewed as a process that in an essential way is not restricted to Berkeley. In any community where disabled people live, their determination for an independent life, however it is expressed, is one seminal force in putting the "Berkeley process" into effect. What remains to be done is to establish the linkages between these separate but determined people.

What attitude should the designer adopt in taking part in this process? If use is made of the strategies already discussed, the designer can work from a position of insightfulness and thus make more reasoned choices in designing for accessibility. With each design problem, however, a major question must be kept in mind. Is the objective to assimilate the disabled person into the environment, or is it to accommodate the environment to the person? Though the answer is probably to balance these two concepts, a few more words of discussion are necessary.

Currently, the emphasis is on assimilation, for this seems to assure that the disabled person, once "broken-in," will be able to operate in society as a "regular person" and that the environment will not undermine his natural agenda to "improve" himself.

As we have shown, this assumption can be counter-productive when designing for accessibility. It may serve only to obscure the fact that the disabled person may have a point of view about the design that challenges what the designers would consider good design. Many designers have, in fact, expressed a certain fear that pressure to accommodate disabled people will jeopardize good design and weaken the design vocabulary. Though certain aspects of the contemporary design vocabulary may have to be reconsidered in making accessible environments, one must also look forward to new items in the vocabulary that will develop in response to these human needs—ultimately leading toward more humane concepts of what makes for good design.

If we remember that at some time in *all* lives there are periods of vulnerability—certainly in infancy and in old age—we cannot but find what disabled people have to say personally meaningful. For several decades designers have tried to understand what it is like for the child or elderly person to operate in a world designed almost exclusively for the able-bodied adult, in order to design more sensitively from that other perspective. Now there emerge other spokespersons for vulnerability—physically disabled people. They are truly articulate about their needs and expectations, and we do not have to second-guess their meaning. They offer a view of being in the world that truly challenges the designer's imagination.

Catalogue

Ways and Means of Adapting the Environment

Designers need not only to listen to their clients when planning new environments, but also to look carefully at what these clients and others who share their particular way of life have engineered for themselves. In this catalogue of largely ad hoc solutions to environmental problems, the physically disabled person reveals real skill in translating personal needs into environments and equipment. The selected examples fall into several groupings.

Nonconforming Uses

At the one extreme of design solutions are *nonconforming* uses of the environment—a term used by Herbert Gans[1] to denote a way of using an environment programmed for one purpose, for another purpose, in order to derive a certain personal advantage otherwise unavailable. These uses are not readily noticed because although the way in which the environment is used is unusual, the environment itself does not undergo change.

Although such environments can offer valuable information for the designer, a disabled person may be reluctant to reveal these practices, which might be considered deviant or make the user appear unseemly. For example, when an able-bodied person sees a person in a wheelchair, he usually assumes that when not in the wheelchair, the disabled person is probably in bed—that he is so physically immobilized or frail that chair or bed are his only environmental alternatives. But this is not necessarily true. Many physically disabled people, though not capable of walking, can crawl or use other body motions to move themselves about on the floor. Some disabled people have come to accept this *ability* and their environment reflects this: furniture and other household equipment have been modified to make them accessible from floor level. But others have not accepted this ability in themselves, for various reasons. Some who could use their environment in this nonconforming way may not do so because it has never occurred to them; others may not because they feel that to do so would be socially unacceptable—to themselves and others. (For a disabled person to be rigidly fixed in wheelchair or bed has become an accepted image in our society even

though it is equated with being ill.) But if such a person were taken to Japan or the Middle East, where floor culture is commonplace, how readily they would fit in! So where alternative environmental experiences are potential, they should be explored and promoted.

Ad Hoc Designs

A second category of design solutions might be called *adhocism*, a term used by Charles Jencks and Nathan Silver to denote "a principle of action having *speed* or economy and *purpose* or utility. Basically, it involves using an available system or dealing with an existing situation in a new way to solve a problem quickly and efficiently. It is a method of creation relying particularly on resources which are already at hand."[2]

Many examples from the catalogue of *ad hoc solutions* could be cited. One is the use of the conventional country club golf cart by physically disabled people as an intermediate-scale vehicle (between wheelchair and automobile) for moving about the city. Crutches or folding wheelchair fit behind the driver in the space which normally carries golfing equipment. The advantages are numerous: the cart is good on both hard and soft lawn surfaces; it can be weatherized; it can make a closer approach to building entrances than automobiles; it can be parked either in regular vehicular parking areas or in spaces set aside for bicycles. At an entirely different scale is the improvisation of a styrofoam drinking cup as the speaker in a frequency-sensitive device that switches an electric appliance on or off by voice command.

Adaptations

A third grouping of design solutions is devoted to *adaptations*, devices usually built by others to meet the special needs of an individual. Most of these items are electrical systems that allow the disabled person, for example, to operate equipment in the dwelling from bedside, thus lessening one's dependency upon others. Adaptations are made to answer telephones, open and close doors automatically, turn lights on or off, or raise and lower the bed. Other adaptations help one get in and out of bed or on and off the toilet unassisted. Some are exceedingly sophisticated in makeup, such as the electronic retrofitting of vehicles to be driven by an individual with specific disabilities and abilities.

Tools

A fourth grouping includes items of modest economy and high-satisfaction yield. In every household of a physically disabled person who lives an independent life one finds cord, string, wooden sticks, Velcro tape, rubber and plastic tubing, pieces of carpeting and plastics shaped or fashioned to do a specific job. These "tools" make it possible for disabled people to use standard products and with little expense make these products work for them. These humble tools are the interface between user and other equipment—extending one's reach, the ability to pull, push, or turn, in effect to manipulate the world about one according to one's abilities.

One of the informants carries several such instruments around with her. These include a ¼-inch (0.6-centimeter) wood dowel 3 feet (0.9 meters) long with a nonslip rubber tip for punching elevator buttons; a metal rod of similar length, but with a handle grip on one end and house key rigidly fixed to the other, for unlocking her front door; and another dowel with a hook attached, for pushing and pulling objects on tables and on her drawing board.

Some interface equipment has the character of Rube Goldberg inventions, especially those rigged to open and close doors. To a designer they may lack "design," but two factors must not be overlooked: the satisfaction of the designer-user who envisions a solution to his own problem and sees it built, and the day-to-day pleasures that come with independent, albeit small, acts. In addition, the capability of the user to produce such tools should alleviate a certain amount of the architect's or interior designer's concern to cover all bases when designing for accessibility.

A final remark is needed about the catalogue. No attempt has been made to be all-inclusive, even if it were possible to do so. The primary intention is to whet the appetite and suggest a typology for organizing and thereby making memorable what one observes as a resource for solving the problems confronted. A secondary observation is that the kinds of designs catalogued here occur in the dwelling or workplace or as part of the wheelchair—environments that can be manipulated and made somehow "complete" through physical adaptations. But in the world outside these discrete environments, a different kind of engineering must take place.

At some point in time and place—usually in the public realm—the physically disabled person will have to ask others, probably strangers, for assistance, instead of relying on the kinds of means cited here. Approaching strangers may be difficult for the physically disabled person, just as it is difficult for many sensitive able-bodied people to offer help to a physically disabled person who may need it. The problem is largely one of attitides, and with time and familiarity it should lessen.

Making the public environment generally accessible to physically disabled people is of paramount importance in the process of familiarization and changing attitudes. Once the public environment is more accessible, physically disabled people will be able to play a more normal role as public figures; their presence will become commonplace, and they may begin to feel less conspicuous, less the intruder. If physically disabled people are able to negotiate the public environment without too much assistance from others, a certain burden of discomfort will be lifted from disabled and able-bodied individuals alike. Disabled people would feel less strongly that they are imposing on others, and able-bodied people would feel less guilt or confusion as to their role in assisting those who are less able. This has been one of the major lessons learned from Berkeley.

People using power chairs often report the dilemma of not knowing whether to consider themselves pedestrians or vehicles. Some defer this decision to the situation. On sidewalks they move at the pace and with the protocol of the pedestrian; but in the street they find it safest and most expedient to adopt a nonconforming pattern and drive against traffic in order to be clearly visible to oncoming vehicles.

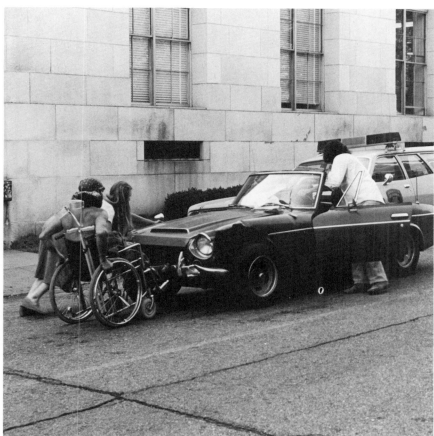

The wheelchair becomes a "tow truck" when giving a shove to a stalled car.

The steady hum and regular movement of the power chair facilitate a walk side by side of two persons with different physical disabilities, one confined to a wheelchair and one blind.

Supermarkets are set up for use by shopping bags and carts, here replaced by lap and power chair.

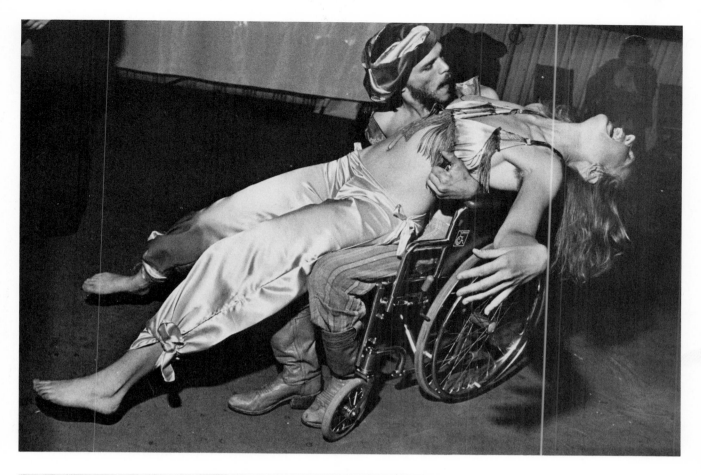

At social occasions—like dances—the physically disabled person does not necessarily have to experience isolation as a wheelchair user.

Friends and couples double up and travel considerable distances in a power wheelchair.

The living room, the most accessible part of the household both physically and socially, makes an ideal bed–sitting room for someone who prefers to be at the center of things.

A sunny private garden becomes a place for bathing out of doors.

The foot of the bed, because exposed to the center of the room, forms one side of a conversational area, bringing the bed's occupant into close, face-to-face contact with others seated there. A small table, placed at the foot, provides a surface for books, papers, drinks.

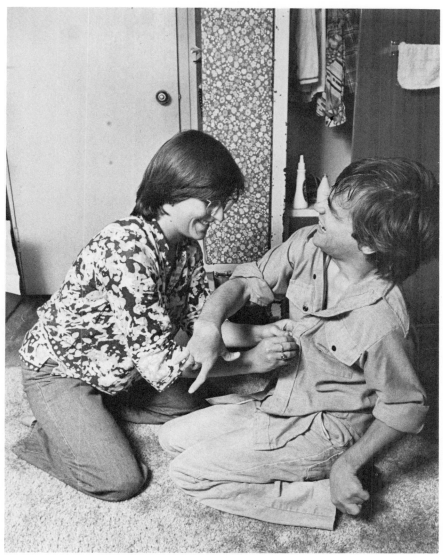

Many people who cannot walk and who use a wheelchair in public can move about with considerable ability on the floor when at home. Given the proper design, the floor has great potential as an accessible and pleasurable environment.

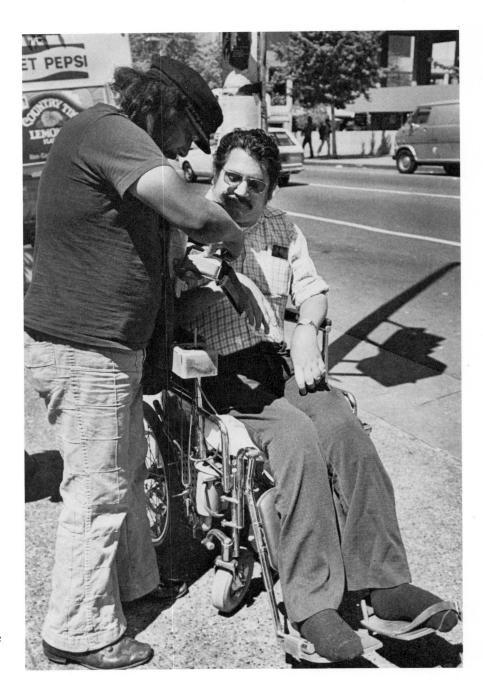

Since handling money in public places is often a problem if one has to rely on strangers for assistance, a conveniently located wallet or purse can facilitate getting the aid one wants without confusion.

Golf carts take on another meaning as intermediate-scale transportation between wheelchair and automobile. The storage section behind the driver's seat, large enough for several laden golf bags, holds one or two folding wheelchairs easily.

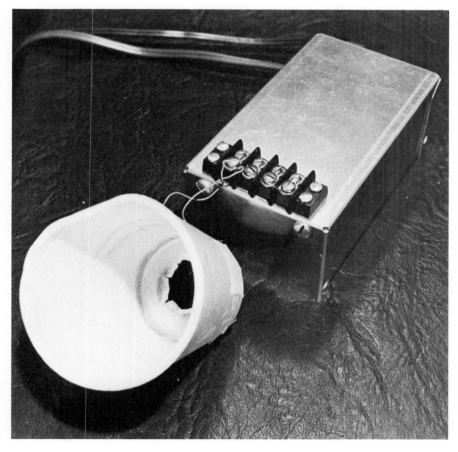

An appliance plugged into this adapted switchbox is activated by a human whistle tone. The frequency-sensitive device discriminates all by one frequency. One whistle turns on the appliance; a second turns it off.

Ready-made kitchen appliances are used in an ad hoc arrangement to make a complete, movable kitchen tailored to individual needs. Here two basic tables are set up in a corner of a standard kitchen. The lower table allows downward action and vision for stirring food on the portable electric range. This table also accommodates a Rubbermaid turntable, Rubbermaid roll-out storage drawers for silverware and utensils, and an adapted water dispenser. The higher table holds a table oven, a Rubbermaid twin turntable for spices, and a Rubbermaid dinnerware rack.

The door to the Farberware Turbo-Jet oven opens to the left rather than downward and is therefore out of the way when sliding the rack or baking pans in and out of the oven. The oven can be used for baking and broiling.

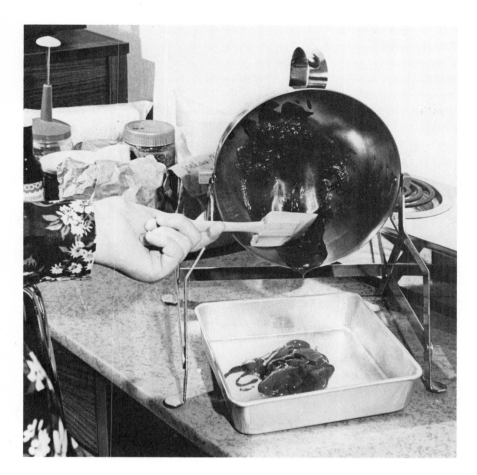

The stand for the mixing bowl is notched to allow the adapted bowl to be fixed in either a stirring or a pouring position. The cook can scrape contents into a baking pan with one hand.

In this ad hoc arrangement surfaces at three different heights adapt to the needs of a specific individual, providing spaces for a two-burner plate, a Toastmaster tabletop oven, an electric frying pan, and a slow cooker. The oven can both bake and broil, and a cook with limited finger dexterity can use the adapted metal extender on the temperature dial. Utensils are equipped with adaptive grips for someone with limited hand-grip.

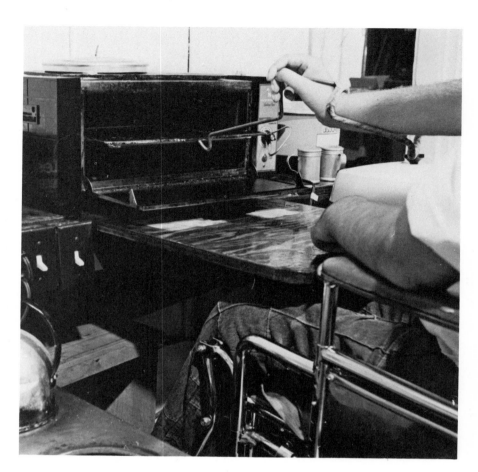

The cook can maneuver a lever on a rotating stand for easy and safe handling of the oven rack.

A multilevel, U-shaped kitchen has been put together as a single unit suited to this person's needs. The design gives the unit an overall appearance of permanence. The program for the design, however, emerged out of a long period of trial and error while using the movable more "portable" types of arrangement described previously.

This water dispenser is a thermos adapted with rubber tubing. Water is released through the tubing by pressing lightly on the wooden extender. The tubing can also run directly into a pot on the burner. This is especially useful when a standard sink faucet is too high to reach.

Rubbermaid pull-out drawers enable a person with limited reach to make better use of a cupboard. The drawers are easily installed and slide smoothly.

A key feature of the ad hoc kitchen is the arrangement and design of switches that permit easy, safe use. Here, fixed switches installed on a horizontal surface are accessible without the need of arm reaches or finger dexterity.

In this arrangement, in which all surfaces are at the same height, it is possible for someone with limited strength to easily slide utensils from hot to cold surfaces.

Two nails driven through the cutting board hold vegetables, bread, and so on for slicing by a person with limited hand-arm function.

This lady's wand, normally used as a tool for a variety of housekeeping chores, takes on another meaning when making an emphatic domestic statement.

165

The body, too, can take on ad hoc uses: here the chin is a useful stabilizing element in opening a jar of spices when cooking.

A meat fork with a special fitting for the hand is used to open sealed packages when finger function is limited.

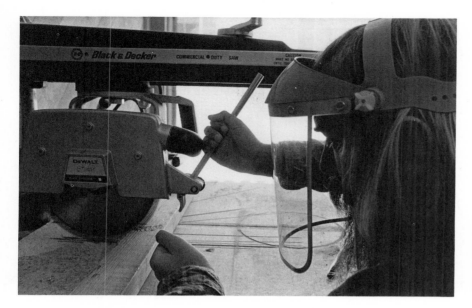

The antikick device, used when ripping lumber to keep the sawed half from flying off the machine, is also useful as a convenient handle for guiding the blade of the saw when there is limited finger function.

A hospital table is given expanded uses as an easily adjusted, rolling desk at home.

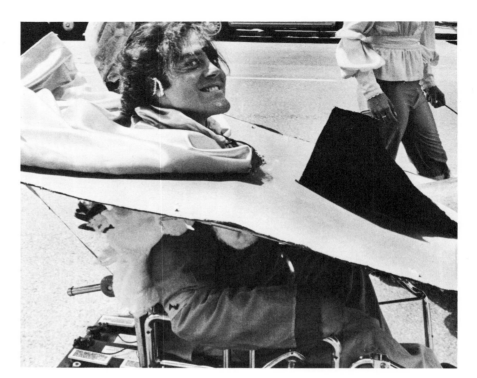

This wheelchair becomes the setting for the Red Baron seated in the cockpit of his plane in Berkeley's Fantasy Day parade.

The beauty of an ad hoc solution is often in the great economy exercised for maximum results. A parking meter is the prop used to stake out a position along the public sidewalk.

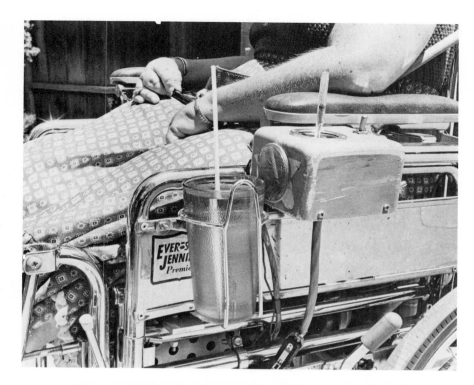

A beverage holder, bolted to the side of the wheelchair, is especially convenient for those who require an ongoing supply of liquids during the day.

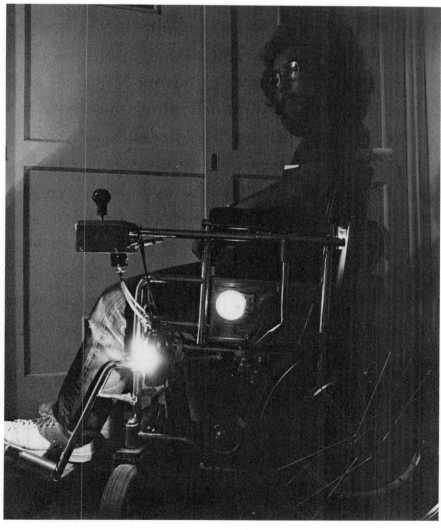

The wheelchair can be adapted for nighttime use by adding lights and reflectors for safety.

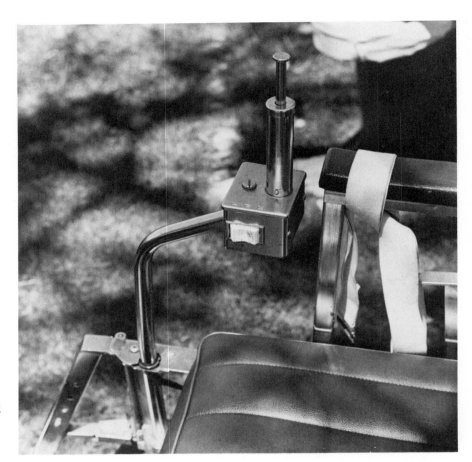

Each electric wheelchair is controlled by a device suited to the abilities of its user. Here an elevated finger control is provided.

On this wheelchair the driving mechanism has been moved to a position directly in front of the operator.

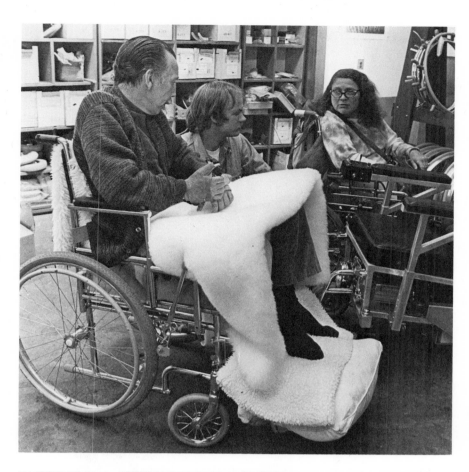

The cold metallic surfaces of a wheelchair can be softened and warmed by the addition of sheepskin rugs and seatcover.

A wand attached to a headpiece, when matched to an elevated receptaclelike switch (right), can be used to drive the wheelchair.

This motorized office stool is well suited for use on smooth surfaces or under a desk. It provides a large range of small motions (turning, moving short distances between office equipment) in places perhaps too tight for the wheelchair.

Specially equipped vans can greatly increase the range of places accessible to disabled people who are able to move about unassisted.

This electric tailgate can be folded and unfolded, raised and lowered, with pushbutton controls.

A folding ramp is permanently attached inside this van. The ramp folds vertically for compact storage while traveling.

Custom-made ramps are usually constructed of wood and provided with a nonskid surface, such as sand and paint mixtures. This ramp integrates its form well with the existing pathway.

Ramps can be designed to fit the style of the residence as well as the needs of its occupants. This ramp is particularly successful in the way it is integrated into the landscaping of the front of the house.

A ramp in a small, tight area can double back for economic use of space.

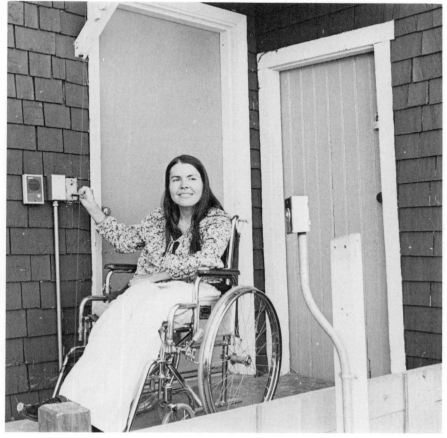

This house entrance has been adapted to contain an electrically operated door. At the entrance there are two switches. The control panel to the left of the door is for locking when leaving; the switch on the right is for unlocking upon arrival.

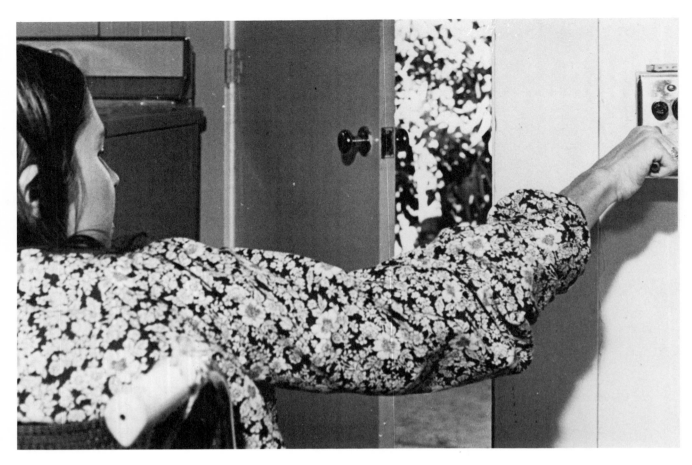

The control panel inside the house includes an automatic door opener.

The unlocking device for the door shown on the bottom of page 175 is within easy arm's reach. The key is bolted to an extender for grasping.

Pieces of carpeting tacked to lower door jambs prevent damage from a wheelchair.

Security is a major concern of disabled people, who are far more vulnerable than able-bodied people if an intruder actually gains entrance. This control panel includes an intercom to both front and back doors permitting screening of visitors—from bedside, if this is the situation—before they are admitted.

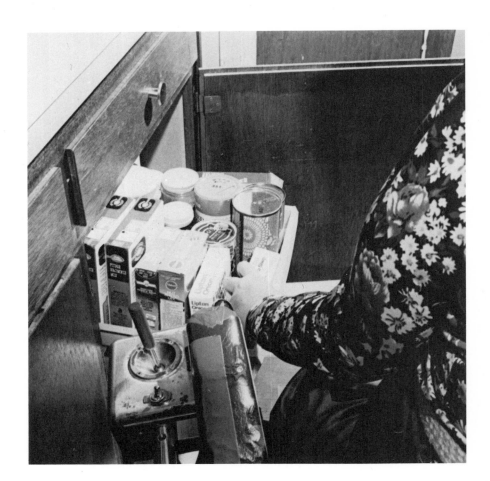

Drawer storage is provided with hardware that allows full extension without tipping.

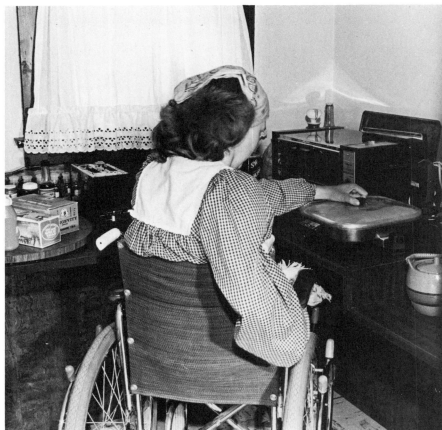

Another storage adaptation is the countertop with a fixed Lazy Susan (left) that arranges many small items together and places each in reach as needed.

The TeleDialer is a touch-tone machine that is hooked up to the telephone. Its memory bank can be fed frequently used numbers. The machine connects the caller with the desired party when a button is pushed next to the space in which the party's name and number are written.

On this hands-free telephone a push of buttons or levers with fingers or mouth-stick summons a special telephone operator who will place calls in Berkeley for the physically disabled person.

Remote-control extension cords can be attached to any appliance. Switches can be placed within easy reach, enabling a person to use lights, radio, television, and other electrical appliances unassisted.

A portable, multiunit box, here set up at bedside, provides easy centralized access to electrical controls.

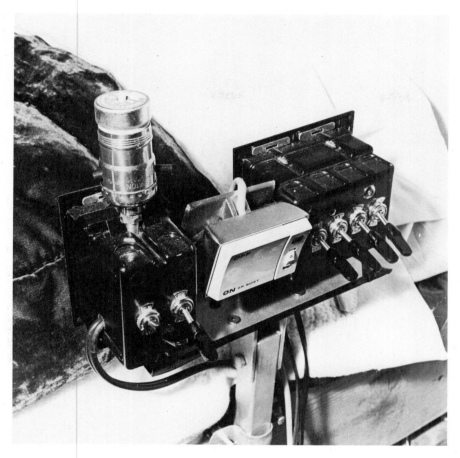

Appliances can be controlled by easy-to-reach switches, here mounted on a post attached to the bed frame. The device is like a series of wall sockets, each independently operated from the rear by toggle switches.

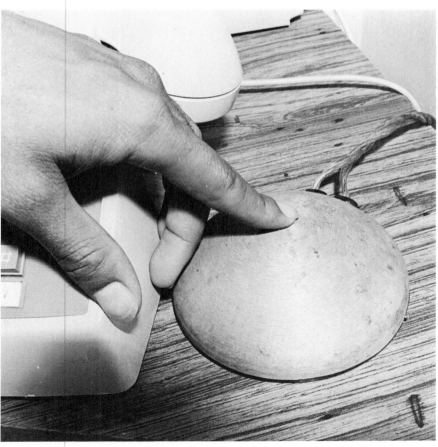

This skin-sensitive appliance switch responds to touch for on-off control.

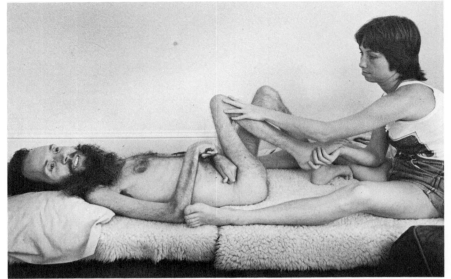

A setting for exercise and massage is made on the floor by using a 6-inch (15.4-centimeter) foam pad covered with sheepskin. Sheepskin is a desirable surface for those who are in bed a lot as it permits air to circulate under the body and thus minimizes the risk of bedsores.

The Hoyer lift allows one to gently lift and transfer a physically disabled person up to 350 pounds (158 kilograms) in weight with little or no effort. The lift is set up here to transfer the person from wheelchair to raised bed. It can also be used for transfer from chair to bathtub, toilet, or automobile.

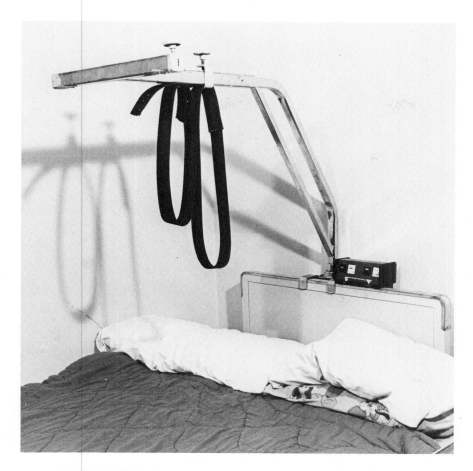

A metal frame attached to the bed (or to the wall over it) allows a disabled person to change position in bed unassisted.

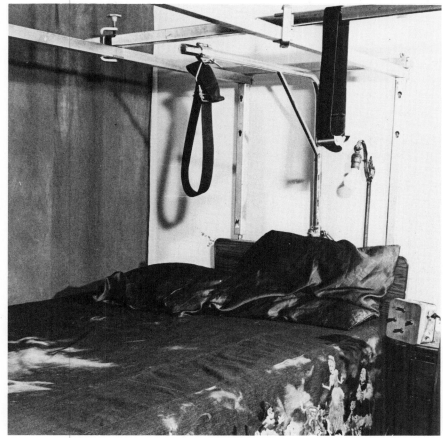

A metal frame suspended above the bed can be extended to facilitate getting into and out of bed unassisted.

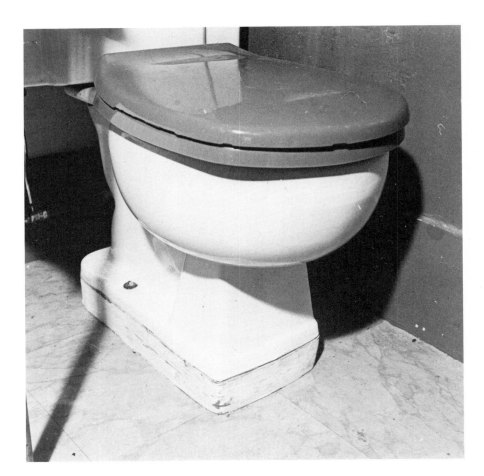

For individuals who can use a regular bathroom, this small modification of a raised wooden base makes the toilet accessible.

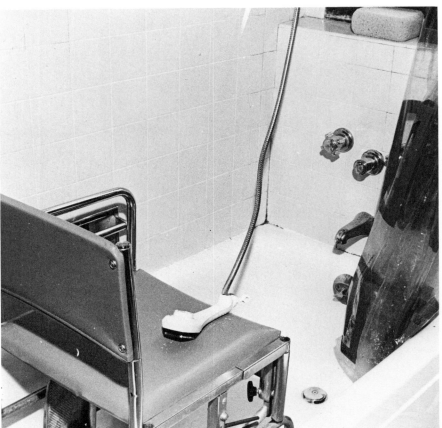

Chairs or benches can fit into showers. (Note the hand-held shower head.) Transfer to it can be made with slideboard, Hoyer lift, or the help of an attendant.

San Francisco architect Sally Swanson designed this bathroom for a physically disabled client. The free-standing toilet with grab bar and hand-held shower alongside respond to the client's needs.

Items in this gift shop are displayed on open glass shelves that go to the floor. This makes it easier for those who use wheelchairs and who perhaps have limited or no arm function to inspect goods at close range.

Tools

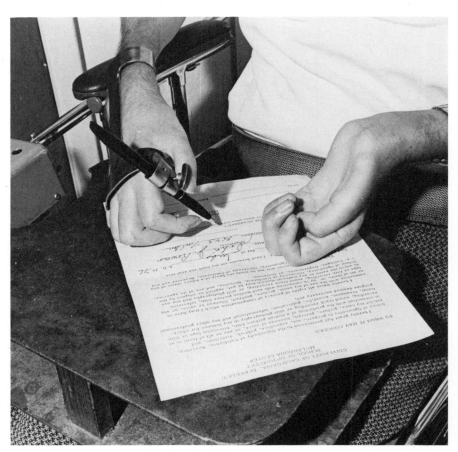

Some of the most personal tools are those extensions of the hand that substitute for small-muscle control in the fingers. The handclasp here has a rubber-tipped metal dowel welded to it; this is used for typing or using a pushbutton telephone.

The ability to sign your own name signals legal maturity; a splint that holds a writing device extends this possibility to those with impaired hand-wrist function.

Wheelchairs can be equipped for many specialized needs. A lapboard resting on the arms of a wheelchair can become a desk and is often detailed with special pockets and trays to carry specialized equipment used by the person in everyday interactions.

This lapboard, hinged in the center, folds easily for storage on a back pouch.

This lapboard is made of Plexiglas, to allow a clear view of the feet and ground ahead. It is designed with compartments for a drinking glass, a tape recorder, a wallet, and note-books.

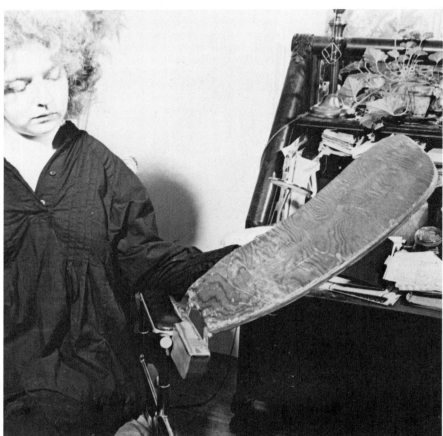

A plywood lapboard is hinged to the armrest of this wheelchair. It swings down to the side when not in use and does not interfere with the operation of the chair.

Sewing is a creative, satisfying activity for a sedentary person. This specially designed splint permits grasping a tiny needle and manipulating it.

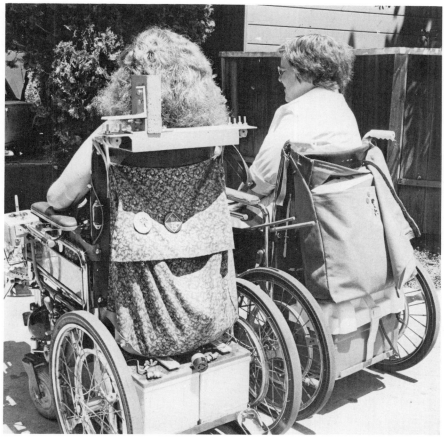

Manufactured or custom-made pouches and backpacks hung on the backs of wheelchairs carry the day's necessities.

Drinking through a straw is easy when the table height is designed for your needs.

Tubing taped to the mouth of this water jug allows a person to drink without assistance.

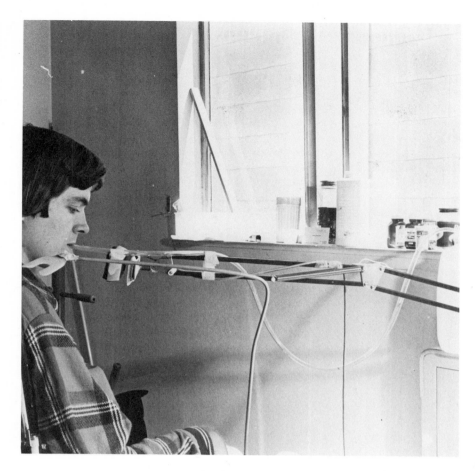

This arrangement for obtaining water without assistance is made of plastic tubing taped along an extender.

A Velcro-fastened loop is used to pull a cupboard door open.

Simple adaptations like this string pull make many standard lamps accessible.

The cord pull of this drawer allows a person to pull the drawer open unassisted.

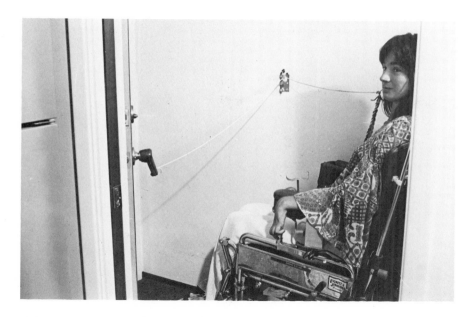

A cord attached to a door and running through a pulley is pulled downward to close the door.

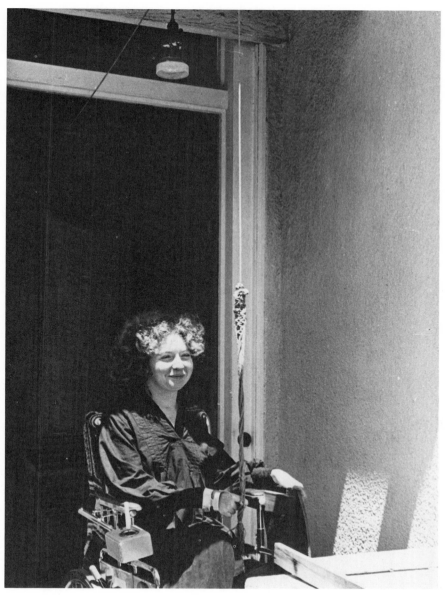

The combination of a rubber door-handle extender, a cord, and a pulley at mouth height permit this door to be opened without the use of the hands.

The metal extender bolted to this key makes it possible to unlock or lock the door with limited finger function.

When a narrow corridor does not permit maneuvering, an extra-long key extender may be required.

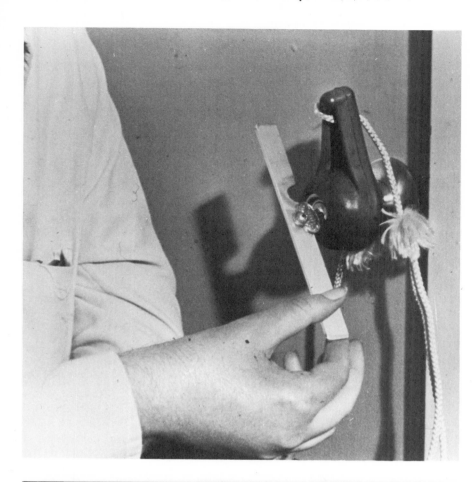

A key bolted to a 6-inch (15.4-centimeter) extender improves leverage for a person with limited grip.

A metal handle may be more easily grasped than a plastic telephone receiver, and the pushbutton telephone is more accessible to those with limited finger-hand-wrist function than the dial system.

This letter board, mounted so others can see it, permits this person, who cannot speak, to convey his thoughts through words, phrases, and an alphabet indicated with his head wand.

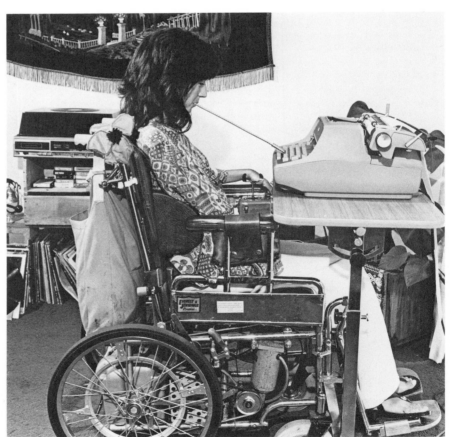

A light-touch typewriter, equipped with an extra-long sheet of paper, allows typing with a mouth wand with a special weighted tip.

Plastic extenders on the control keys permit this cassette tape recorder to be operated by a mouth wand with a special weighted tip.

With the use of varied wands the mouth can substitute for hands in many situations.

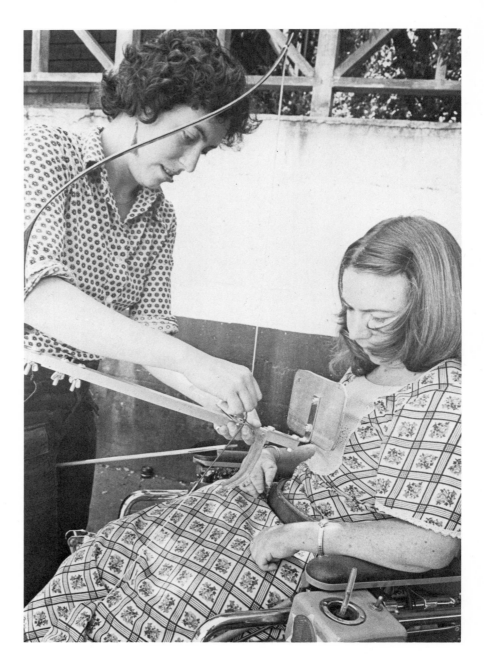

Assistance and ingenuity in rigging the equipment permit participation in a wide variety of activities, even archery.

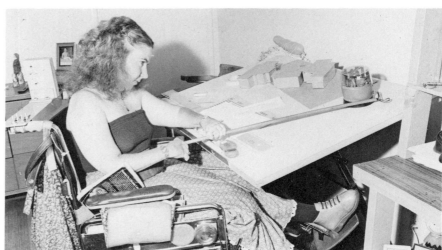

Tools that extend the reach can greatly increase the amount accomplished without assistance. This device both lifts and pulls and is carried as part of the paraphernalia attached to the wheelchair.

198

A 3-inch (7.6-centimeter) metal pin has been inserted in the stereo control knob for easier turning.

A 2-inch (5-centimeter) extender is taped to the on-off knob of the television.

A metal control stick is used to adjust a floor-level heat register.

The wooden railing at one side of this baby crib has been restructured with a spring-hinge device, which allows it to be easily opened or closed by pulling on the cloth strap attached at its center.

200

Notes

Introduction

1. Charlotte Painter, *Seeing Things* (New York: Random House, 1976), p. 10.

2. Ruth Grimes and David Konkel, *Estimating Demand for a Rehabilitation Services Facility* (Berkeley: Research and Evaluation Division, Center for Independent Living, October 1973).

Part 1: Disclosing an Ongoing World

1. A basic discussion of interactionism is in Herbert Blumer, *Symbolic Interactionism: Perspective and Method* (Englewood Cliffs, N.J.: Prentice-Hall, 1969), based on the work of George Herbert Mead. Mead's position is partially presented in George Herbert Mead, *Mind, Self and Society,* ed. Charles W. Morris (Chicago: University of Chicago Press, 1934). As Blumer States:

> Human beings live in a world of objects, and their activities are formed around objects. This bland statement becomes very significant when it is realized that for Mead objects are human constructs and not self-existing entities with intrinsic natures. Their nature is dependent on the orientation and action of people toward them. Let me spell this out. For Mead, an object is anything that can be designated or referred to. It may be physical as a chair or imaginary as a ghost, natural as a cloud in the sky or man-made as an automobile, material as the Empire State Building or abstract as the concept of liberty, animate as an elephant or inanimate as a vein of coal, inclusive of a class of people as politicians or restricted to a specific person as President de Gaulle, definite as a multiplication table or vague as a philosophical doctrine. In short, objects consist of whatever people indicate or refer to (p. 68).

The positional statements that follow in the text and that are adapted to our phenomenon of human-environment relationships are drawn from:

> The first premise [in symbolic interactionism] is that human beings act toward things on the basis of the meanings that the things have for them. . . . The second premise is that the meaning of such things is derived from, or arises out of, the social interaction that one has with one's fellows. The third premise is that these meanings are handled in, and modified through, an interpretative process used by the person in dealing with the things he encounters (pp. 68–69).

In the development of research strategies, too little attention is paid to the actual presence and selectivity of the researcher in the world. While it is acknowledged that his appearance or physical condition affect research results, such obvious signs tell us nothing about his being in the world, his sense of the world, or his mood or "atness" in the world. If presence or being is primordial in human existence, it could be an acknowledged and important, even primal, research tool.

2. Carl R. Rogers, "Empathic: An Unappreciated Way of Being," *The Counseling Psychologist* 5, no. 2 (1975), p. 7.

3. Key informant, as we use the term, is clearly related to what Norman Denzin defines as an informant in *The Research Act* (Chicago: Aldine, 1970):

> By informant I refer to those persons who ideally trust the investigator; freely give information about their problems and fears and frankly attempt to explain their own motivations; demonstrate that they will not jeopardize the study; . . . The primary functions of the informant are to act as *de facto* observer for the investigator; provide a unique inside perspective on events that the investigator is still "outside" of; serve as a "sounding board" for insights, propositions, and hypotheses developed by the investigator; open otherwise closed doors and avenues to situations and persons; and act as a respondent. Informants serve multiple purposes for the investigator, acting simultaneously as expert witnesses and as transmitters of information, and finally as informal sociologists in the field. . . . Furthermore, they will be knowledgeable in that they are exposed to the situations and topics central to the study (p. 202).

4. Mayer Spivack, "Archetypal Places," *Architectural Forum,* October 1973, pp. 43–48.

Part 3: Networks

1. Such a designation process is in keeping with the interactional framework and antithetical to environmental determinism, which we want to avoid. Disabled people determine their world as active agents, they are not determined by it.

2. The distinction between imposed and grassroots networks is similar to the distinction between heteronomy and autonomy in relation to housing in John F. C. Turner, *Housing by People: Towards Autonomy in Building Environments* (New York: Pantheon Books, 1977).

3. The role of the individual in social interaction and the development of identity is presented in Anselm Strauss, *Mirrors and Masks: The Search for Identity* (Glencoe, Ill.: Free Press, 1959).

4. Attendants were observed and interviewed extensively and in different ways to find out about their work and their role from different points of view. Interviews were held with individuals both in their work settings and in clients' homes. We spent a great deal of time speaking informally with attendants while they worked with clients. On occasion we interviewed an attendant and his client at the same time, usually at the request of one or the other. This was insightful as to their relationship. Group interviews of five to eight attendants were held in which they were encouraged to talk among

themselves about questions we raised and thus to articulate their experience in relationship to that of others. We attended the few but intense meetings held by attendants who sought to organize politically during the summer of 1977.

Part 4: Places

1. Mayer Spivack, "Archetypal Places," *Architectural Forum,* October 1973, p. 46.

2. Ibid.

3. Clare Cooper, "House as a Symbol of Self," *Design for Human Behavior: Architecture and the Behavioral Sciences,* ed. Jon Lang et al. (Stroudsburg, Pa.: Dowden, Hutchinson, and Ross, 1974), p. 144.

4. The concept "places of power" derives from Carlos Castaneda, *The Teachings of Don Juan: A Yaqui Way of Knowledge* (New York: Pocket Books, 1968).

5: Alexander Kira, *The Bathroom* (Ithaca, N.Y.: Center for Housing and Urban Studies, Cornell University, 1966).

6. Jeremy Hewes, *Build Your Own Playground* (Boston: Houghton Mifflin, 1974), p. 10.

7. Gaston Bachelard, *The Poetics of Space,* trans. Maria Jolas (New York: Orion Press, 1969).

Part 5: How to Research

1. David N. Aspy, "Empathy: Let's Get the Hell on with It," *The Counseling Psychologist* 5, no. 2 (1975), pp. 10-14.

2. Carl R. Rogers, "Empathic: An Unappreciated Way of Being," *The Counseling Psychologist* 5, no. 2 (1975), p. 6.

3. Ibid., pp. 6-7.

4. Rollo May, *Love and Will* (New York: Norton, 1969), p. 230.

5. Ibid., p. 231. May quotes William James.

6. Peter Prangnell, in a lecture on the subject of Le Corbusier presented in Architecture 200A, a course given in the Department of Architecture, University of California at Berkeley, Fall Quarter 1976.

7. Aldo van Eyck, *Team 10 Primer,* ed. Alison Smithson (Cambridge, Mass.: MIT Press, 1968), pp. 100-104.

8. Ibid.

9. Raymond Lifchez with Barbara Knecht, "A Film Journal: The Environment of Physically Disabled Persons," unpublished manuscript, Department of Architecture, University of California at Berkeley, 1977, pp. 12-13.

10. Alfred Adler, quoting an anonymous English author, as cited in Robert L. Katz, *Empathy: Its Nature and Uses* (London: Free Press of Glencoe, Collier-Macmillian Ltd., 1963), p. 1.

11. *Rehabilitation Literature* is published by the National Easter Seal Society for Crippled Children and Adults, Chicago, Ill.

12. Gina Laurie, *Housing and Home Services for the Disabled: Guidelines and Experiences in Independent Living* (New York: Harper & Row, 1977).

13. The American Society of Landscape Architects Foundation and the U.S. Department of Housing and Urban Development, *Barrier Free Site Design* (Washington, D.C.: Government Printing Office, April 1976).

14. Julian Tarrant and Alice Subiotto, Planning Research Unit, Department of Urban Design and Regional Planning, University of Edinburgh, *Planning for Disabled People in the Urban Environment* (London: Central Council for the Disabled, 1969).

15. Sarah P. Harkness and James N. Groom, Jr., *Building without Barriers for the Disabled* (Whitney Library of Design, 1976).

16. Isabel P. Robinault, *Functional Aids for the Handicapped* (New York: Harper & Row, 1973).

17. Edward W. Lowman and Judith L. Klinger, *Aids to Independent Living: Self-Help for the Handicapped* (New York: McGraw-Hill, 1969).

18. Julia Hale, Anne Duecy Norman, Jane Bogle, and Susan Shaul, Task Force on Concerns of Physically Disabled Women, *Within Reach: Providing Family Planning Services to Physically Disabled Women* (Everett, Wash.: Planned Parenthood of Snohomish County, 1977).

19. Susan Shaul, Jane Bogle, Julia Hale, and Anne Duecy Norman, Task Force on Concerns of Physically Disabled Women, *Toward Intimacy: Family Planning and Sexuality Concerns of Physically Disabled Women* (Everett, Wash.: Planned Parenthood of Snohomish County, 1977).

20. Michael J. Bednar, ed., *Barrier-Free Environments* (Stroudsburg, Pa.: Dowden, Hutchinson and Ross, 1977).

21. *Like Other People* is available from Perennial Films, 1825 Willow Rd., Northfield, Ill.

22. *The Surest Test* is available from the Easter Seal Society, 521 2d Ave. W., Seattle, Wash. 98119.

23. *A Day in the Life of Bonnie Consolo* is available from Barry Spinelllo Films, 7831 Claremont Ave., Oakland, Calif. The film describes the everyday life of a woman born without arms.

24. *Daily Routine in the Life of Dave Harvey,* also available from Barry Spinello Films, describes the everyday life of a paraplegic.

25. Richard Brickner, *The Broken Year* (New York: Doubleday, 1972).

26. Richard Brickner, *My Second Twenty Years* (New York: Basic Books, 1976).

27. Ron Kovics, *Born on the Fourth of July* (New York: McGraw-Hill, 1976).

28. Norman Denzin, *The Research Act* (Chicago: Aldine, 1970), p. 202.

29. Raymond Lifchez, Linda Rhodes, Thomas McLellan, and Kenneth Copenhagen, *Barrier-Free Study: Identification of Physical Obstacles and Recommended Improvements for the Plant Engineering Department, Lawrence Berkeley Laboratory* (Berkeley, Calif.: Lawrence Berkeley Laboratory, 1977); 600 pages, illustrated.

30. Galen Cranz, in lectures given in

Architecture 140, "Social and Cultural Factors in Architecture and Urban Design," Department of Architecture, University of California at Berkeley, Spring Quarter 1977.

31. James P. Spradley and David W. McCurdy, *The Cultural Experience: Ethnography in Complex Society* (Chicago: Science Research Associates, IBH, 1972).

32. Irving Kenneth Zola, Department of Sociology, Brandeis University, in conversation with the authors, Berkeley, Calif., Winter Quarter, 1977.

33. Clare Cooper Marcus, in lectures given in Architecture 240, "Contemporary Issues in Housing Form," Department of Architecture, University of California, Berkeley, Winter Quarter 1977, and in Landscape Architecture 240, "Personal and Societal Environmental Values," Department of Landscape Architecture, University of California at Berkeley, Spring Quarter 1977.

34. Florence C. Ladd, "Residential History: You Can Go Home Again," *Landscape* 21, no. 2 (Winter 1977), p. 15.

35. Paul Byers, "Photography and Anthropology," *Afterimage*, April 1977, p. 9.

36. John Collier, Jr., *Visual Anthropology: Photography as a Research Method* (New York: Holt, Rinehart and Winston, 1967), p. 66.

37. Raymond Lifchez, "From Inside to Outside: A Journey to Architecture" (Department of Architecture, University of California at Berkeley, 1974), pp. 10–11.

38. Raymond Lifchez, "Teaching a Social Perspective to Architecture Students," *Journal of Architectural Education* 31, no. 3 (1978), p. 11–15.

39. I am indebted to Peter Prangnell for this concept, the element of which in his own vocabulary are termed "support," "fill," and "action."

40. Lifchez, op. cit., "From Inside to Outside."

Epilogue

1. Irving K. Zola, "The Consciousness of the Disabled: Why It Is Difficult to Ask or Listen to the Needs of the Handicapped Person" (Lecture delivered in the Department of Architecture, University of California at Berkeley, Apr. 19, 1978).

Catalogue

1. Herbert Gans, *People and Plans: Essays on Urban Problems and Solutions* (New York and London: Basic Books, 1968).

2. Charles Jencks and Nathan Silver, *Adhocism: The Case for Improvisation* (Garden City, N.Y.: Doubleday, 1972).

Selected Bibliography

Fiction, Biography, and Autobiography

Bernstein, Burton. *Thurber.* New York: Ballantine Books, 1975.

Brickner, Richard P. *My Second Twenty Years.* New York: Basic Books, 1976.

———. *The Broken Year.* New York: Doubleday, 1972.

Brightman, Alan J. *Ginny's Backyard.* Syracuse, N.Y.: Human Policy Press, 1978.

———. *Hollis Being Me.* Syracuse, N.Y.: Human Policy Press, 1978.

Cook, Marjorie. *To Walk on Two Feet.* Philadelphia: Westminster Press, 1978.

Dick, Philip K. *Dr. Bloodmoney.* New York: Grossett & Dunlap, 1965.

Glatzer, Nahum, N. *Franz Rosensweig: His Life and Thought.* New York: Schocken Books, 1962.

Heinlein, Robert A. *Waldo and Magic, Inc.* New York: Doubleday, 1950.

Hirsch, Ernest A. *Starting Over: The Autobiographical Account of a Psychologist's Experience with Multiple Sclerosis.* North Quincy, Mass.: Christopher Publishing House, 1977.

Hugo, Victor. *The Hunchback of Notre Dame.* New York: Dodd, Mead, 1976.

Jones, Ron. *The Acorn People.* San Francisco: Zephyros, 1976.

Keller, Helen. *Story of My Life.* New York: Doubleday, 1954.

Kovics, Ron. *Born on the Fourth of July.* New York: McGraw-Hill, 1976.

Lawrence, D. H. *Lady Chatterley's Lover.* New York: Grove Press, 1969.

Mann, Thomas. *The Magic Mountain.* New York: Random House, Vintage Books, 1969.

Maugham, Somerset. *Of Human Bondage.* New York: Pocket Books, 1973.

McCullers, Carson. *The Heart Is a Lonely Hunter.* New York: Bantam Books, 1953.

Rossner, Judith. *Looking for Mr. Goodbar.* New York: Pocket Books, 1976.

Solzhenitsyn, Alexander. *Cancer Ward.* New York: Bantam Books, 1969.

Sturgeon, Theodore. *More Than Human.* New York: Ballantine Books, 1953.

Thayer, Alexander Wheelock. *Thayer's Life of Beethoven,* rev. by Elliot Forbes. Princeton: Princeton University Press, 1973.

Tillyard, E. M. W. *Milton.* New York: Collier Books, 1967.

Trumbo, Dalton. *Johnny Got His Gun.* New York: Bantam Books, 1967.

West, Nathanael. "Miss Lonelyhearts" in *Miss Lonelyhearts and the Day of the Locust.* New York: New Directions, 1969.

Wright, David. *Deafness.* New York: Stein & Day, 1975.

Commercial Films
(Arranged chronologically)

The Hunchback of Notre Dame, 1923

The Phantom of the Opera, 1925

Freaks, 1932

The Hunchback of Notre Dame, 1939

The Light That Failed, 1939

Of Mice and Men, 1940

The Best Years of Our Lives, 1946

Johnny Belinda, 1948

The Stratton Story, 1949

The Men, 1950

With a Song in My Heart, 1952

Moulin Rouge, 1952

Reach for the Sky, 1956

Sunrise at Campobello, 1960

The Miracle Worker, 1962

Whatever Happened to Baby Jane?, 1962

Dr. Strangelove, 1964

A Patch of Blue, 1965

Ship of Fools, 1965

Wait until Dark, 1967

Charly, 1968

The Heart Is a Lonely Hunter, 1968

Midnight Cowboy, 1969

Long Ago Tomorrow, 1971

Longstreet, 1971

El Topo, 1971

The Last Picture Show, 1971

Butterflies Are Free, 1972

The Glass Menagerie, 1973

It's Good to Be Alive, 1974

Death Be not Proud, 1975

Tommy, 1975

The Boy in the Plastic Bubble, 1976

Something for Joey, 1977

The One and Only, 1977

Coming Home, 1978

Documentary Films

Artists' Fantasy. Multimedia Resource Center, 1525 Franklin Street, San Francisco, Calif. 94109.

Daily Routine in the Life of Dave Harvey. Barry Spinello Films, 7831 Claremont Avenue, Oakland, Calif. 94618.

A Day in the Life of Bonnie Consolo. Barry Spinello Films, 7831 Claremont Avenue, Oakland, Calif. 94618.

Don't Tell the Cripples about Sex. Multimedia Resource Center, 1925 Franklin Street, San Francisco, Calif. 94109.

Just What Can You Do? Multimedia Resource Center, 1925 Franklin Street, San Francisco, Calif. 94109.

Like Other People. Perennial Films, 1825 Willow Road, Northfield, Ill. 60093.

Mimi. Billy Budd Films, 235 East 57 Street, New York, N.Y. 10022.

Touching. Multimedia Resource Center, 1925 Franklin Street, San Francisco, Calif. 94109.

Bibliographies

Annotated Bibliography. 1st draft. New York: The National Arts and the Handicapped Information Service, February 1978. ARTS, Box 2040, Grand Central Station, New York 10017.

Resource Guide to Literature on Barrier-Free Environments (with selected annotations). Washington, D.C.: Architectural and Transportation Barriers Compliance Board, January 1977. Washington, D.C. 20201

Works Dealing with Physically Disabled People and with Barrier-Free Environmental Design

Bednar, Michael J., ed. *Barrier-Free Environments,* Stroudsburg, Pa.: Dowden, Hutchinson and Ross, 1977.

Bruck, Lilly. *Access: The Guide to a Better Life for Disabled Americans.* New York: Random House, David Obst Books, 1977.

Cary, Jane Randolph. *How to Create Interiors for the Disabled.* New York: Pantheon Books, 1978.

Fallon, Bernadette. *So You're Paralysed. . . .* London: Spinal Injuries Association, 1975.

Foott, Sydney. *Handicapped at Home.* London: Disabled Living Foundation, Design Council.

Gilbert, Arlene E. *You Can Do It from a Wheelchair.* New Rochelle, N.Y.: Arlington House, 1973

Goffman, Erving. *Stigma: Notes on the Management of Spoiled Identity.* Englewood Cliffs, N.J.: Prentice-Hall, 1963.

Goldsmith, Selwyn. *Designing for the Disabled.* 2d ed. New York: McGraw-Hill, 1968.

Harkness, Sarah P., and James N. Groom, Jr. *Building without Barriers for the Disabled.* New York: The Whitney Library of Design, 1976.

Laurie, Gini. *Housing and Home Services for the Disabled: Guidelines and Experiences in Independent Living.* New York: Harper & Row, 1977.

Levitin, Teresa E. "Deviants as Active Participants in the Labeling Process: The Visibly Handicapped," *Social Problems* 22, No. 4 (April 1975).

Robinault, Isabel P. *Functional Aids for the Handicapped.* New York: Harper & Row, 1973.

Sontag, Susan. *Illness as Metaphor.* New York: Farrar, Strauss & Giroux, 1978.

Spock, Benjamin. *Caring for Your Disabled Child.* New York: Macmillan, 1965.

Wright, Beatrice A. *Physical Disability—A Psychological Approach.* New York: Harper & Brothers, 1960.

Photo Credits

Andrea J. Bernstein: 184, bottom

Henry Bowles, Jr.: 154, bottom; 186, top

Center for Independent Living: 148

George Dibble: 144; 145; 146, top, left and right; 147

Dyche Emory: 153, bottom

Pat Goudvis: 41

Michael Henry: 141

Deborah Hoffman: 10; 154, top

Barbara Knecht: 168, bottom; 170, bottom; 172, top

Raymond Lifchez: 43; 89; 100; 128; 140; 146, bottom, right and left; 155, bottom; 157, top

Colleen Mahoney: 153, top; 158

Lydia Mechanic: 95; 108; 124; 156, top; 185, bottom; 188, top

Multimedia Center: 159, bottom; 160-164; 165, top; 167, top; 169, bottom; 172, bottom; 173; 174-181; 182, bottom; 183; 184, top; 185, top; 186, bottom; 187; 188, bottom; 189-195; 196, bottom; 197, top; 198, bottom; 199; 200, top

Ken Okuno: 52-54; 76; 84-85; 117; 125; 159, top; 166; 167, bottom; 169, top; 170, top; 171, top; 198, top

Rhodes and Lifchez/Architecture and Planning: 136

Jane Scherr: 2; 14; 18; 23; 28; 31; 33; 35; 38; 45; 48; 55-56; 58-59; 60; 71; 73-74; 79; 86; 92; 96; 98; 103; 109; 112; 115; 118; 121; 154, bottom; 155, top; 157, bottom; 165, bottom; 168, top; 171, bottom; 182, top; 196, top; 197, bottom; 200, bottom

Index

Edited by Sarah Bodine and Susan Davis
Designed by Jay Anning
Composed in 11 point Times Roman